Computer-Based Testing and the Internet

Computer-Based Testing and the Internet
Issues and Advances

Edited by

Dave Bartram
SHL Group plc, Thames Ditton, Surrey, UK

Ronald K. Hambleton
University of Massachusetts at Amherst, USA

John Wiley & Sons, Ltd

Copyright © 2006   John Wiley & Sons Ltd, The Atrium, Southern Gate, Chichester,
West Sussex PO19 8SQ, England
Telephone   (+44) 1243 779777

Chapter 9 Copyright © 2006 National Board of Medical Examiners
Chapter 11 Copyright © 2006 Educationl Testing Service

Email (for orders and customer service enquiries): cs-books@wiley.co.uk
Visit our Home Page on www.wiley.com

Other Wiley Editorial Offices

John Wiley & Sons Inc., 111 River Street, Hoboken, NJ 07030, USA

Jossey-Bass, 989 Market Street, San Francisco, CA 94103-1741, USA

Wiley-VCH Verlag GmbH, Boschstr. 12, D-69469 Weinheim, Germany

John Wiley & Sons Australia Ltd, 42 McDougall Street, Milton, Queensland 4064, Australia

John Wiley & Sons (Asia) Pte Ltd, 2 Clementi Loop #02-01, Jin Xing Distripark, Singapore 129809

John Wiley & Sons Canada Ltd, 22 Worcester Road, Etobicoke, Ontario, Canada M9W 1L1

Wiley also publishes its books in a variety of electronic formats. Some content that appears in print may not be available in electronic books.

Library of Congress Cataloging-in-Publication Data

Computer-based testing and the internet: issues and advances/edited
    by Dave Bartram, Ronald K. Hambleton.
        p. cm.
    Includes bibliographical references and index.
    ISBN-13: 978-0-470-86192-9 (cloth : alk. paper)
    ISBN-10: 0-470-86192-4 (cloth : alk. paper)
    ISBN-13: 978-0-470-01721-0 (pbk. : alk. paper)
    ISBN-10: 0-470-01721-X (pbk. : alk. paper)
    1. Psychological tests—Data processing.   I. Bartram, Dave, 1948-
II. Hambleton, Ronald K.
BF176.2.C64 2005
150'.28'7—dc22   2005011178

British Library Cataloguing in Publication Data

A catalogue record for this book is available from the British Library

ISBN-13   978-0-470-86192-9 (hbk)   978-0-470-01721-0 (pbk)
ISBN-10   0-470-86192-4 (hbk)   0-470-01721-X (pbk)

Typeset in 10/12 pt Palatino by Thomson Press (India) Limited, New Delhi
Printed and bound in Great Britain by Antony Rowe Ltd, Chippenham, Wiltshire
This book is printed on acid-free paper responsibly manufactured from sustainable forestry in which at least two trees are planted for each one used for paper production.

Contents

About the Editors

Dave Bartram is Past President of the International Test Commission and is heading ITC projects on international guidelines for standards in test use and standards for computer-based testing and the Internet. He is Chair of the British Psychological Society's Steering Committee on Test Standards and Convenor of the European Federation of Psychologists' Associations Standing Committee on Tests and Testing. He is President-Elect of the IAAP's Division 2.

Professor Bartram is Research Director for SHL Group plc. Prior to his appointment with SHL in 1998, he was Dean of the Faculty of Science and the Environment, and Professor of Psychology in the Department of Psychology at the University of Hull. He is a Chartered Occupational Psychologist, a Fellow of the British Psychological Society (BPS) and a Fellow of the Ergonomics Society. In 2004 he received the BPS award for Distinguished Contributions to Professional Psychology. His specialist area is computer-based testing and Internet assessment systems. Within SHL he is leading the development of their next generation of Internet-based delivery systems and the development of a multi-dimensional generic Competency Framework.

He has published large numbers of popular, professional and academic articles and book chapters, and has been the Senior Editor of the BPS Test Reviews. He has been an editor or co-author of several works including the 1992, 1995 and 1997 BPS Reviews of Psychometric Tests; *Organisational Effectiveness: the Role of Psychology* (with Ivan Robertson and Militza Callinan, published in 2002 by Wiley) and the BPS *Open Learning Programme for Level A (Occupational) Test Use* (with Pat Lindley, published by BPS Blackwell in 1994).

Ronald K. Hambleton holds the title of Distinguished University Professor and is Chairperson of the Research and Evaluation Methods Program and Executive Director of the Center for Educational Assessment at the University of Massachusetts, Amherst, in the United States. He earned a B.A. in 1966 from the University of Waterloo in Canada with majors in mathematics and psychology, and an M.A. in 1967 and Ph.D. in 1969 from the University of Toronto with specialties in psychometric methods and statistics. Professor Hambleton teaches graduate-level courses in educational and psychological testing, item response theory and applications, and classical test theory models and methods, and offers seminar courses on applied measurement topics. He is co-author of several textbooks including (with H. Swaminathan and H. Jane Rogers) *Fundamentals of Item Response Theory* (published by Sage in 1991) and *Item Response Theory: Principles and Applications* (published by Kluwer in 1985), and co-editor of several books including *International Perspectives on Academic Assessment* (with Thomas Oakland, published by Kluwer in 1995), *Handbook of Modern Item Response Theory* (with Wim van der Linden, published by Springer in 1997) and *Adaptation of Educational and Psychological Tests for Cross-Cultural Assessment* (with Peter Merenda and Charles Spielberger, published by Erlbaum in 2005). His research interests are in the areas of item response model applications to educational achievement and credentialing exams, standard-setting, test adaptation methodology, score reporting and computer-based testing. He has received several honors and awards for his more than 35 years of measurement research including honorary doctorates from Umea University in Sweden and the University of Oviedo in Spain, the 1994 National Council on Measurement in Education Career Award, the 2003 Association of Test Publisher National Award for Contributions to Computer-Based Testing, and the 2005 E. F. Lindquist Award for Contributions to Assessment. Professor Hambleton is a frequent consultant to state departments of education, national government agencies and credentialing organizations.

Contributors

Dave Bartram, SHL Group, The Pavilion, 1 Atwell Place, Thames Ditton, Surrey, KT7 0NE, UK

Randy Bennett, Educational Testing Service, Rosedale Road, MS 17-R, Princeton, NJ 08451, USA

Krista J. Breithaupt, American Institute of Certified Public Accountants, Harborside Financial Center, 201 Plaza Three, Jersey City, NJ 07311-3881, USA

Brian E. Clauser, National Board of Medical Examiners, 3750 Market Street, Philadelphia, PA 19104-3190, USA

Fritz Drasgow, Department of Psychology, University of Illinois, 603 East Daniel Street, Champaign, IL 61820, USA

Ronald K. Hambleton, University of Massachusetts at Amherst, Center for Educational Assessment, Hills South, Room 152, Amherst, MA 01003, USA

Michael Harris, College of Business Administration, University of Missouri, 8001 Natural Bridge Road, St Louis, MO 63121-4499, USA

Lutz Hornke, University of Aachen, Department of Psychology, Aachen Technical University, D-52056 Aachen, Germany

Charles Johnson, Competence Assurance Solutions Ltd, 9 Lawford Road, Rugby, CV21 2DZ, UK

Martin Kersting, University of Aachen, Department of Psychology, Aachen Technical University, D-52056 Aachen, Germany

Richard Luecht, Curry Building 209/ERM, University of North Carolina at Greensboro, P.O. Box 26170, Greensboro, NC 27402-6170, USA

Krista Mattern, Department of Psychology, University of Illinois, 603 East Daniel Street, Champaign, IL 61820, USA

Gerald J. Melican, American Institute of Certified Public Accountants, Harborside Financial Center, 201 Plaza Three, Jersey City, NJ 07311-3881, USA

Donald Melnick, National Board of Medical Examiners, 3750 Market Street, Philadelphia, PA 19104-3190, USA

Craig Mills, American Institute of Certified Public Accountants, Harborside Financial Center, 201 Plaza Three, Jersey City, NJ 07311-3881, USA

Tom Oakland, University of Florida at Gainesville, 1403 Norman Hall, Gainesville, FL 32611-7047, USA

Wim J. van der Linden, University of Twente, P.O. Box 217, 7500 AE Enschede, The Netherlands

INTRODUCTION

The International Test Commission and its Role in Advancing Measurement Practices and International Guidelines[1]

Thomas Oakland
University of Florida, USA

We reside in various communities and live in one world. Although we may reside in Beijing, China, on a kibbutz in Israel, or in Muleshoe, Texas, we are aware of the impact of world events on our lives.

This has not always been true. Throughout most of history, life generally was impacted by dominant qualities in one's community or a region reachable within one day. Important events that impacted the lives of those living thousands of miles away generally were unknown and had little impact outside that immediate area. Now, however, knowledge of events that occur throughout the world can be received in real time and can impact others' lives greatly.

Electronic technology accounts for much of this change. The use of telephones, radios, televisions, and computers has drawn people who live hundreds, even thousands of miles away into a common neighborhood by enabling them to have improved access to information, establish and maintain relationships, and in other ways engage in activities beyond their communities and nations.

---

[1] Portions of this chapter appear in Oakland, T., Poortinga, Y., Schlegel, J., & Hambleton, R. (2001). International Test Commission: Its history, current status, and future directions. *International Journal of Testing*, **1**(1):3–32.

Computer-Based Testing and the Internet: Issues and Advances.
Edited by D. Bartram and R. K. Hambleton. © 2006 John Wiley & Sons, Ltd.

People increasingly are never away from their phones. Cameras transmit pictures showing the flow of cars and people. Credit card use requires digitized information be sent to satellites and then returned to the earth, perhaps to a location thousands of miles from where the card was used. TVs convey pictures of warfare in real time. The use of technology is pervasive.

Computer use may account for more change during the last two decades than any other form of technology. Our use of computers has shaped the ways we work, attend school, bank, invest, pay taxes, acquire and disseminate information, plan vacations, order food, and date—to name only some of the more obvious areas.

The development, use, and availability of any technology, to be acceptable, must serve the public good and should assist professionals, as needed, in their efforts to serve the public.

Change that follows the introduction of new technology may be beneficial or harmful to society. Technology generally is intended to enhance the quality of life for a large number of people by providing needed services at lower costs. However, if unregulated and used inappropriately, technology can adversely impact lives. For example, the viewing of violence and sex by children and youths contributes to behaviors and attitudes that often are narcissistic and do not serve the public. Unregulated technology can be harmful. Thus, efforts are needed to help insure technology serves people well.

Technology also should serve professionals well. The introduction of new technology impacts the manner in which professionals can be expected to conduct their work. Professionals incorporate various forms of electronic technology into their practices when they increase effectiveness and efficiency. Their use of technology is preceded by study that informs them of the best ways to shape and apply this technology.

Tests constitute some of psychology's most important technology. Their use is universal, often starting with newborns and extending through the elderly. Their use is intended to serve the public by improving the ability to describe important behaviors, identify personal strengths, diagnose disabling conditions, assist in making administrative decisions, and help predict future behaviors. However, test use, if unregulated and used inappropriately, can adversely impact lives.

Computer use is shaping the ways tests are constructed, normed, validated, administered, and scored. The reach of this technology on test practices is broad and international. Thus, involvement of organizations that transcend one community, even one nation, is needed to envision, create, promote, regulate, and in other ways assist in forming and reforming test-related services that serve the professions responsible for test development and use as well as the public.

Many issues pertaining to test development and use are international in scope and thus need to be addressed at this level. The International Test Commission, International Association for the Evaluation of Educational Achievement, International Association of Applied Psychology, International Union of Psychological Sciences, Organization for Economic Cooperation and

Development, World Bank, and World Health Organization are among those providing leadership internationally. The work of the International Test Commission is becoming particularly prominent in this endeavor and is summarized below.

This introductory chapter reviews some historical features of test development and use and highlights the role of the International Test Commission in furthering these efforts. Thus, a goal of this chapter is to describe the context for forming the International Test Commission, initiating the 2002 Winchester ITC Conference on Computer-Based Testing and the Internet, as well as the contents of this book.

SOWING THE SEEDS OF TEST DEVELOPMENT AND USE

The first widespread use of tests occurred in China more than 3000 years ago. Measures of problem solving, visual spatial perception, divergent thinking, and creativity were used somewhat commonly. Later, under the Sui dynasty (581–618), a national civil service examination system was established that assessed three broad and important areas: cultural knowledge, planning and administration, and martial arts (Wang, 1993). Forms of this examination system continued in China to the end of the 19th century. However, few if any other countries seemingly duplicated these assessment practices or developed others on a national scale until the 20th century. A discipline of psychology, devoted to the study of individual differences in human behavior, was needed to initiate and sustain advocacy for these developments.

Psychological science first emerged from laboratories established by Fechner, Weber, and Wundt in Germany, by Galton in England, and by other pioneers who helped establish the scientific foundation for this fledging discipline. These early efforts to develop and use various tests and other measures, largely for research purposes, set the stage for later efforts that lead to the creation of psychometrics and other test-related specializations within psychology.

Before World War II, leadership in psychology rested among those who saw psychology as an academic discipline, one that was not sufficiently prepared to offer professional services at the same level as well established professions. Tests were developed and used mainly to conduct research and assess educational attainment. Thus, most psychology departments initially resisted pressure to offer programs that prepared practitioners to develop and use tests.

World War I provided one of the first large scale opportunities to evaluate the use of tests in applied settings. Within the United States, group tests of mental abilities were developed, found to be useful in selecting soldiers, and found to be psychometrically sound. Later efforts to develop other group and individually administered tests relevant to issues in psychology and education also proved to be effective. World War II expended the scope of test use, thus supporting its use in the selection, training, and placement of military recruits. By the 1950s, the viability of applied uses of tests was becoming widely accepted.

Following WWII, testing technology was new and generally unregulated. As noted above, the development, use, and availability of any technology, to be acceptable, must serve the public good and should assist professionals, as needed, in their efforts to serve the public. However, during the late 1940s and early 1950s, standards for test development and use had not been developed, and ethical issues regarding test use had not been addressed. Thus, there was little assurance that the emerging testing technology would serve the public and assist professionals.

THE EMERGENCE OF TEST DEVELOPMENT, PURCHASE, AND USE AND THUS THE NEED FOR REGULATIONS

During the 1960s, Swiss psychologists resembled their colleagues in many nations. Most worked in universities and had little interest in or commitment to preparing students for applied careers in psychology. Some believed the discipline of psychology had not matured sufficiently to warrant the professional practice of psychology and its use of tests. Thus, lacking opportunities to acquire needed knowledge and skills within universities, applied psychologists interested in test use often were self-taught or took courses elsewhere.

Although separate Swiss psychological associations were formed for those who had scholarly and applied interests, they united to address two common and inter-related issues: a desire to protect the title *psychologist* as well as methods psychologists developed and used, including tests. At that time, anyone could purchase tests. The Swiss expressed considerable concern when learning that the *Rorschach Inkblot Test*, one developed by a Swiss, as well as other assessment measures, could be purchased without restrictions in bookstores by persons unqualified to use them.

In 1968, Jean Cardinet, a Swiss psychologist, discussed applications of ethical standards in testing at the Swiss Psychological Society. He and others were concerned with the use of important tools to make life-changing decisions by people who lacked sufficient training and experience. In addition, tests were used that lacked adequate psychometric qualities and diagnostic value. Cardinet together with his Swiss colleagues discussed possible solutions to these test-related difficulties. Although these problems were apparent in Switzerland, they were also apparent in other countries. For example, a restriction on the sale of tests in Switzerland would be ineffective if the same tests could be purchased in neighboring countries. Thus, regional and international remedies were needed to address this and other test-related issues.

Cardinet and his colleagues saw the need to create test commissions in all countries charged with two responsibilities: to decide who is authorized to use various types of test and to scrutinize their sales to insure they do not bypass needed controls (Cardinet, 1974a, 1974b, 1974c, 1975, 1995). Cardinet envisioned each national commission designing a program of work in light of its national needs and conditions and cooperating with other national commissions through their association in an international test commission.

Upon contacting all national psychological societies, Cardinet became aware that problems experienced by his Swiss colleagues were international in scope and that some countries addressed them better than others. Fifteen countries had established test commissions, and additional countries expressed interest in forming one. Support for an international association devoted to test-related issues was also expressed.

FORMATION OF THE INTERNATIONAL TEST COMMISSION

Cardinet expressed hope that an international test commission would develop an ethics code and standards for test construction and evaluation, create a journal to promote an exchange of information, and assist colleagues working in developing countries to improve conditions governing the development and use of tests.

In 1974, leadership for forming a fledging international test commission transferred from Cardinet to Ype Poortinga, a leader of the Dutch Test Commission. During the next four years, Poortinga's efforts were directed toward developing an administrative infrastructure, including drafting a constitution, establishing a newsletter, and forming an advisory committee. A constitution for the International Test Commission (ITC) was approved in 1976, at which time Poortinga assumed the office of president. Articles of Incorporation for the International Test Commission, Inc. were filed in 1999 as a not-for-profit corporation within the state of Florida, thus establishing the ITC as a legal entity.

International Test Commission's Primary Goals

The ITC's primary goal has been to assist in the exchange of information on test development and use among its members and affiliate organizations as well as with non-member societies, organizations, and individuals who desire to improve test-related practices. Consistent with Cardinet's vision (i.e. to create an ethics code and standards for test construction and evaluation and a journal to promote an exchange of information, and assist colleagues in developing countries to improve conditions governing the development and use of tests), the ITC has worked to promote its goals through expanding membership, working cooperatively with other organizations, developing and promoting guidelines for test development and use, and engaging in other forms of publications and communication.

International Test Commission Membership

The ITC's constitution initially identified two membership categories: full members consisting of national test commissions recognized by a national psychological association and affiliate members consisting either of international associations that had an interest in assessment or national groups from countries not full members of the ITC. Revisions to the constitution expanded membership to include testing companies, universities, organizations interested in tests including those unable to pay yearly dues (e.g. psychological associations from developing countries), and individuals involved in test development and use. The increased breadth of membership reflects the ITC's desire to further increase and broaden its membership base and to include as members all persons with legitimate interests in test development and use, including non-psychologists.

As of March 2003, the ITC had 127 members. Most national psychological societies in Europe and North America, a number of national societies from other continents, nearly all major test publishers, together with many research departments in educational and psychological measurement are ITC members.

Working Cooperatively with Other Organizations to Achieve Common Goals

The ITC's limited resources require it to work in concert with other organizations that have complementary goals. International conference initiatives exemplify this commitment to work with others. The efforts of the ITC have been furthered through its association with the following: American Psychological Association, Arab Council for Childhood and Development, Association of Test Publishers, British Psychological Society, Canadian Nursing Association, CAT*ASI, Collegio de Psicologos, Educational Testing Service, European Association for Psychological Assessment, Europe Federation of Psychologists Association, European Test Publishers Group, International Association of Applied Psychology, International Association for the Evaluation of Educational Achievement, International Association for Cross-Cultural Psychology, International Language Testing Association, International Union of Psychological Sciences, National Council on Measurement in Education, National Institute for Educational Measurement, National Institute for Education Measurement in the Netherlands, NCS Pearson, NFER Nelson, Psychological Assessment Resources, Riverside Publishing, SHL Group, Swets & Zeitlinger, The College Board, The Psychological Corporation, and Thomson Prometric.

Development and Promotion of Guidelines for Test Development and Use

ITC's leadership in developing and promoting guidelines for test development and use became more evident in the early 1990s, when it began sponsoring international and regional meetings on topics that hold special importance to test issues that had a decided international scope. Five ITC-sponsored conferences are described below.

1993 Conference on Test Use with Children and Youth:
International Pathways to Progress

The first international conference independently proposed and organized by the ITC was held in June 1993 at St. Hugh's College, Oxford University, in England (Oakland & Hambleton, 1995). The conference's primary focus was on testing practices of children and youth in developing countries. This focus was consistent with the goals of the World Summit for Children in 1990 and the World Conference on Education for All in 1991. Both underscored the importance of promoting children's educational development though using test results to assist in planning and evaluation efforts. The ITC conference underscored its concerns about a need to improve educational and psychological assessment practices for children and youth. This need was especially apparent in developing countries as underscored in a series of publications (Hu & Oakland, 1991; Oakland & Hu, 1991, 1992) on the status of test development and use in 44 countries.

Guidelines for Adapting Tests

Test use in many countries is characterized by translating tests originally developed elsewhere. This common practice is contrary to common sense and violates laws, ethics codes, and psychometric principles.

The ITC observed a growing interest in avoiding problems associated with the use of translated tests and in pursing proper adaptation of educational and psychological tests. For example, by 1992, some tests developed in the United States had been translated and adapted into more than 50 languages. At the same time, efforts to adapt tests were hindered, in part, because technical guidelines governing test adaptations were unavailable. The ITC, under the leadership of Ronald Hambleton and with the assistance of an international panel, developed guidelines for adapting educational and psychological tests (e.g. Hambleton, 1994; Muniz & Hambleton, 1997; van de Vijver & Hambleton, 1996; Hambleton, Spielberger, & Merenda, 2005; also see the ITC web site).

1999 Conference on Test Adaptations: Adapting Tests for Use in Multiple
Languages and Cultures

The availability of the ITC guidelines on test adaptations, advances in test translation methodology, and considerable international interest in the topic warranted the International Conference on Adapting Tests for Use in Multiple Languages and Cultures, held in May 1999 at Georgetown University in Washington, DC (Hambleton, Spielberger, & Merenda, 2005).

1999 Conference on Cultural Diversity and European Integration

A conference on Cultural Diversity and European Integration, held at the University of Graz, Austria, in June 1999, also featured issues associated with test adaptations. The ITC co-sponsored this pan-European event with the International Association for Cross-Cultural Psychology. Primary motivation for the conference was the widespread immigration taking place throughout Europe and the need for better understanding cross-cultural issues as the European integration process continued.

2000 International Congress of Psychology in Stockholm

The International Union of Psychological Sciences convenes the International Congress of Applied Psychology every four years. It also sponsors advanced research training seminars in conjunction with the congresses. The ITC presented a seminar on psychological test adaptations to diverse cultures and measuring personality cross-culturally during its 2000 meeting in Stockholm (Oakland & Lonner, 2001).

2002 Conference on Computer-Based Testing and the Internet

The ITC leadership recognizes the value of drawing together people with common interests to discuss topics and issues important to test development and use. Somewhat small and well focused conferences can allow everyone to participate, promote an exchange of information, promote lasting relationships, and result in other positive unintended outcomes.

The ITC-sponsored conference on Computer-Based Testing and the Internet was designed with these beliefs. Directed by Dave Bartram and held in Winchester, England, in June 2002, the 250 conferees discussed issues relating to the uses and misuses of electronically transmitted tests and other assessment devices together with methodological, technical, legal, ethical, and professional issues arising from applications of computer-based technology to testing. This conference together with the contents of this book and new Guidelines for Computer-Based Testing and Testing on the Internet (Bartram & Coyne, 2003) launches the ITC's efforts to promote knowledge and understanding of uses and possible abuses in using computers to assist in test development and use.

International Guidelines for Test Use

The ITC's commitment to promote practices that can benefit test use is seen in its original charge. Early records reveal uneasiness as to the presence of unqualified persons using tests, their making important decisions despite having limited preparation and experience, and their use of tests that lack suitable norms and sufficient validity.

The ITC, under Dave Bartram's leadership, developed guidelines for the fair and ethical use of tests (Bartram, 1998, 2001). These guidelines provided an internationally agreed framework from which standards for professional preparation and test user competence and qualifications can be derived. The guidelines were approved by the ITC in 1999 and have been endorsed by the European Federation of Psychologists Associations Standing Committee on Tests and Testing. Psychological societies in a number of countries, including Argentina, Brazil, Croatia, Denmark, France, Germany, Lithuania, the Netherlands, Norway, Portugal, Slovenia, and Sweden, have translated the guidelines for use. The guidelines for the fair and ethical use of tests contribute importantly to the previously approved guidelines for test adaptations.

Publications and Communications

A Newsletter

The need to establish a journal to help promote communication and dissemination internationally has been a long-standing goal. Progress toward this goal was slow but continuous. The *Newsletter* served as the ITC's first vehicle of communication and dissemination. The *Newsletter* later spawned the *ITC Bulletin*, a publication that included articles of a scholarly nature as well as more general membership information. In 1991, the ITC decided to separate the two content areas by developing a more scholarly outlet and re-establishing a newsletter.

Association with the European Journal of Psychological Assessment

The ITC immediately entered into an informal agreement with the *European Journal of Psychological Assessment* that resulted in reserving 16–20 pages of each issue as an ITC-sponsored publication. This relationship continued through the 1999 volume years.

Testing International

The newsletter was re-established, renamed *Testing International*, and made available through the ITC website. Anita Hubley served as its editor through to 2005, when she was succeeded by Jan Bogg.

International Journal of Testing

A long-standing goal to create an ITC-sponsored journal was achieved in 1999. The *International Journal of Testing* was launched, with Lawrence Erlbaum Associates, Inc., Publishers. Norbert Tanzer and then Bruno Zumbo served as its editor through to 2005, when he was succeeded by John Hattie. The *International Journal of Testing* enables the ITC to meet a long-standing need: to create a truly international journal that addresses issues important to test development and use. The creation of the *Journal* is consistent with other efforts to positively impact testing internationally.

ITC Website

The creation of a website (*http://www.intestcom.org*) provided another method to improve communication between members and to communicate ITC's goals and programs internationally. The site provides information about membership, ITC projects, and *Testing International*, and launches documents developed and promulgated by the ITC.

ITC Contributions Through Books

The ITC's long-standing commitment to disseminate information also is found in its members' publishing books as well as sponsoring and presenting papers at national, regional, and international meetings. The first book highlighted advances in educational and psychological testing (Hambleton & Zaal, 1991). The second book focused on issues underscored in the Oxford conference, namely test use with children and youth (Oakland & Hambleton, 1995). Issues central to test adaptations were discussed by Hambleton, Spielberger, and Merenda (2005). Special issues of the *ITC Bulletin* that appeared in the *European Journal of Psychological Assessment* featured topics on computers in psychology in 1994, advances in assessment practices in 1997, and the ITC guidelines for adapting educational and psychological tests in 1999.

Computer-Based Testing and the Internet: Issues and Advances

This current book, edited by Bartram and Hambleton, represents another step forward, given the ITC's mission to advance test development and use internationally. Its contents reflect the leadership of the co-editors together with the continued dedication by the ITC to engage in scholarly activities intended to help promote test development and use internationally. It builds upon and extends contributions derived from the ITC-sponsored 2002 Winchester conference on Computer-Based Testing and the Internet.

A key theme of the Winchester conference was to provide the background to the development of guidelines on computer-based testing and testing on the Internet. The development of these guidelines has progressed in parallel with the production of this book and we expect both to be published at about the same time. These guidelines, like all the other ITC guidelines, can be found on the ITC's website.

REFERENCES

Bartram, D. (1998). The need for international guidelines on standards for test use: A review of European and international initiatives. *European Psychologist*, **3**:155–163.

Bartram, D. (2001). The development of international guidelines on test use: The International Test Commission Project. *International Journal of Testing*, **1**:33–53.

Bartram, D., & Coyne, I. (2003). ITC's International Guidelines on Computer-Based and Internet-Delivered Testing. *Testing International*, **13**(1):13.

Cardinet, J. (1974a). De Liège à Montréal. *Bulletin de la Commission Internationale des Tests*, **1**:6.

Cardinet, J. (1974b). Rapport sur la mise en application des recommandations de Liège. *Bulletin de la Commission Internationale des Tests*, **1**:8–10.

Cardinet, J. (1974c). Conclusions de la session de Montréal. *Bulletin de Commission Internationale des Tests*, **1**:14–25.

Cardinet, J. (1975). International Test Commission: Application of the Liege recommendations for the period 1971–4. *International Review of Applied Psychology*, **2**(1):11–16.

Cardinet, J. (1995). A prehistory of the International Test Commission. *European Journal of Psychological Assessment*, **11**(2):128–132.

Hambleton, R. K. (1994). Guidelines for adapting educational and psychological tests: A progress report. *European Journal of Psychological Assessment*, **10**:229–244.

Hambleton, R. K., Spielberger, C., & Merenda, P. (Eds.). (2005). *Adapting educational and psychological tests for cross-cultural assessment*. Mahwah, NY: Erlbaum.

Hambleton, R. K., & Zaal, J. N. (Eds.). (1991). *Advances in educational and psychological testing*. Boston, MA: Kluwer.

Hu, S., & Oakland, T. (1991). Global and regional perspectives on testing children and youth: An international survey. *International Journal of Psychology*, **26**(3):329–344.

Muniz, J., & Hambleton, R. K. (1997). Directions for the translation and adaptation of tests. *Papeles del Psicologo*, August, 63–70.

Oakland, T., & Hambleton, R. (1995). *International perspectives on academic assessment*. Boston, MA: Kluwer.

Oakland, T., & Hu, S. (1991). Professionals who administer tests with children and youth: An international survey. *Journal of Psychoeducational Assessment*, **9**(2):108–120.

Oakland, T., & Hu, S. (1992). The top ten tests used with children and youth worldwide. *Bulletin of the International Test Commission*, **19**:99–120.

Oakland, T., & Lonner, W. (2001). Report on the Advanced Research Training Seminar (ARTS) on psychological test adaptations to diverse cultures and measuring personality cross-culturally. *International Journal of Psychology*, **36**(3):199–201.

Van de Vijver, F. J. R., & Hambleton, R. K. (1996). Translating tests: Some practical guidelines. *European Psychologist*, **1**:89–99.

Wang, Z. M. (1993). Psychology in China: A review. *Annual Review of Psychology*, **44**: 87–116.

CHAPTER 1

Testing on the Internet: Issues, Challenges and Opportunities in the Field of Occupational Assessment[1]

Dave Bartram
SHL Group plc, UK

This chapter starts by considering what the Internet is and what it can it offer in relation to testing and assessment in the work and organisational field. It then goes on to take a look into the future and consider a range of practical and good practice issues. In considering testing on the Internet we need to consider both the technical strengths and weaknesses of the Internet itself (as a transport medium) and the limitations that the WWW technology imposes on the design of tests and control over their delivery. Throughout the chapter, the emphasis will be on the use of computer-based and web-based testing in the field of occupational assessment. Other chapters in this volume consider applications in other fields, notably educational testing and testing for licensing and certification.

COMPUTER-BASED TESTING (CBT) BEFORE THE INTERNET

The main value of CBT historically has been in the area of report generation. Some of the earliest systems (back in the days before personal computers) were designed to automate the scoring and interpretation of instruments such as the MMPI. With the advent of the personal computer, we saw the development of computer-administered versions of paper and pencil tests. These provided some advantages over paper and pencil, in terms of control of administration, and some disadvantages (e.g. the need for sufficient hardware

---

[1] Based on a keynote presentation to the ITC Winchester Conference, 13 June 2002.

to test groups of people). They also raised the question of equivalence with their paper and pencil counterparts. Most research (see Bartram, 2005; Mead & Drasgow, 1993) has tended to show that equivalence was not a major problem so long as the tests were not speeded measures of ability.

Bartram (1997) commented on the fact that, despite the potential offered by technology for novel forms of assessment, the literature on computer-based assessment (CBA) within occupational assessment settings has been largely confined to a small number of issues. These have been dominated by the issues relating to the parallel use of computer-based and paper-based versions of the same tests and use of computers to generate descriptive and inter-pretative reports of test results (for reviews, see Bartram and Bayliss, 1984; Bartram, 1987b, 1989, 1993, 1994, 2005).

INNOVATION IN COMPUTER-BASED TESTING

Despite the increasing sophistication of computer-based assessment systems, within the field of occupational assessment the tests they contain are, typically, computer implementations of old paper-and-pencil tests. Nevertheless, there has been innovation in the field and the consequences of that innovation are increasingly finding their way into commercial practice. Tests can be innova-tive in a number of different ways. The most obvious is where the actual test content is innovative. However, innovation can also occur in less obvious ways. The process used to construct the test may be innovative and rely on computer technology and the nature of the scoring of the items may be innovative. In practice there is an interaction between these different aspects of innovation, in that some of the most interesting developments in test content also involve innovation in how that content is created.

For computer-based testing, the most obvious examples of content innova-tion can be found where tests use sound or video to create multi-media items. Drasgow, Olson-Buchanan and Moberg (1999) describe a full-motion inter-active video assessment, which uses video clips followed by multiple choice questions. Simulations can also be run on computer to provide realistic work-sample assessments. Hanson, Borman, Mogilka, Manning, and Hedge (1999), for example, describe the development of a computer-based performance measure for air traffic control selection and Bartram (Bartram & Dale, 1983; Bartram, 1987a) describes the use of a simplified landing simulator for use in pilot selection.

Innovation in content also relates to the use of more dynamic item types, for example, where drag-and-drop or other familiar Windows-based operations are used rather than the simple point-and-click simulation of paper-and-pencil multiple-response. A review of this area of innovation in item types is presented by Drasgow and Mattern in Chapter 3.

Innovation in content, however, is often associated with novel methods of content generation. Item generation techniques have provided the potential for a whole host of new item types as well as more efficient production of conventional items. Bartram (2002a), and Goeters and Lorenz (2002) describe the use of generative techniques to develop a wide range of task-based and item-based tests for use in pilot selection. It is worth noting, however, that most of the developments in this area of innovation have occurred in areas where selection leads to very high cost training or into high risk occupations or both (as is the case for trainee military pilot selection). Innovation is expensive, and the sort of tests described in the papers referred to above have required extensive research and development programmes. However, as in all areas of testing, the lessons learned from this work will result in benefits in due course for the general field of occupational assessment.

Computer software provides for the recording of very detailed information about a test-taker's performance. In addition to the response given to an item, we can record how long the person took to respond. We can also record information about choices made and changed during the process of responding. For more complex item types we can track the performance of the person as they work their way through a task or series of subtasks. Bartram (2002b) reported validation data from the use of a set of computer-based ability tests that were administered without any time limit. These were designed for use in a diagnostic mode for people entering further education training courses. Time to respond was normed independently for each item and response latency was scored together with accuracy to produce a measure of efficiency. This efficiency score had higher validity than the traditional number correct score.

While there has been some experimentation in the use of response latency data for checking response stability (Fekken & Jackson, 1988) and socially desirable responding (Holden & Fekken, 1988; George & Skinner, 1990a, 1990b), these approaches have not been developed into practical applications for general use in personnel selection or other areas of I/O assessment as yet.

Item Response Theory (IRT) has been with us since the 1980s (Lord, 1980), but its application has tended to be confined to educational and some large-scale occupational uses. It has not been generally applied in the area of occupational assessment until relatively recently. IRT has the considerable advantage of approaching test construction from the item level. Its application to routine occupational assessment has become possible with the advent of better data collection and data management procedures. IRT has many advantages over traditional methods; however it also comes with some costs: the need for larger samples of data with which to determine the properties of items. Although computer technology has provided the possibility of implementing adaptive testing using (in particular where it is based on IRT models) the impact of this on general test practice has been slight in the occupational field. The main reason why traditional classical fixed-item-set tests have held sway for so long has been one of infrastructure. Neither paper and pencil nor PC-based testing is well suited to adaptive testing and the use of large item banks. The Internet potentially changes all of this. There are clear signs that attitudes to CBA are changing as people come to appreciate the real benefits of technology for assessment, and as the technological infrastructure needed to support these applications becomes increasingly ubiquitous.

Development of Computer-Based Testing and Growth of the Internet

The use of computer-based testing is increasing rapidly. It has been helped not only by the development of better interfaces, but by the dramatic increases in volume of and accessibility to hardware. Access to the Internet is now available to you in your home for a few hundred pounds of capital outlay. In addition we have seen the advent of email and restricted Internet services on digital TV systems. The new millennium heralded the appearance of the first generation of WAP mobile phones, with their ability to access the Internet in a wireless environment and the promise of broadband 3G systems becoming available in the next few years. However, the pattern of development is not uniform around the world. Even where the technology is present, some users are more conservative than others in their adoption of that technology.

Computer networks have existed for a long time. The first use of a hyperlinked network by the US military occurred in 1957. Academic institutions in the UK joined in 1973 when University College London set up the first connection. The first commercial UK IP network was set up in 1989. At the start of the 1990s, Tim Berners Lee proposed the idea of using a standard graphical browser and a communication standard to provide access to data from any source, and so 'invented' the World-Wide Web (WWW). The Mosaic browser, the first of the WWW browsers, appeared in 1992. In 1994, Netscape was founded and a year later, Microsoft embraced the Internet, having previously dismissed it.

In many ways we can look on 1995 as the real beginning of widespread use of the Internet, the time at which it started to become part of the fabric of many people's everyday lives. In the few years since then, the range of applications and volume of use have mushroomed. For all practical purposes, while the potential of the Internet has been known for many years, it has only just reached the stage of development at which that potential can begin to be realised. We are now at a significant watershed in its development for a number of reasons.

Within North America, Europe and Asia–Pacific, we now have widespread availability of inexpensive, high-powered computer systems. As the hardware has become more widespread, so the range of service providers has increased. Now it is as easy to get onto the net as it is to have a phone installed. Indeed, wherever a phone or a cable TV connection has been installed, an Internet connection can be made. Once on the net, you have access to information and services that were previously restricted to expert users or specialists. You can be your own travel agent; you can buy books and other goods from anywhere in the world; you can consult experts, read government reports, or find a new job.

The convergence towards common standards has made it commercially viable for service providers to offer users more and more sophisticated applications. The advances in technology have provided us with standard features we would hardly have dreamt of a few years ago: minimum screen resolutions of 1024×768 and 32-bit colour resolution; real-time animation, video and sound capabilities; multi-tasking and so on.

Finally, we have also witnessed an increase in reliability. This is the key to the use of computers in testing. Though computer systems are still prone to crashes, hang-ups and network failures, we are moving rapidly closer to the point where the user expectation is that computers should operate reliably.

Tests and documents are essentially 'soft' products. As such they can be downloaded over the Internet to users. This means that the Internet can be used as a complete commercial solution for test publishers. There is no longer any need for printing and production, warehousing and postal delivery services.

More significant for testing, however, is the shift in locus of control provided by the Internet from the 'client side' to 'server side'. For paper and pencil testing, publishers have had to provide users with test items, scoring keys and interpretation algorithms. As these are 'public', the danger of compromise and security breaches is high. Test users can (and do) pass these materials on to people who are not authorised to use them. All the test data also resides with the user. The process of developing norms, checking the performance of test items and carrying out validation studies is dependent upon costly procedures for recovering data from users. For the Internet this situation is reversed. The data and the intellectual property reside on the publisher's server. The user has access only to those parts of the process that they need.

Time for a Revolution!

The infrastructure is now being built to support a radical change in the way testing is done. We are seeing the widespread availability and acceptance of computers; standardisation on operating systems and interfaces and the growth of the Internet as the generic communication medium.

Ipsos-Reid in their annual 'Face of the Web' survey (reviewed by Pastore, 2001c) actually claim that the revolution is over and that we are entering a 'post-revolutionary' phase as growth of the Internet market starts to level off in most of the developed regions around the world. Global Internet population was estimated at around 350 million at the end of 2000. For 2005 it is estimated that it will be around 500 million. The US still has more people online than any other country, but its share of global users is shrinking. Western Europe plus the remainder of the English speaking world (UK, Australia, Canada and South Africa) now rivals the US as a bloc. In 2000, 65% of the population in Sweden used the Internet in a 30-day period, while in Canada it was 60%. This surpassed the US (59%), for which the percentage remained constant from 1999 to 2000. However, in a poll conducted in 2002 (Ipsos, 2002), the percentage of US Americans going online in a 30-day period had jumped to 72%. Very rapid growth was also noted in Korea, urban China, urban India, France, Germany and the UK (where usage increased from 35% in 2000 to 50% in 2002).

Awareness of the Internet is now almost universal in North America, Australia, Europe and Japan. While awareness levels are low in urban areas of China, India and Russia, they are increasing rapidly. The 2002 Ipsos study, for example showed an increase from 9 to 19% in urban India usage (over a 30-day period) and from 21 to 30% in urban China between 2000 and 2002. Internet use in Asia–Pacific is expected to surpass that in the US by 2005 (Pastore, 2001d, quoting an International Data Corp. study). Asia–Pacific (excluding Japan) is forecast to exceed 240 million users from the 2001 base of 64 million, with a fundamental shift in the position of China.

While predictions are always dangerous, by 2010 I believe that in the field of occupational assessment we will see computer-managed and computer-delivered assessment becoming the default and paper-and-pencil testing the exception.

WHAT CAN THE INTERNET OFFER NOW?

In this section some current areas of application of the Internet are considered, and illustrated. The applications covered include:

- using the Internet to support test users
- assessment for development
- test practice and familiarisation
- recruitment and selection
- post-hire applications, including online 360-degree feedback and development.

Supporting Test Users

Most discussion of the Internet tends to focus around the delivery of tests to test takers online. However, the Internet also provides a new medium for distribution of test materials, reports and manuals, and for the automated collection of data. Even traditional paper and pencil materials can be delivered online as PDF format files using e-book publishing technologies.

Many publishers now use the Internet as a major source of support for test users. SHL, for example, delivers updates for its offline PC-based test systems over the Internet, together with norm updates and other technical data to support paper-and-pencil test users. As a medium, the Internet also provides a channel for users to communicate with each other (through user-groups) and with the publishers of materials. This communication is not just for traditional support purposes, but also provides the potential for supplier and client to have more of an ongoing dialogue through which the supplier can better target future research and development.

Self-Assessment and Practice

It is widely acknowledged (e.g. Kellett, 1991; Callan & Geary, 1994) that we should provide people who are to be assessed with the opportunity for practice, such that when the final assessment is taken they are all performing at or close to their asymptotic level. In the past, this has not been possible. Until recently, the only practical mechanism for giving people experience of testing has been through the use of practice tests or dissemination of information leaflets that provide examples of test items.

The Internet provides an ideal mechanism for making practice test materials available to people. Indeed, where testing is being used in this 'formative assessment' mode, the complex issues of test user authentication and supervision are of lesser importance, so long as the test content is different from that used for selection testing. For example, the SHL Direct for Students site[2] provides sample items for verbal, numerical and diagrammatic tests as well as personality inventory items in both Likert-rating and ipsative (forced-choice) format. In addition, complete timed practice tests are available for potential test takers.

A range of other test publishers now provides Internet-based practice (though these generally do not include timed test items). Such systems provide the test taker with potentially useful feedback and are widely used to provide career advice, especially on web-based job boards.

Recruitment on the Internet

A major consequence of the rapid growth of the Internet and its accessibility is that increasing numbers of organisations are recruiting and selecting applicants for jobs online (see Bartram, 2000, and Lievens & Harris, 2003, for reviews of this area). Applicants for jobs and job-seekers are increasingly expecting to find work through the Internet rather than more traditional means. The Electronic Recruiting Index (ERI, 2000) showed a substantial increase in spending on e-recruiting in 1999. For 1998 the total was about $4.5 billion, while in 1999 it jumped to over $15 billion. The ERI forecasts steady growth from around $18 billion in 2000 to nearly $40 billion by 2005.

The Association of Graduate Recruiters in the UK (AGR, 2000) reported the results of a survey that showed that the number of recruiters recruiting online doubled in the year 1999 to 2000, from one-third to two-thirds of them. Nearly 90% of graduates were seeking their first jobs on the Internet and nearly 50% were applying online. What is more interesting is that employers report that the quality of applicants who applied online was higher than that of those who applied by traditional methods. Interestingly, the major change envisaged by the respondents as a consequence of growing use of the Internet was the

---

[2] See *http://www.shldirect.com/shldirect-homepage/SHLDirect-1.asp*

demise of the hand-written application form. This reflects the growing trend to move away from the posting of CVs and resumes to the use of structured application forms systematically covering biographical data, experience, skills etc.

The Internet provides more than just a replacement for the traditional recruitment process. Online applicants can be responded to very quickly (within minutes by automated email, and within hours by recruiting managers). They can access sites where there is information about the company, the jobs it has, realistic job previews and so on. It is not just an online application process.

Internet recruitment has clear advantages for both applicants and recruiters. For recruiters, it provides the following:

• Larger applicant pools.
• Job profiling tools to set competency benchmark profiles against which to assess candidate fit.
• Very significant reductions in time to hire. Typically, times are reduced from four to eight weeks down to two weeks or less.
• Reduced cost per hire.
• The capability to email to candidates invitations to attend an interview or further assessment within hours of completing an application. This speed of response is likely to be critical for success in hiring for organisations competing for a limited talent pool.
• The potential for higher validity early sift leading to more cost-efficient selection.

For applicants, the advantages are:

• better feedback and advice on career and company choice
• good information about the available jobs and organisations
• access to a wider range of jobs and employers
• more rapid feedback and the ability to track one's progress.

Well designed sites can help candidates make sensible decisions about whether they are qualified to apply and therefore increase the average suitability of the pool that go on to submit an application.

Candidate management and tracking are key features of Internet-based recruitment systems. These allow both candidates and hiring managers to know where a person is in the process and what their status is. People no longer have to post off an application form and then wait for weeks for a possible reply.

The key to making best use of the Internet for recruitment lies in using the new technology to apply valid objective assessment techniques to the initial sift process. Despite the fact the majority of large organisations now recruit over the Internet, most of them sift on the basis of purely demographic criteria and simple checks on relevant experience (Stanton & Rogelberg, 2001). What is more, in a large number of cases they do this by printing out an applicant's CV or resume, and then carrying out a traditional paper sift!

Future Trends

The future lies in developing structured assessments that can be completed online by job seekers and that can be shown to be job relevant. By doing this, it becomes possible to re-position online recruitment as a process of matching the competencies and capabilities of the applicant to the requirements of the job vacancy, and so produce a high quality shortlist.

Changes in technology need to be considered together with changes in recruitment practice. A major trend in personnel management has been the decentralisation of many operational responsibilities to staff at business unit, departmental or line-management level. A survey by the UK Institute for Personnel and Development (IPD, 1999) showed that in the UK line-managers are involved in determining recruitment criteria 97.4% of the time. The figures for central personnel staff (55.2%) and local personnel staff (36.6%) are much lower.

This trend to shift responsibility for recruitment and selection out to line management has implications for the design of selection systems. It is no longer safe to assume that a small number of highly trained personnel professionals will oversee the recruitment and selection procedures within their organisation. Thus, while needing to increase the sophistication of the recruitment and selection tools (to counter the increasing volumes of applicants available through online methods), we also need to 'de-skill' these tools from the point of view of the user. While it may be desirable, it is not practical to expect line managers in organisations to complete formal test user training courses before they begin to recruit personnel. Given such realities, the challenge for occupational psychologists is to design tools that are objective and job relevant but also easy and safe to use by relatively unskilled users.

Post-Hire: Main Applications

The most widely used application of the Internet for assessment within organisations is probably 360-degree feedback. There is now a wide range of systems available both for use over the Internet and for use on company Intranets. The major benefits are logistical. By its very nature 360-degree feedback is an administrative nightmare to manage. People involved in the process tend to be geographically dispersed but also need close supervision in order to ensure that the ratings are carried out to schedule and that sufficient raters are obtained for each focus of the assessment.

Good online systems focus on managing the workflow associated with the 360-degree process (Bartram et al., in press), from initial set-up and preparation of the people involved, through the management of the rating process (including delivery and scoring of questionnaires), to the production of reports and their delivery to feedback providers. Features of such systems will include:

- either candidate self-service or HR control over the administration
- users can choose their own raters
- task notifications, reminders and report delivery all automated
- either generic competency models can be used or they can be tailored to the organisation's needs.

'Good practice' in carrying out a 360-degree feedback process can be built into the system by providing certain constraints on what users can do.

In addition to 360-degree feedback, there are a host of other applications where we are seeing the Internet becoming more widely used:

- organisational surveys
- multi-rater job analysis
- competency profiling
- individual development planning and tracking of development action plans
- performance appraisal
- performance management.

In addition, all the assessment procedures used in selection can be applied to post-hire development as well (e.g. through the use of virtual development centres).

FUTURE INTERNET APPLICATIONS

As noted earlier, there have been interesting developments in occupational testing within the military field and in the fields of education testing that have yet to impact significantly upon routine occupational testing. Certainly, we are starting to see developers and publishers move beyond traditional multiple-choice questionnaires (MCQs) and the use of classical test theory. There are a number of areas that are being developed.

Internet Interviews

Use is already made of the telephone for structured interviewing (Edenborough, 1994). However, the face-to-face interview serves a range of social functions other than the collection of information about the applicant (see, e.g., Herriot, 1989). One of the defining elements of a job interview is that it is an interactive dialogue between at least two people. It provides the opportunity for the applicant to learn about the potential employers and acts as a forum in which negotiation can take place between the parties.

Wide band G3 video-phone will provide a halfway house between the telephone interview and the 'live' face-to-face interview. Video-conferencing provides the employer with the opportunity to conduct single, pair or panel interviews without having the cost of transporting applicants to a common interview site. Certainly for overseas applicants, video-conference interviewing provides a major saving in cost and (for the applicant) time. By 2010 we can expect to see domestic digital TVs with built-in cameras being used as video-phones as part of their role as general-purpose multi-media entertainment and information centres. This will enable high fidelity interviewing to take place without applicants having to leave their homes.

It is likely that for certain jobs there will remain a final stage at which the job applicant and the employer need to meet face to face before entering into a formal employment contract. However, the role of this final meeting could shift away from that of an assessment process (as the information can be collected more efficiently online) towards that of discussing and agreeing the contract between applicant and employer. We could then see the interview become an event that occurs between the formal job offer being made and the applicant's acceptance or rejection of it.

Reference Checks

It is already quite common to seek and transmit references by phone and by email. The use of the Internet to deliver structured and adaptive reference checks will add to the range of ways in which this information can be collected. It will also provide an effective means of providing a higher level of control over the administration of the reference-checking instrument. The same techniques can be used as are currently used in the systematic collection of information for 360-degree feedback.

Formal checking (subject to the necessary search and access permissions having been obtained) of medical, criminal and credit records will become very highly automated, as all the relevant data will be held on databases with (secure) Internet access.

Assessment and Development Centres

It is in the area of both group and individual assessment exercises that some particularly exciting new possibilities emerge. One of the earliest applications of the Internet (well before the advent of the World Wide Web) was for multi-user games such as Dungeons and Dragons. It is now possible to create multi-user exercises (e.g. business simulations) that can be closely monitored and assessed. The users need not be brought together to a single location, but could form part of a virtual assessment or development centre. While such procedures may have a greater part to play in training and development, they could also be used in a selection context.

For single-user exercises, web-based in-basket exercises are already available. These can be designed as relatively simple systems, for non-experienced users, or use software such as MS Outlook. In either case, people can be provided with emails, phone messages and background information, and have to work to obtain a set of objectives within some pre-defined constraints. The user can set tasks, make appointments, send emails and so on. All the actions and events can be logged, analysed and assessed.

The potential advantage of making such tasks Internet based is that it removes the geographical constraints on having to bring people together to take part in an assessment.

Cognitive Ability Testing

Excellent descriptions of the advances made in computer-based cognitive testing are provided in other chapters of this book and in reference books such as that by Wainer *et al.*, (1990). For now we focus attention on the potential afforded by the Internet for remotely supervised cognitive ability testing. Use of the Internet for the deliver of cognitive ability tests is technically straightforward. Java or Flash applets, for example, can be written that provide high levels of control over the presentation of material and the timing of tests and responses. The use of downloaded applets also ensures that tests are not affected by denials of service from the user's ISP occurring during a test session.

An example of an application of this new technology is provided by the SHL online Numerical Reasoning Test (Baron, Miles, & Bartram, 2001). The software developed for this test enables unique tests to be created for each individual, while ensuring that the difficulty level of the test is known and controlled. Standardised scoring is achieved through item calibration and then tests are constructed by constrained random generation from a large item bank. As a result of the fact that each test is unique, the issue of test security no longer arises. This test has been used by a number of organisations in an unsupervised mode as part of an initial screening sift in graduate recruitment. Research of the data subsequently collected from those candidates who proceeded to the second stage of the selection process showed high correlations with re-assessment data (collected under supervised conditions) and a substantial increase in the overall quality of the sifted applicants (twice as many passed the assessment centre as did before this sift tool was introduced).

PRACTICAL AND GOOD PRACTICE ISSUES

As the market for Internet-delivered computer-based testing develops, and as the technological sophistication of the products increases, so the issue of ensuring that those who use such tests and assessment tools follow good practice will increase in importance.

In this section we will consider a range of inter-related issues:

- Performance characteristics and technical limitations of the Internet as a test delivery medium: speed, network integrity, reliability, bandwidth etc.
- Security: protecting the publishers' IPR; controlling test access and distribution, keeping scoring and rules confidential.
- Privacy: controlling access to test results, legal issues relating to data protection, privacy and storage.
- Fairness: equality of access for all groups to the net—closing the 'digital divide'.

Performance

It is in the area of performance that the major current limitations of the Internet are to be found. Testing makes two main requirements of the delivery medium. First, it should provide the means of controlling the timing of delivery. Second, it should be robust and not fail mid-way through a test. Rapid delivery of pages to the user cannot be relied upon at present for a number of reasons. Many users are still on the end of a slow modem connection. While publishers can ensure that their servers deliver pages faster than users can call for them, slow connections at the user end, or other delays caused by the Intranet itself, can result in the actual appearance of pages on the user's browser appearing to be very slow.

Even if the user has a broadband connection and there are no delays on the Internet, the most rapid delivery is only of value if it can be relied upon. Hang-ups and lost Internet connections can potentially terminate a test session in mid-stream. For some tests it is not practical simply to resume from the point at which a break occurred. For example, at present it is not safe to rely on the integrity of the Internet to the extent we would require for timed testing, even if we could be sure the page flow rate could be fast enough.

The easiest way to overcome these performance issues is to download any time critical material as an applet. This at least will ensure that the test administration is not dependent on the Internet for its timing and integrity. However, from the user's point of view this may create another problem: if the connection is a slow one or the applet is large, the applet may take a considerable time to download. Furthermore, many organizations will not allow applets through their corporate fire-walls.

Consistency of Appearance

The Internet poses some of the same problems as stand-alone computer-based testing. For example, the test distributor has no direct control over the user's screen size or resolution. For standalone systems software controls can be used to mitigate and control some of the extremes of variation in screen settings. For browser-based testing, however, the level of control is rather less. Browsers are designed to leave the user in control of navigation around the Web and to be able to examine and modify the page display parameters in ways that we would wish to prevent in a normal test-taking situation.

Furthermore, there is no one 'standard' browser. Currently, two browsers dominate the market: Internet Explorer and Netscape Navigator. Unfortunately, these do not display information in exactly the same way. As a result, a test will look different and may behave differently depending upon the browser you are using. This problem is exacerbated by the fact that each of the browsers exist in a range of versions which also differ in how they render information.

Again, the solution to these problems, where they are likely to compromise the integrity of a test, is to create the test within an applet that can be downloaded and run on the user's computer.

Security

Security concerns tend to be very high on the list of those worried about the use of the Internet for testing. The concerns over security need to be considered in relation to various sets of data:

- The test itself (item content, scoring rules, norms, report-generation algorithms, report content etc).
- The test taker's identity—both authenticating the person's identity and preserving confidentiality.
- Test results—ensuring that only those eligible to access the test scores are able to do so.

While all the above are areas of concern, it is important to put these into perspective by considering how the Internet, as a testing medium, compares with the current alternatives: paper-and-pencil and stand-alone computer-based testing.

Test Security

The key feature of the Internet is that, apart from the browser software itself, all the application software and all the data resides on the server, not on the user's computer. Herein lie some of the main advantages of Internet based testing:

- All the important intellectual property associated with a test (scoring rules, norms, report-generation algorithms etc) remains on the server under the control of the distributor.

- This level of control provides the distributor with detailed knowledge about the use of their products: who is using what, and when. This has enormous potential commercial benefits.
- The test software and reference data set only exists in one location. This ensures that all users have access to the most up-to-date version. It also greatly simplifies the process of making changes, fixing 'bugs', updating norm tables and so on.

Authentication of Users

There is a range of levels of authentication that can be used. The distributor can either make a test open access, or exercise full control over who can access the test content, when they can access it and from where. Control can be exercised by requiring a username and password, or access can be limited to specific machines on the Internet (by only allowing those with particular IP addresses to use the test). By combining IP address checking with user passwords, a very high level of control can be exercised. Such a level of control was never possible for paper-and-pencil testing or for stand-alone computer-based testing.

While this level of authentication would be more than sufficient for managing access to personal banking information, it is not sufficient for ensuring that people are not cheating in a high-stake testing situation. For such a situation, a person could pass their identification to another person who would actually take the test, or they could have a group of helpers with them while they complete the test. Further advances in identification technology (fingerprint recognition and retinal eye-pattern recognition) would not really solve the problem of security in this sort of high-stake testing situation.

For this reason, it is likely that high-stake tests will continue to require the presence of a test administrator to confirm the identity of the test taker and ensure the test is completed under the correct conditions. While this is often noted as a disadvantage of Internet testing, it is really no different to other forms of testing technology.

Data Privacy

All the data generated by test takers resides on the central server. By applying best practice to the management of the server, the security of all aspects of the data can be far better assured than would be the case if the data were distributed amongst the various test users. While some people still have concerns about their data being held centrally, these concerns will decrease in the future as standards of security and good practice become more clearly established. In many ways worrying about having your data held on a professionally managed server is like worrying about your money being held in a bank—it is really a lot safer than keeping it at home!

Not only does the centralisation of data storage make it easier to manage but it also makes all test data potentially available for research and development purposes. This in turn can raise concerns in some people that they may be losing control over their data. Clearly, if the data are to be used for research and development purposes then this should be agreed with the data providers in advance. The service providers should have clear policies on how individual data are to be kept, for how long and who is allowed access to them. These details must be made clear to the test taker and be agreed to by the test taker before the data are collected. Of course, such policies must take account of, and be consistent with, national and international law on data privacy (for example, the European Union has a Directive relating to data privacy that is binding on all member countries of the Union).

Fairness—and the Digital Divide

There has been much concern expressed about the Internet creating a 'digital divide' between those with access to computer technology and those without (Keller, 1996). This is currently true on a geographical basis, with nearly all of the infrastructure and development of business taking place in North America, Europe and Asia–Pacific. This will change over the coming decade, but for some time we will not be able to use the Internet as the sole source of recruitment and selection in countries outside these three main areas.

However, if we consider just those areas where the infrastructure is well developed, does everyone have equal access to it? In considering any selection and recruitment process we need to consider its potential for adversely impacting on one or more particular groups within the population. From the viewpoint of litigation, the main 'protected' groups are ethnic minorities, women, and people with disabilities. More generally we should be concerned about equality of access in terms of geographical dispersion (rural versus urban), age, educational background and any other factors that may not be directly job relevant, but have an effect on access to the recruitment process.

In his review of Internet usage data, Bartram (2000) suggested that we are now seeing a second generation of Internet users and a move towards the equalisation of access. This view is supported by more recent data that shows a 35% growth rate from April 2000 to April 2001 in the number of African-American households online (Pastore, 2001a), bringing the total to over 50% of all such households. Pastore also quotes research showing that home Internet access for blue-collar workers surged by 52% in the year March 2000 to March 2001. In relation to age, the 55–64 age range experienced the second largest increase in the age demographic, growing by 20% to reach 52% of all households. Averages for the US in 2001 ranged from around 51 to 68% of all households for various demographic groups. Pastore (2001b) also quotes the results of a survey showing that Hispanics and Asians in the US are now more likely to be online at home that Caucasians and African-Americans, and that the growth rate for Hispanics has been over 80% in the past two years.

The first generation users are those who were there in the early days, who transitioned from pre-WWW Internet to the WWW in the mid-1990s and who are predominantly computer-skilled, young, white, male users. The second generation users are those who have come to use the WWW as it has become a part of the fabric of their work and home life (typically in the last two or three years). The latter generation are pretty equally divided between males and females, reasonably balanced in terms of ethnic mix, are older than first generation users and do not aspire to the higher levels of technical user-skill of the earlier generation. In terms of age, the main under-represented group is now unemployed people over 50.

TEST ADMINISTRATION OVER THE INTERNET

Exercising Control

Internet technology provides the opportunity for exercising much greater control over distribution of materials and intellectual property than traditional media. It provides us with the potential for:

- control over materials—immediate updating, ensuring that everyone is using the same versions
- control over prior practice—enabling test takers to start from a level playing field
- control over test takers—authentication: knowing who is taking the test
- control over test conditions—ensuring conformity to good practice.

However, it also provides us with the freedom to reduce or remove levels of control. Sometimes this may be desirable (e.g. providing large numbers of people with open access to good guidance on career choices), sometimes it may not (e.g. giving access to test materials that should be kept secure).

Much of the concern over Internet testing relates to issues of good practice. These concerns relate to three main areas:

- Ensuring that there is adequate control over the management of the assessment process.
- Ensuring that feedback and reporting is of high quality and contained within procedures that reflect good practice in assessment.
- Controlling the quality of tests delivered over the Internet.

Managing the process of assessment is a major topic and one that illustrates both how much control we can exercise and the dangers of not matching the levels of control to the requirements of the assessment process.

Management of the Assessment Process

Testing is a process involving a number of participants, each with differing roles. The exact nature and number of participants will vary depending on the nature of the test and the reason for testing. Typically the roles include:

- the initiator or 'sponsor' of the testing process
- the person responsible for managing the process
- the test administrator
- the test taker
- the person who will provide feedback to the test taker
- third parties who will be provided with information consequent upon the testing.

In addition to involving various people playing various roles, testing follows a sequence of events:

- the tests are chosen
- the arrangements are made for who is to be tested, when and where
- the tests are administered
- the scores are derived and reports generated
- the reports are delivered to the designated recipients
- feedback is provided to the test taker and/or relevant others.

The Internet provides the ideal medium for managing both the participants and the process. For example, some systems manage the process as a project that requires certain resources, in terms of people and materials, and has a time-line with a sequence of tasks and milestones. The workflow is managed using project templates that users can configure by entering the names of the various participants, selecting the instruments to be used and setting mile-stone dates for key points in the sequence of events that make up the testing process. The process is automatically managed by assigning tasks to people and communicating with participants by automated emails and hyperlinks. The level of control that can be exercised in this way over each participant is potentially configurable by the user. In this way, for example, it is possible to ensure that only qualified test users will have access to reports that require an understanding of a particular instrument or that only qualified test adminis-trators are allowed to log test candidates onto the system.

Modes of Test Administration

Four modes of test administration have been defined (Bartram, 2001c). These modes form the basis for the guidelines on computer-based testing and the Internet developed by the ITC.

1. *Open mode.* These are conditions where there is no means of identifying the test taker and there is no human supervision. Examples of this include tests that can be accessed openly on the Internet without any requirement for test taker registration.
2. *Controlled mode.* This is similar to the open mode in that no human supervision of the test session is assumed. However, the test is only made available to known test takers. For the Internet this is controlled through the requirement for the test taker to be provided with a logon username and password.
3. *Supervised mode.* For this mode, a level of human supervision is assumed, whereby the identity of the test taker can be authenticated and test-taking conditions validated. This mode also provides a better level of control over dealing with unexpected problems or issues. For Internet testing, this mode is achieved by requiring the test administrator or proctor to log-in the candidate and to confirm that the testing was completed correctly at the end of the session.
4. *Managed mode.* This is a mode where a high level of human supervision is assumed and there is also control over the test-taking environment. For computer-based testing this is achieved through the use of dedicated testing centres. The organisation managing the testing process can define and assure the performance and specification of equipment in test centres. They can also generally exercise more control over the competence of the staff. In addition to standard 'thin-client' Internet applications, managed mode also provides the opportunity for delivering 'thick-client' applications under highly controlled conditions.

Test Session Supervision Functions

Supervision or proctoring has six functions.

1. Authenticating the identity of the test taker (i.e. establishing who is actually taking the test).
2. Establishing a positive rapport with the test taker (i.e. making sure that an appropriate climate is created for the test taking session and that the test taker is not unduly anxious).
3. Ensuring that instructions regarding standardised conditions are followed (e.g. making sure that timing conditions are adhered to, that calculators or other aids are used or not as instructed).
4. Dealing with unexpected conditions or problems that arise prior to or during the administration process (managing problems with equipment, hardware, disruptions during the test session, test taker disabilities etc).
5. Validating the test results (i.e. ensuring that the results obtained are what they appear to be, and were the product of the authenticated test taker operating unaided).
6. Ensuring that test materials are kept secure (i.e. making sure that no copies of test booklets or items are removed by the test takers).

The degree to which administration of an instrument requires the presence of a human supervisor will depend on the importance of direct supervision for each of these functions. This in turn depends on the nature and format of the test and the reasons why testing is taking place: for example, the type of test being administered (maximum versus typical performance); the format of the test (physical versus virtual); and the consequences of assessments (high versus low stakes).

One of the main reasons for requiring human supervision of testing is to manage the level of exposure that the item content has. Item generation techniques (Irvine & Kyllonen, 2002) provide us with the opportunity of developing a whole new range of tests for which this aspect of test security become less of a problem. This is a particular issue for high-stake tests where the item content needs to be re-used or where it might otherwise become known before the test session occurs. It is generally not an issue where tests of typical performance are concerned.

The management of test-taker honesty within a high-stakes assessment process is not just a matter of supervision. It is also a matter of the design of the whole process and the extent to which cheating or dishonest behaviour is likely to be detected. The assessment processes for job selection can be backed by an explicit 'honesty policy' to which candidates are asked to sign up. This is supported by the process of re-assessing, under controlled supervised conditions in the final stages of the selection process, any key competencies which formed the basis for the sift. Such agreements are used to 'click-wrap' the application. While such contracts are not legally binding or able to guarantee that the applicant has actually abided by them, they do help provide a clear set of expectations and explain that failure to abide by these conditions could have undesirable consequences.

At present we have very little hard data to show the impact of such approaches on test taking strategies. What we do know, however, is that the use of an unsupervised randomly generated numerical reasoning test during the sift stage of a recruitment procedure can dramatically improve the quality of the candidates who pass that sift (Baron et al., 2001).

Feedback and Reporting

Just as it is necessary in some conditions to ensure that there is a human test administrator or proctor present to ensure that high-stake assessments are carried out properly, so there will also be conditions where it is important to ensure that feedback is provided to a test taker by a qualified person rather than over the Internet. The question of when this is necessary is a matter of professional judgement. Generally, one can argue that in any situation where the feedback is complex and needs careful explanation face-to-face feedback should be given. An in-between option is to provide simple feedback online with a phone-in 'help-line' for people to get more in-depth feedback.

Most computer-generated test reports are designed for the test user rather than the test taker (Bartram, 1995a). Considerable care and attention needs to be given to reports that are intended to provide the sole source of feedback for the test taker.

In practice, the situations where feedback needs to be provided on a face-to-face basis will tend to be the same ones as where the assessment itself needs to be supervised. As such, providing for this is no more of a problem than it would be for traditional paper-and-pencil testing. With well designed Internet testing process-management software, the logistics of arranging for test sessions and feedback appointments are much simpler than for traditional assessment.

Test Quality

The effect on a test's psychometric properties of delivering it over the Internet must be considered. Examples of bad practice abound. For example, some people have taken timed, supervised, paper-and-pencil tests and put them onto the Internet as un-timed and unsupervised. Clearly, in such cases, one cannot regard the Internet version as the 'same' test as the original.

In general, when a test is presented in some medium other than the one in which it was developed, it is necessary to check the equivalence of the new form. In practice this is most likely to be an issue for timed ability and aptitude tests. Most research suggests that the data obtained from un-timed self-report inventories are not affected by whether the test is administered on paper or on computer (see Bartram, 1994; Bartram & Brown, 2004; Mead & Drasgow, 1993; Salgado & Moscoso, 2003).

In summary, the main concern over the use of unsupervised modes of test administration is that such administration will adversely affect validity and, therefore, utility. In addition, lack of supervision can result in the compromising of test security. This may be a critical issue for traditional ability tests, which have a fixed set of items. Once these become widely known, the test will be of little value. However, this is far less of an issue for self-report personality measures or for tests where item content is continually modified.

CONCLUSIONS

It has been argued that the Internet actually allows us to exercise far more control than we have been able to do in the past over distribution of materials, management of the assessment process and the collection of data.

The key advantage, as the medium matures, will lie in test producers and publishers being able to assume the availability and accessibility of a ubiquitous infrastructure through which to deliver new products and services. Test users and test takers will have access to a wider range of services, better matched to their needs and better supported. Test designers will be able to consider new possibilities for assessment design: real-time interactive virtual group exercises using emails or videophone conferencing; realistic in-tray tasks and so on.

The advantages of the Internet are also its dangers. Anyone can now set up a home-page and 'publish' a test. Assessment authoring systems are already available for producing and delivering simple tests and questionnaires on the Web. Dozens of 'tests' can be found that provide interesting looking reports (a quick search of the web for measures of Emotional Intelligence, for example, found more than a dozen questionnaires). However, there is typically no indication of the quality of these and the unwary user can be forgiven for failing to distinguish between serious assessment and trivia.

From the test user and test taker's points of view, it is becoming increasingly difficult to discriminate between good tests and bad. In testing, the medium is not the message, as the quality of the test is always hidden in the technical data. As a result, the emphasis placed by the major publishers on technical and ethical standards and good practice will become increasingly important.

We need to consider the implications of the new technology on standards and good practice in assessment (Bartram, 1995b, 1998, 2001a). In particular, though, we need to do this at an international level. National professional associations and national publishers can no longer operate as closed systems. The presence of international networks, globalisation of industry and communications means that testing is now an international activity and individual nations need to be prepared to work as open systems within agreed international standards frameworks.

In the next few decades we will see the availability of Internet technology with which one can create fully immersive virtual realities (sound, touch, vision and smell) for single- and multi-person assessments. The opportunities this will provide for assessment are almost without limit. However, with each new step advance in technology come associated new issues for best practice.

The work of the International Test Commission on test adaptation (Hambleton, 1994; Hambleton, Merenda & Spielberger, 2005; International Test Commission, 2001a) and test user guidelines (Bartram, 1998, 2001b; International Test Commission, 2001b) provides a valuable starting point for future developments at the international level. However, more needs to be done if standards are to keep pace with the changes in technology, and those involved in recruitment and selection procedures are to be protected from bad practice and poor assessment tools. The International Test Commission embarked on a new project in 2001 to develop guidelines for computer-based testing and testing on the Internet. The ITC Conference in Winchester in 2002 and the resulting chapters in this book have been major contributions to this development. In the time it has taken to develop this book, these guidelines have also been developed. They have been through a number of cycles of international consultation and will be published, as befits guidelines on this subject, on the International Test Commission website: *http://www.intestcom.org* by the time this chapter is published.

We are in the middle of a very exciting revolution. We need radically to review our conception of assessment as a process and to reconsider the relationships between the various stakeholders in the assessment process: test developers, test publishers, test users, test takers, consumers of test results, professional bodies and lawmakers. While the essential principles of best practice will not change, as they are independent of assessment technologies, actual standards do need to be reviewed and re-considered in terms of the relationships between virtual tests and roles in cyber-space, rather than material tests and people in real geographical space.

REFERENCES

Association of Graduate Recruiters (AGR). (2000). *Going to work on the Web: Web-based graduate recruitment* (AGR Briefing No. 11). Warwick, UK: AGR.

Baron, H., Miles, A., & Bartram, D. (2001, April). *Using online testing to reduce time-to-hire.* Paper presented at the 16th Annual Conference of the Society for Industrial and Organizational Psychology, San Diego.

Bartram, D. (1987a). The development of an automated pilot testing system for pilot selection: the MICROPAT project. *Applied Psychology: an International Review*, 36:279–298.

Bartram, D. (1987b). Future directions in Computer Based Assessment. *Bulletin of the British Psychological Society*, 40:A27.

Bartram, D. (1989). Computer-based assessment. In P. Herriot (Ed.), *Handbook of assessment in organisations*, London: Wiley.

Bartram, D. (1993). Emerging trends in computer-assisted assessment. In H. Schuler, J. L. Farr, & M. Smith (Eds.), *Personnel selection and assessment: Individual and organizational perspectives* (Chapter 17, pp. 267–288). Englewood Cliffs, NJ: Erlbaum.

Bartram, D. (1994). Computer Based Assessment. *International Review of Industrial and Organizational Psychology*, 9:31–69.

Bartram, D. (1995a). The role of computer-based test interpretation (CBTI) in occupational assessment. *International Journal of Selection and Assessment*, 3:178–185.

Bartram, D. (1995b) The development of standards for the use of psychological tests: The competence approach. *The Psychologist*, 8:219–223.

Bartram, D. (1997). Distance assessment: Psychological assessment through the Internet. *Selection Development Review*, 13:10–14.

Bartram, D. (1998). The need for international guidelines on standards for test use: A review of European and international initiatives. *European Psychologist*, 3:155–163.

Bartram, D. (2000). Internet recruitment and selection: Kissing frogs to find princes. *International Journal of Selection and Assessment*, 8:261–274.

Bartram, D. (2001a). Guidelines for test users: A review of national and international initiatives. *European Journal of Psychological Assessment*, 17:164–177.

Bartram, D. (2001b). The development of international guidelines on test use: The International Test Commission Project. *International Journal of Testing*, 1:33–53.

Bartram, D. (2001c). *The impact of the Internet on testing for recruitment, selection and development.* Keynote paper presented at the Fourth Australian Industrial and Organizational Psychology Conference, Sydney.

Bartram, D. (2002a). The Micropat pilot selection battery: Applications of generative techniques for item-based and task-based tests. In S. H. Irvine & P. Kyllonen (Eds.), *Item generation for test development* (pp. 317–338). Mahwah, NJ: Erlbaum.

Bartram, D. (2002b). Power and efficiency: expanding the scope of ability measures. *Proceedings of the BPS Occupational Psychology Conference, Blackpool* pp. 116–121.

Bartram, D. (2005). Computer-based testing and the Internet. In A. Evers, O. Smit-Voskuyl, & N. Anderson (Eds.), *The handbook of selection*. Oxford: Blackwell.

Bartram, D., & Bayliss, R. (1984). Automated testing: Past, present and future. *Journal of Occupational Psychology*, **57**:221–237.

Bartram, D., & Brown, A. (2004). Online testing: Mode of administration and the stability of OPQ32i. *International Journal of Selection and Assessment*, **12**, 278–284.

Bartram, D., & Dale, H. C. A. (1983). *Micropat Version 3: A description of the fully automated personnel selection testing system being developed for the Army Air Corps* (Ministry of Defence Technical report ERG/Y6536/83/7).

Bartram, D., Geake, A., & Gray, A. (in press) The Internet and 360-degree feedback. In M. Scherm (Ed.), *360-Grad-Beurteilungen. Diagnose und Entwicklung von Fuhrungskompetenzen*. Gottingen: Hogrefe.

Callan, A., & Geary, B. (1994). Best practice—putting practice testing to work. *Selection and Development Review*, **10**:2–4.

Drasgow, F., & Mattern, K. (2006). New tests and new items: Opportunities and issues. In D. Bartram & R. Hambleton (Eds.), *Computer-based testing and the Internet: Issues and advances*. London: Wiley.

Drasgow, F., Olson-Buchanan, J. B., & Moberg, P. J. (1999). Development of an interactive video assessment: Trials and tribulations. In F. Drasgow & J. B. Olson-Buchanan (Eds.), *Innovations in computerized assessment* (pp. 177–196). Mahwah, NJ: Erlbaum.

Edenborough, R. (1994). *Using psychometrics*. London: Kogan Page.

Electronic Recruiting Index (ERI). (2000). *2000 Electronic Recruiting Index: Performance and the emergence of the middle market*. Executive Summary. Retrieved May 27, 2005, from *http://www.interbiznet.com/2000ERI*

Fekken, G. C., & Jackson, D. N. (1988). Predicting consistent psychological test item responses: A comparison of models. *Personality and Individual Differences*, **9**:381–387.

George, M. S., & Skinner, H. A. (1990a). Using response latency to detect inaccurate responses in a computerized lifestyle assessment. *Computers in Human Behavior*, **6**:167–175.

George, M. S., & Skinner, H. A. (1990b). Innovative uses of microcomputers for measuring the accuracy of assessment questionnaires. In R. West, M. Christie & J. Weinman (Eds.), *Microcomputers, psychology and medicine* (pp. 251–262). Chichester: Wiley.

Goeters, K-M., & Lorenz, B. (2002). On the implementation of item-generation principles for the design of aptitude testing in aviation. In S. H. Irvine & P. Kyllonen (Eds.), *Item generation for test development* (pp. 339–360). Mahwah, NJ: Erlbaum.

Hambleton, R. K. (1994). Guidelines for adapting educational and psychological tests: A progress report. *European Journal of Psychological Assessment*, **10**:229–244.

Hambleton, R. K., Merenda, P., & Spielberger, C. D. (2005). *Adapting educational and psychological tests for cross-cultural assessment*. Mahwah, NJ: Erlbaum.

Hanson, M. A., Borman, W. C., Mogilka, H. J., Manning, C., & Hedge, J. W. (1999). Computerized assessment of skill for a highly technical job. In F. Drasgow & J. B. Olson-Buchanan (Eds.), *Innovations in computerized assessment* (pp. 197–220). Mahwah, NJ: Erlbaum.

Herriot, P. (1989) Selection as a social process. In M. Smith and I. T. Robertson (Eds.), *Advances in selection and assessment* (pp. 171–189). London: Wiley.

Holden, R. R., & Fekken, G. C. (1988). *Using reaction time to detect faking on a computerized inventory of psychopathology*. Paper presented at the Canadian Psychological Association Annual Convention, Montreal.

Institute of Personnel and Development (IPD). (1999). *IPD Survey Report 5: Recruitment*. London: IPD.

Ipsos (2002). *Internet use continues to climb in most markets*. Retrieved December 10, 2003, from Ipsos News Center: *http://www.ipsos-na.com/news/pressrelease.cfm?id=1690*

Irvine, S. H., & Kyllonen, P. (Eds.). (2002). *Item generation for test development*. Mahwah, NJ: Erlbaum.

International Test Commission. (2001a). *Guidelines for adapting educational and psychological tests*. Retrieved May 27, 2005, from *http://www.intestcom.org*

International Test Commission. (2001b). International guidelines on test use. *International Journal of Testing*, **1**:95–114.

Keller, J. (1996). Public access issues: An introduction. In B. Kahin & J. Keller (Eds.), *Public access to the Internet*. Cambridge, MA: MIT Press.

Kellett, D. (1991). Practice tests in occupational selection—further steps. *Guidance and Assessment Review*, **7**(5):1–3.

Lievens, F., & Harris, M. M. (2003). Research on internet recruitment and testing: Current status and future directions. In C. L. Cooper & I. T. Robertson (Eds.), *International review of industrial and organizational psychology* (Vol 18, pp. 131–165). Chichester: Wiley.

Lord, F. M. (1980). *Application of Item Response Theory to practical testing problems*. Hillsdale, NJ: Erlbaum.

Mead, A. D., & Drasgow, F. (1993). Equivalence of computerized and paper-and-pencil cognitive ability tests: A meta-analysis. *Psychological Bulletin*, **114**:449–458.

Pastore, M. (2001a). *Minority, low-income Internet use increases*. Retrieved May 17, 2001, from *http://Cyberatlas.internet.com/big_picture/demographics/article/0,,5901_768141,00.html*

Pastore, M. (2001b). *Hispanics increase PC adoption*. Retrieved February 15, 2001, from *http://Cyberatlas.internet.com/big_picture/demographics/article/0,,5901_590991,00.html*

Pastore, M. (2001c). *US share of Internet users continues to shrink, 'Hypergrowth' over*. Retrieved May 21, 2001, from *http://Cyberatlas.internet.com/big_picture/geographics/article/0,,5911_76945,00.html*

Pastore, M. (2001d). *Internet users in Asia–Pacific to surpass US users in 2005*. Retrieved May 16, 2001, from *http://Cyberatlas.internet.com/big_picture/geographics/article/0,,5911_767371,00.html*

Salgado, J. F., & Moscoso, S. (2003). Paper-and-pencil and Internet-based personality testing: Equivalence of measures. *International Journal of Selection and Assessment*, **11**:194–295.

Stanton, J. M., & Rogelberg, S. G. (2001). *Challenges and obstacles in conducting employment testing via the Internet*. Paper presented at the 16th Annual meeting of the Society for Industrial and Organizational Psychology, San Diego, CA.

Wainer, H., et al. (1990) *Computerized adaptive testing: A primer*. Hillsdale, NJ: Erlbaum.

CHAPTER 2

Model-Based Innovations in Computer-Based Testing

Wim J. van der Linden
University of Twente, The Netherlands

Though the arrival of the computer in educational and psychological testing has been a relatively recent event, it has already completely revolutionized our conception of testing. For one thing, the computer has exchanged the idea of a test item as a few lines of text for one of an item as an assignment presented to an examinee in an environment with graphics, video, application software, databases, and sound. Also, the examinee's response need no longer be a handwritten response or an ink bubble on an answer sheet. Computers can record such actions as an examinee maneuvering a cursor on the screen, clicking a hot spot, giving input to an application program, and manipulating a device with built-in sensors. At the same time, they automatically record the speed at which those actions are executed.

Though the changing of the stimulus and response formats is the most visible aspect of the computer revolution in testing, behind the scenes there are other psychometric developments aided by the great power of the computer, and these will be the primary purpose of the chapter. The key feature of these developments is that the computer allows us to apply results from psychometric modeling to testing in real time.

For example, a well known probabilistic model for the response of an examinee to a test item is the three-parameter logistic (3PL) model in item-response theory (IRT) (see, e.g., Hambleton & Swaminathan, 1985). This model defines the probability of a correct response $U_i = 1$ to item i as

$$\Pr(U_i = 1 \mid \theta) = p_i(\theta) = c_i + (1 - c_i) \frac{e^{a_i(\theta - b_i)}}{1 + e^{a_i(\theta - b_i)}} \tag{2.1}$$

Computer-Based Testing and the Internet: Issues and Advances.
Edited by D. Bartram and R. K. Hambleton. © 2006 John Wiley & Sons, Ltd.

where U_i is the response variable for item i and $\Pr(U_i = 1 \mid \theta)$ is the probability of a correct response on the item by an examinee with ability level $\theta \in [-\infty, \infty]$. In addition, parameter $b_i \in [-\infty, \infty]$ can be interpreted as the difficulty item i, parameter $a_i \in (0, \infty]$ as its discriminating power, and $c_i \in [0, 1]$ as a parameter that represents the probability of success for an examinee who guesses without any knowledge. Even for this relatively simple dichotomous response model, not too long ago the scoring of examinees by estimating the value of the ability parameter θ from their responses was a timeintensive activity. The same held for the use of its item parameters in assembling a test from a pool of items.

Nowadays, however, we are able to execute such procedures in real time. As a consequence, we can produce interim estimates of an examinee's ability at any time during the test, use these estimates in refined methods of item selection, diagnose the response behavior of an examinee while (s)he is on line, and immediately update item-parameter estimates after each item in continuous computer-based testing (van der Linden & Pashley, 2000). This is not only possible for the model in (2.1) but also for models for more involved response formats and models for response times.

The message in this chapter is that, though the new stimulus and response formats made possible by the computer have been breathtaking, the true revolution in CBT may very well be this marriage between the current computing power of PCs and recent developments in psychometric modeling. In a fortunate twist of history, computing power became plentiful and cheap in the 1990s, just when fundamental models in psychometrics had matured and become statistically tractable for use on a routine basis. Another fortunate coincidence is that the same type of modeling now helps us solve various practical problems that did not exist in the pre-computer era in testing, for example, the need to minimize the number of items that are stolen and to eliminate other forms of security breaches.

In this chapter, we will illustrate our claim by reviewing a few applications of psychometric modeling to problems in CBT. We begin with an application for computer-based tests with an adaptive format. For a description of computerized adaptive tests (CATs), see, for instance, Wainer (2000). The problem we address is how to build tests on line that are not only based on the principle of adaptation but also meet the numerous content and other statistical specifications we may have in mind. The next two applications deal with threats to test integrity and are for any type of individualized computer-based testing. In one application, we show how to build individual tests without overexposing some of the items in the pool. In the other, we use response times recorded during testing to diagnose examinee behavior on line for possible aberrances due to flaws in the test design or cheating by the examinee. The final application deals with the problem of item shortage in adaptive testing. One of the proposed solutions is item cloning, that is, generating a family of new items from an existing item or an item structure. We will discuss a psychometric model for calibration and adaptive testing from a pool with such item families.

BUILDING CATs TO LARGE NUMBERS OF CONTENT SPECIFICATIONS

A fundamental dilemma in testing is that if we knew the examinee's ability level, θ, we could easily assemble a test that would be statistically optimal, but the very reason we need a test is that the examinee's ability level is unknown.

How to assemble a test if θ were known follows directly from quantities known in IRT as the item and test information function. For the model in (2.1), Figure 2.1 gives the information functions for five items. Their curves show

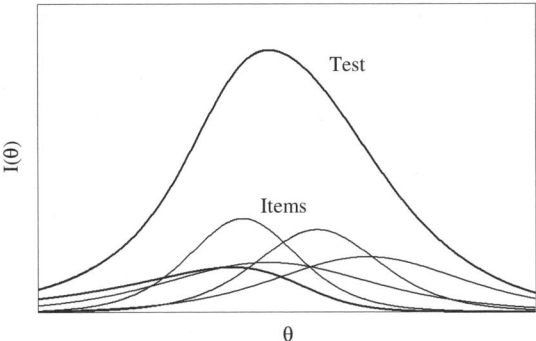

Figure 2.1   Item and test information functions for a five-item test

how much information on the unknown parameter θ the responses to these items contain. The figure also illustrates the additivity of the information functions. Let $I_i(\theta)$ be the information in the response to item i on θ and $I(\theta)$ the information in the responses all n items in the test. It holds that

$$I(\theta) = \sum_{i=1}^{n} I_i(\theta). \tag{2.2}$$

Hence, if we knew that examinee j has ability θ_j, a straightforward approach would be to pick the n items in the pool with the largest values for $I_i(\theta_j)$.

In the absence of any knowledge about the values of θ for a population of examinees, it is customary to assemble a test to have an information function that reflects a target for the entire population. For a target to be realistic, it has to compromise between the potential ability levels of the examinees. Since the introduction of CBT, however, the need to compromise has become obsolete, because the items can be selected adaptively. As already indicated, it is now possible to estimate the ability of the examinee on line. In computerized adaptive testing (CAT), the test begins with an initial ability estimate which is updated after each response by the examinee. Each subsequent item is then selected to have maximum information at the last estimate. Extensive simulation studies have shown that to reach the same level of statistical information as a fixed test adaptive tests need only some 40–50% of the items.

Application of the statistical principle of adaptation is not enough to build a CAT though. Each test has also to be built according to an (often extensive) set of content specifications. In fact, when the first large-scale testing programs became adaptive in the 1990s, their developers were actually after a shorter test with exactly the same look and feel as the previous paper-and-pencil version of the test. The first attempts to have the computer produce such tests were based on heuristic modifications of the basic CAT algorithm. For example, instead of selecting the best items from the entire pool, the idea was to rotate the selection of the items over sections of the pool with items that shared a common content attribute. However, for tests with larger sets of content specifications, such approaches lead to patchwork algorithms with *ad hoc* procedures and decisions that do not guarantee optimal results.

A more flexible approach is to *model* the adaptive test assembly problem as an optimization problem with each test specification represented by an explicit constraint. This modeling can easily be done using 0–1 decision variables for the items. We first illustrate the idea for a fixed test and a known ability θ, and then extend the formulation to adaptive tests.

Let $i = 1, \ldots, I$ denote the items in the pool. Decision variables x_i are defined to take the value units if item i is selected in the test and the value zero if it remains in the pool. The objective is to maximize the information in the test at ability level θ. The additional specifications are modeled as constraints. We use $V_g, g = 1, \ldots, G$, as a generic symbol to denote subsets of items that share a categorical attribute in the test specifications. Examples of categorical attributes are item content and format. These attributes are categorical in that their values are unordered and they classify the item pool into subsets of items with the same value. In addition, we use q_i as a generic symbol for the value of item i on a quantitative attribute. Examples of quantitative attributes are word counts, expected response times and statistical parameters. These attributes are quantitative because they take numerical values.

A useful representation of a test assembly problem is

$$\text{maximize} \sum_{i=1}^{I} I_i(\theta) x_i \tag{2.3}$$

subject to

$$\sum_{i=1}^{I} x_i = n \tag{2.4}$$

$$\sum_{i \in V_g} x_i \le n_g^{(\text{max})} \quad g = 1, \ldots, G \tag{2.5}$$

$$\sum_{i \in V_g} x_i \ge n_g^{(\text{min})} \quad g = 1, \ldots, G \tag{2.6}$$

$$\sum_{i=1}^{I} q_i x_i \le b_q^{(\text{max})} \tag{2.7}$$

$$\sum_{i=1}^{I} q_i x_i \ge b_q^{(\text{min})} \tag{2.8}$$

$$x_i \in \{0, 1\} \quad i = 1, \ldots, I. \tag{2.9}$$

The objective function maximizes the test information at the examinee's true ability value. The first constraint defines the test length. The next two sets of constraints require the number of items from category set V_g to be between a maximum number $n_g^{(max)}$ and minimum number $n_g^{(min)}$. Likewise, the next two constraints require the sum of values of quantitative attribute q_i to be between upper bound $b_q^{(max)}$ and lower bound $b_q^{(min)}$. The final set of constraints defines the range of the decision variables.

The model in (2.3)–(2.9) is only a restricted example of types of model that are possible. For more realistic models with a much larger selection of types of attribute and specification that can be formulated as objective functions and constraints, see the work of van der Linden (2005). Because the model is linear in its variables, it belongs to the class of 0–1 linear programming (LP) models. In practice, it is not unusual to have models for a pool of 500–1,000 items with hundreds of constraints needed to represent existing test specifications. Using a commercial solver for these problems, for example, the one in the software package CPLEX 9.0 (ILOG, Inc., 2003), such models can easily be solved for optimal values of the variables $x_1, \ldots, x_I$, which identify the best test in the pool.

Shadow-Test Approach

In CAT, the items are selected one at a time, and each next item has to have maximum information at the current interim estimate of θ. An effective way to solve the assembly model for adaptive tests is through a shadow-test approach (van der Linden, 2000, 2005, chapter 9; van der Linden & Reese, 1998). In this approach, before the selection of each item, the model in (2.3)–(2.9) is solved for a full-size fixed test (known as a shadow test) at the current ability estimate with the decision variables of the items already administered fixed at the value units. Each shadow test is required to meet all constraints. The CAT algorithm then picks the optimal item at the ability estimate from the free items in the shadow test for administration, upon which the remaining items are returned to the pool and the procedure is repeated.

More specifically, the steps of item selection are as follows.

Step 1. Choose the initial ability estimate.
Step 2. Assemble a shadow test with maximum information at the current ability estimate that meets all constraints.
Step 3. Administer the free item in the shadow test with maximum information.
Step 4. Use the response to update the ability estimate.
Step 5. Add the constraint $x_i = 1$ to the model for the item that has been administered.
Step 6. Repeat steps 2–5.

The addition of the constraint in step 5 guarantees that the items already administered are always in the test. Therefore, the model automatically takes

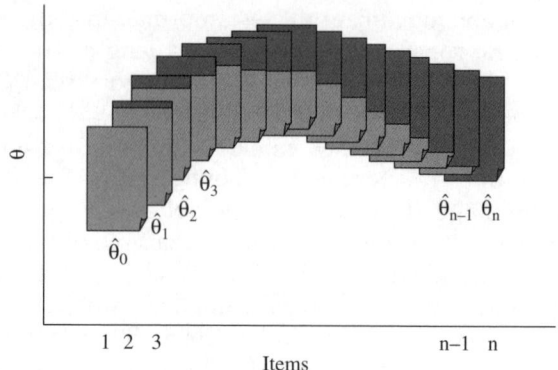

Figure 2.2   Graphical representation of the shadow-test approach in CAT

the attributes of this item into account when the next shadow test is required
to meet the constraints. A graphical illustration of the shadow-test approach is
given in Figure 2.2. The darker portion of each shadow test represents the
items already administered. The vertical dimension represents the size of
ability estimates during the test; an increase or decrease in the height of a new
shadow test shows an increase or decrease in the ability estimate as the result
of a correct or incorrect answer.

Because each shadow test meets the constraints, the set of items that is
administered adaptive test automatically meets them. Likewise, because each
shadow test has maximum information at its ability estimate and the item that
is administered at the estimate is always the best free item available, the
adaptive test is maximally informative. Figure 2.3 shows the mean-squared
error (MSE) for 20- and 30-item adaptive versions of the Law School Admission Test (LSAT) found in a simulation study with a pool of 753 items. In this

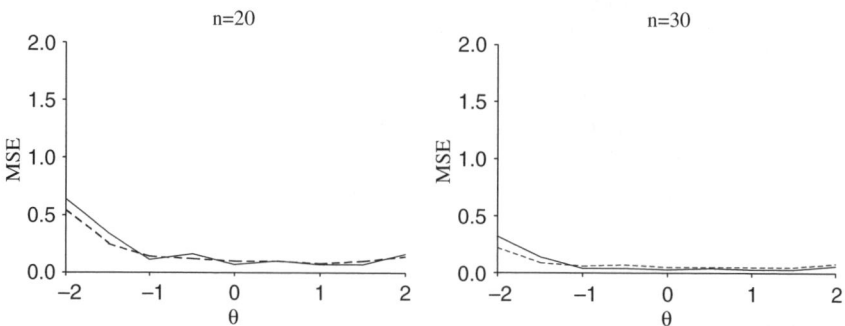

Figure 2.3   Mean-squared error (MSE) functions for the ability estimator in an
adaptive test without (dashed line) and with 433 content constraints (solid line) (left
panel, $n = 20$; right panel, $n = 30$)

study, we compared the shadow-test approach with CAT without any content constraints as a baseline. The addition of the 433 constraints needed to model the content specifications of the LSAT did not have any noticeable impact on the estimation error.

The time for a commercial integer solver to find a shadow test of realistic size is a split second. This is possible because each shadow test can be calculated using the previous test as initial solution. The most important advantage of the shadow approach is that it can deal with any type of content specification that can be applied formulated as a constraint for a fixed test. If a testing program becomes adaptive, all existing test specifications for its previous paper-and-pencil version can thus be continued automatically.

CONTROLLING ITEM EXPOSURE

One of the attractive features of CBT is the possibility to offer examinees continuous opportunity to take the test. The first experiments with continuous testing, however, led to new types of cheating by the examinees. Instead of attempts to copy answers from each other, some of the examinees conspired and tried to memorize and share the items in the pool that was used. An effective measure against this behavior is to reduce the exposure of the items by building a random component in their selection. We discuss this problem for CBT with an adaptive format, but the same line of defense is possible for CBT with a linear test, for example, in so-called linear on-the-fly testing (LOFT).

Suppose the task is to keep the probability of an item being administered below a certain level. Let A_i be the event of item i being administered and r_{max} the maximum level for this probability. That is, for the items in the pool it is required that

$$P(A_i) \leq r_{max}. \tag{2.10}$$

A standard method of item-exposure control in CAT is the one introduced by Sympson and Hetter (1985). In their method, the CAT algorithm selects the item and then executes a probability experiment to decide whether the item is actually administered or removed from the pool and another item is selected. The exposure rates for the pool are controlled by the (conditional) probabilities with which the selected items are administered. The values of the probabilities are found through a series of CAT simulations in which the computer selects the items and generates the response for the examinees. If the exposure rates of the items appear to be too high, their conditional probabilities of administration are lowered in the next simulation. Because of the dependences between all these parameters, this process is time intensive. If the exposure rates are controlled conditionally on a selection of θ levels (Stocking & Lewis, 1998, 2000), typically we have to run more than 100 CAT simulations before the exposure rates settle below a target value.

Again, a more practical approach appears to *model* the problem more carefully first and then use the results to formulate a solution. We will show this and discuss an alternative method of item-exposure control that is based on the idea of controlling for item exposure not each time after an item is selected but before an examinee takes the test. The decisions to be made are which items in the pool are eligible for the examinee. If an item remains eligible it is available for selection and administration by the CAT algorithm for the examinee; if not, it becomes inactive.

Ineligibility Constraints

A natural way to implement item-eligibility decisions is through the shadow-test approach in the preceding section. The decision of item i being ineligible for the current examinee implies the addition of the following simple constraint in the model in (2.3)–(2.9):

$$x_i = 0. \tag{2.11}$$

If item i remains eligible, no ineligibility constraint is added to the model.

The idea is to make these constraints probabilistic, that is, impose them with a certain probability for each item in the pool. The probabilities are chosen to be adaptive; that is, as we will show below, they are updated to a larger value if an item tends to be exposed too frequently and to a lower value otherwise.

For a real-life CAT program, the number of items that need control is invariably small. It is only the items with the largest value of their information function over a certain range of abilities that tend to be overexposed. The probability of ineligibility will therefore be negligible for the majority of the items. Nevertheless, in principle, it is possible that too many ineligibility constraints are imposed for an occasional examinee and the model becomes infeasible, that is, has no solution left. In the empirical study reported below, this never happened, but for the sake of completeness we will consider the possibility of infeasibility in our derivation of the probabilities of eligibility. Our assumption is that if infeasibility does happen, all ineligibility constraints are removed from the model for the examinee, and the shadow test is calculated for this relaxed model. The adaptive nature of the probabilistic experiment our model automatically corrects for an occasional extra exposure of an item due to this measure later in the testing process.

Derivation of Probabilities of Item Eligibility

The process of item administration for a given pool of items and population of examinees is determined by the probabilities of four different events for a random examinee. The events are (1) event E_i of item i being eligible for the examinee, (2) event F of the shadow test remaining feasible after all eligibility constraints have been added to the model for the examinee, (3) event S_i of item i being selected for the examinee, and (4) event A_i of item i being administered to the examinee. We will use a bar over the symbols of these events to denote a complementary event. For example, the event of infeasibility, (and hence of removing the ineligibility constraints from the model) is denoted as $\overline{F}$.

For these four events it holds generally that an item can be administered only if it is selected. Likewise, it can be selected only if it is eligible or all ineligibility constraints have been removed from the model because of infeasibility. In set-theory notation, it thus holds that

$$A_i \subset S_i \subset \{E_i \cup \overline{F}\}. \tag{2.12}$$

For the probabilities of the four events it follows that

$$P(A_i) = P(A_i \mid S_i)P(S_i \mid E_i \cup \overline{F})P(E_i \cup \overline{F}). \tag{2.13}$$

However, the first two factors in the right side simplify as follows:

$$P(A_i \mid S_i)P(S_i \mid E_i \cup \overline{F}) = P(A_i \mid E_i \cup \overline{F}).$$

Therefore, the probability of administering item i can be written as

$$P(A_i) = P(A_i \mid E_i \cup \overline{F})P(E_i \cup \overline{F}). \tag{2.14}$$

Substituting this expression for $P(A_i)$ into the one with the upper bound in (2.10) shows that this upper bound is always met if

$$P(E_i \cup \overline{F}) \leq \frac{r_{\max}}{P(A_i \mid E_i \cup \overline{F})}. \tag{2.15}$$

This inequality does not impose any direct constraint on the probabilities of item eligibility $P(E_i)$, but making a very mild assumption on the (unlikely) event of infeasibility and following the derivation by van der Linden and Veldkamp (2004) it can be shown that the following constraint should be imposed:

$$P(E_i) \leq 1 - \frac{1}{P(F)} + \frac{r_{\max}P(E_i \cup \overline{F})}{P(A_i)P(F)}, \qquad P(A_i) > 0, \qquad P(F) > 0, \tag{2.16}$$

with $P^{(j)}(A_i) > 0$ and $P^{(j)}(F) > 0$.

Thus, if we want to keep the probabilities of item administration $P(A_i)$ below a maximum $r_{\max}$, all we have to do is keep the probabilities of item eligibility below the upper bound in (2.16).

Adaptive Property of Probabilities

The upper bound in (2.16) can be maintained in an adaptive way. The adaptation is at the level of the individual examinees. To show the procedure, we assume that j examinees have been tested. For the last examinee we had a probability of item administration equal to $P^{(j)}(A_i)$, a probability of feasibility equal to $P^{(j)}(F)$, and a probability of item i being available for selection equal to $P^{(j)}(E_i \cup F)$. For examinee $j+1$ the update of the probabilities of item eligibility is given by

$$P^{(j+1)}(E_i) = 1 - \frac{1}{P^{(j)}(F)} + \frac{r_{\max} P^{(j)}(E_i \cup \overline{F})}{P^{(j)}(A_i) P^{(j)}(F)}. \tag{2.17}$$

To show why this update is adaptive with respect to the targets $r_{\max}$, van der Linden and Veldkamp (2004) show that

$$\begin{aligned}
P^{(j+1)}(E_i) &< P^{(j)}(E_i) && \text{if} \quad P^{(j)}(A_i) > r_{\max} \\
P^{(j+1)}(E_i) &= P^{(j)}(E_i) && \text{if} \quad P^{(j)}(A_i) = r_{\max} \\
P^{(j+1)}(E_i) &> P^{(j)}(E_i) && \text{if} \quad P^{(j)}(A_i) < r_{\max}.
\end{aligned} \tag{2.18}$$

Thus, if the probability of eligibility of item i was actually larger than $r_{\max}$ for examinee j, it immediately goes down for examinee $j+1$. If it is exactly at the target, no change is introduced. If it is below the target, the probability of eligibility is actually relaxed.

Implementing the Method

All we need to do to implement the method is to record the events E_i, A_i, and F during the testing program. The probabilities can then be estimated using the counts of these events. For example, if $\alpha_i^{(j)}$ is the count of the events of item i being administrated through examinee j, the probability $P^{(j)}(A_i)$ in (2.16) is simply estimated as

$$\widehat{P}^{(j)}(A_i) = \frac{\alpha_i^{(j)}}{j}. \tag{2.19}$$

The decision to add an ineligibility constraint for item i to the model for the shadow test is based on experiment with the probabilities in (2.16) based on these estimates. Alternatively, we can base the experiment on probabilities that have been smoothed over a time window of, say, 100 examinees. For these smoothed estimates, see the work of van der Linden and Veldkamp (2004).

Unlike the Sympson–Hetter method of item-exposure control, no time intensive computer simulations are needed to adjust control parameters to correct levels before the method can be used in operational testing. The method can immediately be used for a new item pool in a CAT program; the mechanism in (2.18) then automatically adapts the probabilities of item eligibility to their optimal level and keeps them at these levels during the rest of the test. Also, if items have to be removed from the pool or added to it, the method automatically settles at new optimal levels. The only conditions that should be avoided are estimates $\widehat{P}^{(j)}(A_i) = 0$ and $\widehat{P}^{(j)}(F) = 0$; if this happens, $\widehat{P}^{(j+1)}(E_i)$ in (2.19) becomes undefined. A simple way to avoid this condition is to set $\widehat{P}^{(j+1)}(E_i) = 1$ at the begin of a new application until both the counts of events A_i and F are no longer equal to zero.

Figure 2.4 shows the actual item-exposure rates of all items in two CAT simulations for the same pool of 753 items from the LSAT and the same set of

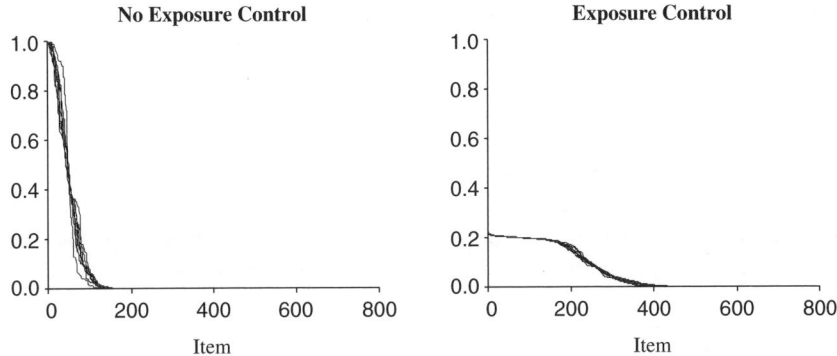

Figure 2.4   Actual item-exposure rates for an adaptive test without (left panel) and with exposure control (right panel) conditional on seven different ability levels

contest specifications as for the simulations with the shadow-test approach reported in Figure 2.3. One simulation was without any exposure control; in the other we used a conditional version of the method of exposure control based on the ineligibility constraints discussed in this section. We controlled the exposure rates at seven different ability levels, $\theta = -2.0, 1.5, \ldots, 2.0$. For each of these levels the target value was set at 0.20. As the results show, for the condition without control, at each level some 10–12% of the items had larger exposure rates than permitted, whereas in the condition with control all items had correct exposure rates (except for minor random variation due to remaining error in the probabilities of eligibility for the first items).

DETECTION OF CHEATING

Even if a CBT program uses an effective exposure-control method, it may still be prudent to have routine checks for possible remaining irregularities during testing. For an IRT model such as the one in (2.1), these checks take the form of person-fit analysis, that is, checks for individual examinees with unexpected responses in their score vector. For example, a correct response on a difficult item for an individual of low ability may point to an item known before the test, or to copying of the response from someone else. For a review of the available statistical techniques for detecting unexpected responses, see Meijer and Sijtsma (1995).

A common feature of all these techniques, however, is the lower statistical power of detecting cheating than desirable due to the binary nature of the responses. For a well-designed test with the difficulties of the items near the true ability of the examinee, the probability of a correct response approximates 0.50. As a consequence, correct and incorrect responses become equally probable, and any statistical test of cheating tends to lose its power entirely. This result is particularly likely for adaptive testing, where the difficulty of the items is adapted to the examinee's ability level.

It seems therefore attractive to look for other potential sources of information on examinee behavior that could be diagnosed for possible irregularities. An obvious source are the response times by the examinees, which are recorded automatically recorded in CBT. These times are continuous and not binary as are the responses themselves. Also, if the test is assembled to have maximum information at the examinee's estimated or anticipated ability level, this selection criterion does not involve any detriment to the power of a test for diagnosing response behavior based on response times.

Lognormal Model for Response Times

The approach we follow is analogous to the one typical of a statistical test based on the responses only. That is, analogous to (2.1) we model the response times by an examinee on an item by a probability distribution with examinee and item parameters, estimate the item parameters during pretesting and check the model for its validity, estimate the examinee's speed, predict the times we expect the examinee to spend on the items, and use a statistical test to determine whether the actual times deviate too much from the prediction. Of course, to have a convincing proof of cheating, we must have such additional evidence as reports by test proctors, seating plan or material confiscated during the test.

As an example, suppose that we have evidence that an examinee might be part of a network that tries to memorize items in a testing program. A statistical test on item preknowledge would then check this examinee for the combination of correct responses on items for which this person has low probability of success and response times that are much shorted than expected given this person's ability and speed estimates.

A useful response-time model is the lognormal model, which models the logarithm of the response time as a normal distribution. The logarithmic transformation allows for the typically skewness in response-time distributions;

because time is on a non-negative scale, its distribution tends to have a short lower tail and a longer upper tail. Lognormal distributions for response times have been applied used successfully by Schnipke and Scrams (1997), Thissen (1982), van der Linden, Scrams, and Schnipke (1999), van der Linden and van Krimpen-Stoop (2003). We will use a parameterization for this distribution similar to the one for the two-parameter logistic version of the response model in (2.1) proposed by van der Linden (in press).

Let T_{ij} denote the response time by examinee $j = 1, \ldots, J$ on item $i = 1, \ldots, I$. The proposed model for the distribution of T_{ij} is

$$f(t_{ij}; \tau_j, \alpha_i, \beta_i) = \frac{\alpha_i}{t_{ij}\sqrt{2\pi}} \exp\left\{-\frac{1}{2}[\alpha_i(\ln t_{ij} - (\beta_i - \tau_j))]^2\right\} \qquad (2.20)$$

which is the probability density for the normal distribution, with $\ln t_{ij}$ substituted for t_{ij} on the original scale (e.g. time measured in seconds).

The model has an parameter τ_j which represents the speed at which this examinee j responds to the items in the test. A larger value of τ_j implies a larger probability for a shorter time. In addition, the model has two para-meters, β_i and α_i, which parallel the item difficulty and discrimination parameters in (2.1). Parameter β_i represents the amount of time item i tends to require from the examinees. The larger this parameter, the larger the amount of time each examinee tends to spend on the item. It is therefore appropriate to call β_i the time-intensity parameter for item i. Parameter α_i can be interpreted as a discrimination parameter. A larger value for α_i means less dispersion for the response-time distribution of each examinee on item i, and hence better discrimination by the item between the distributions of two persons with levels of speed slightly above and below β_i. The model in (2.20) does not have the equivalent of a guessing parameter; it does not need to have one because response times have a natural lower limit at zero.

The scale for parameters τ_j and β_i in the model is not yet determined; an increase in the former can always be compensated by an increase in the latter. We remove this indeterminacy by imposing the following identifiability constraint:

$$\sum_{j=1}^{N} \tau_j = 0 \qquad (2.21)$$

where N is the number of examinees in the analysis. This constraint centers the values of the time-intensity parameters for the items, β_i, at the average response time of the examinees and items in the data set. For more details on estimating the parameters in this model and testing its validity, we refer to the work of van der Linden (in press). This reference also reports a study of the model for a data set from the adaptive version of a test in the Armed Services Vocational Aptitude Battery (ASVAB), which showed perfect fit of the items to the model.

Use of Response Times

It is easy to estimate the item parameters in the response model in (2.20) from the times recorded during the pretesting of the items as part of their usual calibration. If item parameters β_i and α_i can be treated as known as the result of this calibration, it becomes quite easy to estimate the examinees' speed parameters τ_j during the test. For example, after n items the maximum likelihood (ML) of this parameter on the scale defined by the identifiability constraint in (2.21),

$$\widehat{\tau}_j = \sum_{i=1}^{n} (\beta_i - \ln t_{ij})/n. \qquad (2.22)$$

This estimate can be viewed as the actual logtimes by the examinee on the items given to this person corrected for the time intensity of the items. Because of this correction, these estimates of examinees who received different items are automatically on the same scale.

To detect irregularities in testing, we can built up an estimate of τ_j during the test. Because all other time parameters are known for the items in the pool, this estimate translates immediately into estimates of the entire response time distributions in (2.20) for the examinee on these items. It is therefore easy to check the reasonableness of his/her actual times against these distributions.

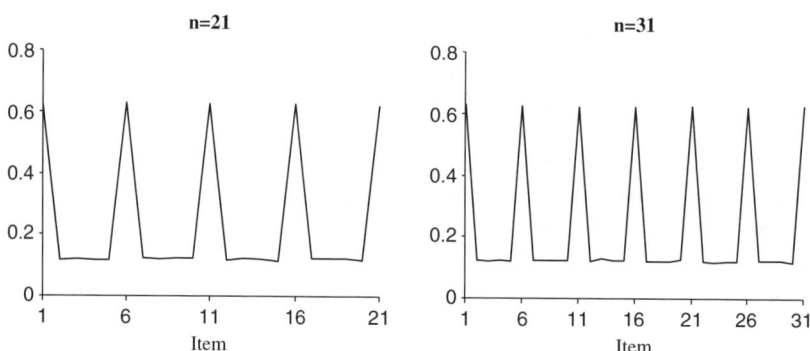

Figure 2.5 Hit rates (every sixth item) and false alarm rates (other items) for a Bayesian test of item preknowledge using the response times in an adaptive test with $n = 21$ items (left panel) and $n = 31$ items (right panel) ($\alpha = 0.05$)

Figure 2.5 shows the results for a more sophisticated Bayesian version of this test based on the posterior predictive distributions for the examinee on the items in the test (van der Linden & van Krimpen-Stoop, 2003). The left panel is for a test of 21 items, where each of the examinees was assumed to have preknowledge of every sixth item. The panel shows the hit rates (= proportion of times the statistical test identified the item as compromised) and the false alarm rates for two different effect sizes (= reduction of response time due to item preknowledge). Both test were executed at a significance level of $\alpha = 0.05$. The left panel was a replication of this study for a longer test (31 items). These hit rates were much larger than the rates for a test based on the (binary) responses by these examinees; in this study the curves for this test actually showed no power at all. As the two panels show, the higher hit rates were obtained at the costs of false-alarm rates larger than nominal. In a practical application, the significance level has to be chosen at a level that guarantees the desired false-alarm rate for the test; for these and other details, see the work of van der Linden and van Krimpen-Stoop (2003).

CBT WITH ITEM CLONING

A critical factor in the costs of running a CBT program is item writing and pretesting. For a low-stake program, such as for the placement of students in a curriculum, the main costs are incurred when setting up the program. Once the item pool has been assembled, it can remain in use for as long as the domain measured by the test remains unchanged. However, for high-stake programs, item pools have to be replaced as soon as the number of administrations considered to be dangerous has been reached for some of the items.

One of the potentially powerful solutions to the problem of periodical item pool replacement is application of techniques of item cloning. This ideas has been pioneered early in work by, for example, Bormuth (1970), Hively, Patterson, and Page (1968) and Osburn (1968). A more recent review can be found in the work of Irvine and Kyllonen (2002).

Several procedures for item cloning have been proposed. Some of these procedures are based on an item form or item template, with placeholders for the elements for which substitution sets are available. Each combination of substitutions defines a new item. Other procedures apply the idea of cloning more literally. They take an exemplary item and use transformation rules to turn it into a set of new items. These rules can be linguistic or rules defined on a formal representation of the item.

From a practical point of view, an important question is whether items in a family generated from the same form or parent have comparable statistical characteristics. If they were statistically identical, they would have identical values for the item parameters in the 3PL response model in (2.1), and it would be sufficient to pretest one item from every family. The savings in the efforts of item pretest and calibration would then be enormous.

The empirical literature on this issue is not ample. The types of item-cloning technique that have been investigated showed small within-family variability, but not small enough to justify the assumption of identical parameter values for items in the same family. This finding seems to suggest that although item cloning leads to the desired reduction in the costs of item writing, all items still have to be pretested to estimate their parameter values.

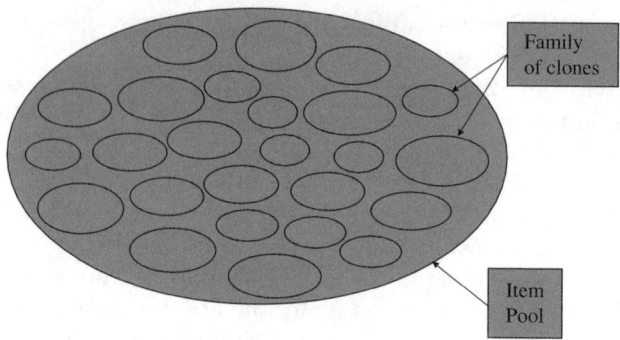

Figure 2.6 Venn diagram of a pool of cloned items, with the size of the sets representing the variability of the item parameters

Glas and van der Linden (2003) show that the second part of this conclusion is not necessary, provided we model the situation appropriately. Their model is based on two-stage (or stratified) selection of a test from a pool of cloned items. The steps are (1) selection of the families of items in the pool from which an item is to be administered, and (2) random sampling of an items from each selected family. A graphical representation of the selection process is given by the Venn diagram in Figure 2.6. The selection of the families is assumed to be based on a statistical criterion; how this can be done is discussed below. However, it is important that the selection of the items from the families is random; the model in the next section is based on this assumption

In the hypothetical case depicted in Figure 2.6, we have much more variability between than within the families. Intuitively, the proportion of the total variability that is between the families is an upper bound to the gain in the precision of ability estimation that can be made by optimizing the first step in the item selection procedure using a statistical criterion. The proportion that is within the families determines the loss in precision due to random item sampling in the second step.

Two-Level Model

The proposed item-selection procedure suggests a two-level IRT model. At the first level, each of the individual items in each family is represented by a regular response model, such as the 3PL model in (2.1). At the second level, the distribution of the item parameters in each family is modeled. These distributions are allowed to vary across families.

Specifically, suppose we have a pool with families $p = 1, \ldots, P$ and individual items $i_p = 1, \ldots, I_p$ for family p. The first-level model is the 3PL model in (2.1), which describes the probability of success on item i_p as a function of ability level θ and the item parameters. For brevity, we denote the parameters as a vector $\xi_{i_p} = (a_{i_p}, b_{i_p}, c_{i_p})$. The distribution of the responses of examinee j to item i_p from family is thus determined by the probabilities

$$\Pr(U_{i_p j} = 1) = p(\theta_j; \xi_{i_p})$$
(2.23)

given in (2.1).

The second-level model describes the distribution of the parameters ξ_{i_p} by a separate trivariate normal distribution for each family p

$$\xi_{i_p} \sim MVN(\mu_p, \Sigma_p),$$
(2.24)

where μ_p and Σ_p are the vector with the mean values of the item parameters and their covariance matrix in family p, respectively. Observe again that we have a different normal distribution of the item parameters for each family. This property allows us to deal with the facts that some item families are more difficult or discriminating on average than others, have less variability in their values for the difficulty or guessing parameter, and so on.

Item-pool calibration now takes the form of estimating the parameters μ_p and Σ_p of each family in the pool. These parameters are estimated from the response data of examinees to items randomly sampled from the families. Procedures for marginal maximum likelihood estimation of the parameters are given by Glas and van der Linden (2003); for more informative Bayesian estimation procedures, see Glas and van der Linden (in press).

Selection of Families of Items

It is obvious that the selection of an entire item family for a test cannot be based on the information function for a single item defined in (2.2), but because the actual items in the test are drawn randomly from the families selected it makes sense to select the family using the average of the information functions of the items in it. Adapting our notation to the case of families of items, the information function for item i_p in family p, with vector of item parameters ξ_{i_p}, is denoted as

$$I_{i_p}(\theta; \xi_{i_p}).$$
(2.25)

The expectation or average of this information function over the item parameters in family p is

$$I_p(\theta) = \int I_{i_p}(\theta; \xi_{i_p}) p(\xi_p | \mu_p, \Sigma_p) \mathrm{d}\xi_p.$$
(2.26)

If the test administered by the computer is fixed, it can be assembled optimally from the pool using a test assembly model such as the one in (2.3)–(2.9). The model then has to be formulated at the level of the families rather than the individual items. That is, we then define decision variables x_p, which take the value units if an item is sampled from family p and the value zero if no item is sampled. In addition, we use n_p to denote the number of items to be sampled from family p if it is selected. The only changes necessary in the model in (2.3)–(2.9) are

(1) replacing x_i by x_p, with $p = 1, \ldots, P$,
(2) reformulating the objective function in (3) as

$$\text{maximize} \sum_{i=p}^{P} I_p(\theta) x_p \tag{2.27}$$

with $I_p(\theta)$ the family information function in (2.26), and
(3) reformulating the constraint in the test length in (2.4) as

$$\sum_{i=p}^{P} n_p x_p = n. \tag{2.28}$$

If the test is to be administered in an adaptive mode, we simply use this reformulated test assembly model as the model for the shadow test in the CAT algorithm depicted in Figure 2.2.

The effect of the approach to calibration of cloned items on the errors in ability estimation in CAT was studied empirically by Glas and van der Linden (2003). Their study showed a small loss of precision of the ability estimates due to the random sampling of the items in the second stage of the two-stage selection procedure relative to the case where all items were calibrated individually, particularly towards the ends of the ability scale. This loss can always be compensated by increasing the length of the CAT somewhat. Given the potentially large numbers of items available, the increase is the small price that has to be paid for a huge reduction in item writing and pretesting if test items are cloned rather than written and pretested individually.

CONCLUSION

The arrival of computers in educational and psychological testing has had a deep impact on the appearance of modern test items and the response modes possible in educational and psychological itesting. As a result, we now have an enormous reservoir of types of item and response mode that can be used to increase the validity of our measurements. At the same time, the use of computers in testing has enabled us to use their gigantic power to work operationally with the models and procedures necessary to score examinees taking different items on the same scale, for on-line assembly of tests in a fixed or adaptive format, to increase the security of the item pools and to reduce the costs of item writing and pretesting. It was the purpose of this chapter to illustrates some of these models and procedures.

It is not our opinion that most of the challenges introduced by the computer have already been met. We are at the beginning of a new era in testing, and exciting times are ahead of us. To mention just one formidable new challenge: before too long we expect large portions of the tests to have test items that are dynamic and take the form of simulations or games with stimuli changing as a function of the examinee's responses. This format is particularly appropriate for measuring professional knowledge and skills in licensing and certification testing. The question of how to infer scores from examinee responses in such a dynamic environment is largely unexplored and no doubt requires more complicated psychometric modeling than the examples in this chapter.

REFERENCES

Bormuth, J. R. (1968). *On the theory of achievement test items*. Chicago, IL: University of Chicago Press.

Glas, C. A. W., & van der Linden, W. J. (2003). Computerized adaptive testing with item clones. *Applied Psychological Measurement*, 27:247–261.

Glas, C. A. W., & van der Linden, W. J. (in press). Modeling item parameter variability in item response models. *Psychometrika*.

Hambleton, R. K., & Swaminathan, H. (1985). *Item response theory: Principles and applications*. Boston, MA: Kluwer–Nijhoff.

Hively, W., Patterson, H. L., & Page, S. J. H. (1968). A 'universe-defined' system for arithmetic achievement test items. *Journal of Educational Measurement*, 5:275–290.

ILOG, Inc. (2003). *CPLEX 9.0* [Computer program and manual]. Incline Village, NV: ILOG.

Irvine, S. H., & Kyllonen, P. C. (Eds.). (2002). *Item generation for test development*. Mahwah, NJ: Elbaum.

Meijer, R. R., & Sijtsma, K. (1995). Detection of aberrant item response patterns: A review of recent developments. *Applied Measurement in Education*, 8:261–272.

Osburn, H. (1968). Item sampling for achievement testing. *Educational and Psychological Measurement*, 28:95–104.

Schnipke, D. L., & Scrams, D. J. (1997). *Representing response time information in item banks* (LSAC Computerized Testing Report No. 97-09). Newtown, PA: Law School Admission Council.

Stocking, M. L., & Lewis, C. (1998). Controlling item exposure conditional on ability in computerized adaptive testing. *Journal of Educational and Behavioral Statistics*, 23:57–75.

Stocking, M. L., & Lewis, C. (2000). Methods of controlling the exposure of items in CAT. In W. J. van der Linden & C. A. W. Glas (Eds.), *Computerized adaptive testing: Theory and practice* (pp. 163–182). Boston, MA: Kluwer.

Sympson, J. B., & Hetter, R. D. (1985, October). Controlling item-exposure rates in computerized adaptive testing. *Proceedings of the 27th annual meeting of the Military Testing Association* (pp. 973–977). San Diego, CA: Navy Personnel Research and Development Center.

Thissen, D. (1982). Timed testing: An approach using item response theory. In D. J. Weiss (Ed.), *New horizons in testing: Latent trait theory and computerized adaptive testing* (pp. 180–203). New York: Academic.

van der Linden, W. J. (2000). Constrained adaptive testing with shadow tests. In W. J. van der Linden & C. A. W. Glas (Eds.), *Computerized adaptive testing: Theory and practice* (pp. 27–52). Boston, MA: Kluwer.

van der Linden, W. J. (2005). *Linear models for optimal test design*. New York: Springer.

van der Linden, W. J. (in press). A lognormal for response times on test items. *Journal of Educational and Behavioral Statistics*.

van der Linden, W. J., & Pashley, P. J. (2000). Item selection and ability estimation in adaptive testing. In W. J. van der Linden & C. A. W. Glas (Eds.), *Computerized adaptive testing: Theory and practice* (pp. 1–25). Boston, MA: Kluwer.

van der Linden, W. J., & Reese, L. M. (1998). A model for optimal constrained adaptive testing. *Applied Psychological Measurement*, 22:259–270.

van der Linden, W. J., Scrams, D. J., & Schnipke, D. L. (1999). Using response-time constraints to control for speededness in computerized adaptive testing. *Applied Psychological Measurement*, 23:195–210.

van der Linden, W. J., & van Krimpen-Stoop, E. M. L. A. (2003). Using response times to detect aberrant response patterns in computerized adaptive testing. *Psychometrika*, 68:251–265.

van der Linden, W. J., & Veldkamp, B. P. (2004). Constraining item exposure in computerized adaptive testing with shadow tests. *Journal of Educational and Behavioral Statistics*, 29:273–291.

Wainer, H. (2000). *Computerized adaptive testing: A primer*. Hillsdale, NJ: Erlbaum.

CHAPTER 3

New Tests and New Items: Opportunities and Issues

Fritz Drasgow and Krista Mattern
University of Illinois at Urbana-Champaign, USA

The technological advances of the last forty years, specifically the advent of the computer and its remarkable improvement in capacity and functionality, have revolutionized almost every aspect of psychological testing and assessment. Before the existence of such technology, tests were restricted in numerous aspects such as the test medium, test and item format, and construct assessed. For example, traditional multiple-choice tests are limited in that they are administered via paper and pencil with all test-takers required to answer the same items in the same order, regardless of their performance on previous items. Furthermore, although traditional paper-and-pencil tests are well suited to assessing the breadth and depth of one's factual knowledge of a topic, it is very difficult, if not impossible, to assess skills and performance abilities.

The capabilities of computerized testing present numerous opportunities to improve psychological testing. Computerizing provides test developers much greater freedom to manipulate the characteristics and features of items and tasks presented to examinees, which allows for richer assessments of a broader array of individual differences. Important aspects of computerized tests include the media employed by a test (i.e. graphics, sound, etc.), the format of a test (i.e. adaptive), the format of items or tasks (i.e. essay, simulations, etc), and the construct that the test assesses (i.e. skills, performance abilities). Test items that utilize the capabilities of a computer in creative ways to either improve measurement of a characteristic already assessed by a traditional paper-and-pencil test or to measure an individual difference that previously was difficult or impossible to measure are referred to as *innovative computerized test items*.

This chapter provides a review of many developments in computerized testing. Of course it is impossible to describe all of the innovations in this rapidly changing field. Nonetheless, we attempt to provide an overview

Computer-Based Testing and the Internet: Issues and Advances.
Edited by D. Bartram and R. K. Hambleton. © 2006 John Wiley & Sons, Ltd.

of important new directions in assessment resulting from advances in computerization.

DIMENSIONS OF INNOVATION

Classifying test items as either innovative or non-innovative is an oversimplification. It is more useful to classify items according to the framework for innovation of Parshall, Davey, and Pashley (2000). Their framework includes five underlying aspects of innovation: item format, response action, media inclusion, level of interactivity, and scoring algorithm.

Item Format

Item format refers to the type of response that is required of the examinee (Parshall et al., 2000). The two major subcategories within this dimension are *selected response* and *constructed response*. When confronted with a selected response item format, the examinee must choose an answer from a list of alternatives, which usually includes from two to five options. The most common forms of selected response items are true–false and multiple choice. Three disadvantages of this format are often discussed. First, even if the examinee does not know the answer, he/she nonetheless has some probability of answering correctly by guessing; on the other hand, scoring this test is very easy and straightforward. Computerizing allows a test developer to reduce the probability of examinees guessing the answer by increasing the number of response options. For example, a test that assesses verbal ability could ask the examinee to locate errors within a passage (see, e.g., Davey, Godwin, & Mittelholtz, 1997). After locating an error, the examinee moves the cursor and clicks on the section that he/she believes should be changed. The computer then provides a list of possible alternatives of revision for the selected section.

A second criticism of selected response items is that the examinee is not required to produce the answer; instead, he/she only needs to recognize it. Third, selected response items have been criticized as assessing decontextualized problem solving. Specifically, such items may become so atomistic that they "yield a task that is abstracted too far from the domain of inference" (Wainer, Bradlow, & Du, 2001, p. 245). On the other hand, constructed response items require the examinee to produce his/her own response (Parshall et al., 2000) and consequently seem less subject to these criticisms. Obviously, examinees must do more than recognize an answer with this format.

Some classic examples of constructed response items are fill-in-the-blank, short answer, and essay. These item formats have had limited roles in large-scale testing programs due to difficulties in scoring. That is, these items need to be scored by trained human graders, which can be time consuming and costly. However, computer scorers such as *e-rater* and computational algorithms are being developed and implemented as solutions to such problems (Powers, Burstein, Chodorow, Fowles, & Kukich, 2002). As a result of these innovations, constructed responses are beginning to play a bigger role in standardized testing; the newly implemented essay section of the GRE provides an example. The major benefits of a test composed of constructed response items are that guessing is almost completely eliminated, examinees must produce their own answer rather than recognize an answer provided by the test developer, and broader questions can be posed to the examinee.

Response Action

In addition to item format, an innovative item can also be characterized in terms of its *response action*, or what the examinee must physically do to answer the item (Parshall et al., 2000). For example, the response action of the traditional paper-and-pencil test requires the examinee to use a pencil to fill in a bubble. With computerizing testing, a variety of response actions may be applicable. For example, examinees may be required to type a response on a keyboard, click on an option with a mouse, or speak their answer into a microphone. This flexibility is an advantage because test developers can ask a wider variety of questions using innovative items; however, test developers should first ensure that examinees have the necessary skills and abilities to successfully interact with the computer before administering tests with these types of item. If they fail to do so, an examinee's score may be a reflection of his/her ability to interact with the computer rather than a score of his/her ability on the latent trait that the test intends to measure.

Media Inclusion

By administering items via computer, test developers are free to include different media in addition to traditional text-based material (Parshall et al., 2000). Media included in some recent tests include audio (Vispoel, 1999), graphics (Ackerman, Evans, Park, Tamassia, & Turner, 1999), and video (Olson-Buchanan et al., 1998). Media inclusion provides numerous benefits. For example, it would be impossible to assess one's listening skills in a foreign language without the inclusion of audio. Furthermore, Chan and Schmitt (1997) found that using video clips to assess an interpersonal skill eliminated the adverse impact towards a US minority group that was present when the test was administered via paper and pencil. The findings by Chan and Schmitt suggest that traditional paper-and-pencil tests confound the measurement of an interpersonal skill (i.e. management skill) with the cognitive factor of verbal ability. Therefore, the video-based assessment is a more authentic measure of the interpersonal skill because it removes a confound caused by paper-and-pencil administration.

Interactivity

Interactivity is the extent to which the computer interacts with, or adapts to, each individual examinee (Parshall et al., 2000). With a traditional paper-and-pencil test, there is zero interactivity between the test and examinee. All examinees receive the same items regardless of their individual performance. In contrast, a computerized test may be completely adaptive, as in computer adaptive tests (CATs), or partially adaptive, as in a computer adaptive sequential test (CAST; Luecht & Nungester, 1998, 2000). In CATs and CASTs, the computer adjusts in accordance with the examinee's performance on each previous item or block of items, respectively, by administering easier questions if the examinee answered incorrectly or harder questions if the examinee answered correctly.

Scoring Algorithm

The final dimension of innovation is the method of scoring the test (Parshall et al., 2000). Tests that lack innovative scoring methods are those that use computers as electronic page turners, recording the examinee's responses as he/she goes through the test and calculating a number-right total score when finished. On the other hand, some computerized tests require sophisticated scoring algorithms. For example, CATs use item response theory to compute a maximum likelihood or Bayesian score based on the examinee's pattern of right and wrong answers as well as the difficulty of the items that were administered. Implementing automated scoring methods for selected res-ponse items is a relatively simple task; however, scoring becomes quite tricky when the test is composed of constructed response items because these items may have many equally correct answers and answers may vary in their degree of correctness. Thus, test developers are faced with the challenge of devising efficient scoring methods for these types of item. Two notable successes are described by Bejar (1991) for the architectural licensing examination and Bennett, Steffen, Singley, Morley, and Jacquemin (1997) for a new constructed response mathematical reasoning item type. Research on scoring constructed response items is currently an active area of research.

HISTORY

Before summarizing the opportunities and risks associated with developing and implementing innovative computerized test items, we give a brief des-cription of the assimilation of the computer into testing and assessment. This background provides a context for understanding computerized testing and, specifically, innovative computerized test items.

As early as the late 1960s, some visionary psychologists realized that com-puters were well suited for the purposes of assessment (Bartam & Bayliss, 1984). However, this insight preceded the technology: psychologists were restricted by the capabilities (or lack thereof) of computers of that era. For example, during the late 1960s, clinical psychologists began to use computers to perform such tasks as conducting interviews and administering psychological tests. However, these early adaptations from pencil and paper to computerized formats were merely a change in test medium. In other words, the two assessment instruments were identical in content with the only difference lying in the administration format: paper-and-pencil versus computer. Furthermore, the role computers played in the field of assessment was limited by the high cost of mainframe computers, lack of memory, use of dumb terminals wired to mainframes, clumsy software, and lack of multimedia capabilities.

In order to capitalize on the potential of the computer for test delivery, test developers needed to devise new formats utilizing the capabilities of the computer rather than simply transforming traditional paper-and-pencil tests to electronic page-turner versions (McBride, 1997). In 1979, the Navy Personnel Research and Development Center launched an extensive research program with the plan of developing and implementing the first CATs (Wolfe, McBride, & Sympson, 1997). These tests, administered via computer, used item response theory to administer test items that matched each examinee's ability level as determined by his/her performance on previous items. Specifically, the computer first administers an item that is intermediate in difficulty. Then, the test interacts uniquely with each individual examinee by branching to a harder question if the examinee correctly answers that item or to an easier question if the examinee answers incorrectly. The test continues to adjust in accordance with the examinee's performance until enough information is gathered to assign a score that reflects the examinee's true ability on the characteristic assessed by the test.

Despite the remarkable gains incurred in test development through the implementation of CATs, innovation throughout the 1980s and the beginning of the 1990s was impeded by the lack of computer capabilities. For example, an early version of the CAT-ASVAB was designed and implemented on a system so slow that only one examinee could be tested at a time (Wolfe, McBride, & Sympson, 1997). In fact, the CAT-ASVAB was not implemented nation-wide until 1993.

In the mid-1990s computers finally became equipped with the necessary capabilities for substantial innovation. Graphical user interfaces became commonplace, memory was continually upgraded, and sound and video cards opened the door to the possibility of multi-media assessment. At this point in time the technology had finally caught up with the creativity of test developers, and the stage was set for a revolution in test development (Drasgow & Olson-Buchanan, 1999).

OPPORTUNITIES

Assessing Skills and Performance Abilities

As noted previously, traditional paper-and-pencil tests provide satisfactory measurement of declarative knowledge but are frequently criticized for inadequate assessment of skills and performance abilities. This has been of great concern to several licensing boards, which used the traditional multiple-choice format as a central component for certification. As a result, several licensing boards instituted research programs aimed at developing innovative computerized tests to measure candidates' skills and performance abilities as well as their knowledge of the field.

A good example is provided by the National Board of Medical Examiners (NBME). In 1999, NBME changed their licensing test to a computerized format (Clyman, Melnick, & Clauser, 1999). This new test includes case simulations, where the test-taker assumes the role of physician. The test-taker is presented with a brief description of the patient's presenting symptoms. The candidate physician can request the virtual patient's medical history, conduct a physical examination, order laboratory tests, and perform procedures to gather information to diagnose and treat the patient. However, while the candidate physician is gathering information, the patient's medical status also progresses and changes in accordance with the treatment provided. For example, the candidate physician may choose to order a certain test, a procedure for which results are known in two hours. To obtain the results of the test, the candidate physician must advance a clock displaying time for the virtual patient by two hours; concurrently, the patient's status advances two hours.

These case simulations provide a highly authentic emulation of the actual work of a physician. Unlike the traditional examinations that primarily measure declarative knowledge of medicine, these case simulations assess skills and abilities relevant to diagnosing and treating patients. It is important to note that the traditional examinations and the case simulation examination really assess different domains: their disattenuated correlation has been found to be only about 0.5 (Clyman et al., 1999). In sum, by delivering the test via computer the NBME improved its certification process by utilizing the computer's capabilities to provide a more authentic test of medical care giving.

In May 2004, the American Institute of Certified Public Accounts (AICPA) began administering their licensing examination via computer. The new version includes case simulations as well as multiple-choice questions. Similar to NBME and its concerns about measuring medical care giving proficiency with multiple-choice test items, the AICPA felt that a test comprised of selected response items did not adequately tap the skills and performance abilities necessary to be a competent accountant.

The AICPA simulations first present the candidate with a brief description of a client and his/her accounting needs. Then, the candidate must work through several sections of the simulation such as completing spreadsheets, searching through the definitive literature for information pertinent to the client's needs, calculating relevant estimates such as gross income, and communicating a final recommendation for the client through a free response section. These simulations more accurately portray the demands and requirements of an accountant and therefore seem better suited for assessing the skills and abilities required for practice as a certified public accountant.

Using Media Inclusion to Improve Measurement

Many tests rely solely on text-based items for assessment; however, measurement can sometimes be enhanced greatly by incorporating media within the test. This is evident in Vispoel's (1999) tonal memory CAT that assesses musical aptitude, the Test of Dermatological Skin Disorders by Ackerman et al. (1999) that assesses the ability to identify and diagnose different types of skin disorder, and the Conflict Resolution Skills Assessment by Olson-Buchanan et al. (1998) that assesses the interpersonal skill of conflict resolution.

Tests of musical aptitude date back to 1919 with Carl Seashore's *Measures of Music Talent* (Vispoel, 1999); however, measuring musical aptitude accurately and efficiently has been an issue for test developers over the years. Vispoel (1999) points out that traditional tests of musical aptitude are inefficient in three important ways. First, enough items to accurately assess all ranges of musical ability levels must be included, which results in very long examinations. Second, because musical aptitude tests require high levels of concentration due to the fact that it is not possible to repeat a question or go back to answer a question later, examinees become fatigued quite quickly. Finally, due to the repetitious nature of these tests, examinees become easily bored or inattentive.

As a solution to these problems, Vispoel (1999) recommended replacing the traditional test with a computer adaptive test (CAT). As mentioned before, CATs administer test items based on the examinee's ability level. As a result, fewer items are required of CATs in comparison to traditional paper-and-pencil tests to obtain the same level of reliability. In addition to fewer test items, by automating musical aptitude tests, the examinee is provided with greater control over the testing environment. For example, in the traditional format that uses audio cassette players, examinees can be disadvantaged by their seat: people seated at the back of the room are farther from the recorder and therefore cannot hear as well. Furthermore, other noises could be distracting and detrimental to one's score. With the tonal memory CAT, each examinee wears a pair of headsets so that distracting noises are reduced or eliminated and volume can be adjusted to the satisfaction of each individual examinee. Moreover, digital sound quality provided by computers is a tremendous improvement over that of cassette tapes. Finally, the examinee sets his/her own pace by advancing to the next question when he/she is ready.

Each item on Vispoel's tonal memory CAT includes two short audio clips. The examinee listens to both and then decides which, if any, tones were changed in the second clip in relation to the first. The tonal memory CAT was able to reach the same level of reliability while administering substantially fewer items in comparison to traditional tests of music aptitude. In fact, the tonal memory CAT required 76–93% fewer items to reach the same levels of reliability as the Seashore test and 73–87% fewer items to reach the same levels as the Wing test which is another traditional test of musical aptitude. Clearly, the computerized version assesses musical aptitude with much greater efficiency.

The problems with test delivery in traditional tests of musical aptitude are analogous to problems with traditional assessments of diagnostic skills for skin disorders. Before the computerized Test of Dermatological Skin Disorders by Ackerman et al. (1999), pictures of different skin disorders were administered via slide projector. Again, examinees at the back of large rooms were disadvantaged because they could not see the image as well. Furthermore, the clarity of slides is of lower quality than high-resolution digital images. Again, the test administrator rather than the examinee had control over the pace of the examination.

As a solution to these problems, Ackerman et al. developed the Test of Dermatological Skin Disorders (1999), which is comprised of *analyzing situation items*, or items that present a visual/audio clip along with text information that examinees use to make a decision or diagnosis (Zenisky & Sireci, 2002). In this test, the examinee is presented with a brief history of a patient along with a digital image of the patient's skin disorder. The examinee then selects the correct name of the skin disorder from a list of possible answers. This test is designed to assess the examinee's ability to recognize and accurately identify several different types of skin disorder such as dermatitis, acne, and pigment alterations. By computerizing the test of skin disorders, the problems described above are eliminated.

Just as tests of musical aptitude and of skin disorders have been improved by the inclusion of media, the assessment of interpersonal skills has also been improved. Businesses have long desired a reliable measure of interpersonal skills as a means of hiring and promoting managers; however, the traditional tests that have been administered are confounded with cognitive ability and/or personality factors. For example, Chan and Schmitt (1997) found that a paper-and-pencil version of a situational judgment task (SJT) correlated 0.45 with reading comprehension; however, a video-based version correlated only 0.05 with reading comprehension. Since then, research has been conducted to design and implement tests that measure only interpersonal skills (i.e. Olson-Buchanan et al. 1998).

The Conflict Resolution Skills Assessment by Olson-Buchanan et al. (1998) incorporates interactive video as a means of assessing conflict resolution skill in a way that is not confounded with cognitive or personality factors. In this test, the examinee watches a short video clip of a workplace conflict. By viewing the scenario, the test developers believe that examinees become more psychologically involved in the situation than if he/she had merely read the scenario. When the clip ends, the examinee is asked to pick the best resolution to the problem from a list of possible solutions. The test then branches to another video clip, which is designed to reflect the results of the examinee's decision concerning the previous scenario, and again the examinee must select a multiple-choice option. Olson-Buchanan et al. (1998) found that examinees' scores on this assessment were correlated with their supervisors' ratings of their conflict management performance on the job; furthermore, scores were not related to measures of verbal or math ability.

Implementing Novel Item Types to Improve Measurement

By administering tests via computer, test developers are provided with more leeway in the types of question they can ask than with traditional paper-and-pencil tests, which are well suited to multiple-choice questions. In a comprehensive review of the literature on computerized testing, Zenisky and Sireci (2002) identified over 20 new types of item format. Some examples of novel item formats for computer testing include *graphical modeling*, *mathematical expressions*, *generating examples*, *multiple numerical responses*, *passage editing*, and *problem-solving vignettes*. In this section, a brief description along with an example will be provided for each of these novel item formats.

Graphical modeling, mathematical expressions, and generating examples can all be classified as novel ways to assess mathematical ability (Bennett, Morley, & Quardt, 2000). Historically, math tests included in large-scale testing programs such as the Scholastic Aptitude Test (SAT) and the American College Testing (ACT) program were composed of selected response items; however, graphical modeling, mathematical expressions, and generating examples represent three alternative assessment formats for mathematical ability that use a constructed response approach. With *graphical modeling* (GM) items, examinees are given a brief description of a mathematical problem and asked to plot this information on a grid so that it represents the information provided. For example, an examinee may be asked to plot points on a grid for a circle with an area equal to 16π. As in this problem, it is possible to have more than one correct answer; consequently scoring becomes a challenge for the test developer.

While completing *mathematical expression* (ME) items, examinees are asked to construct a mathematical equation that represents the problem (Bennett et al., 2000). For example, if n is the arithmetic mean of three numbers 3, 5, and j, what is the value of j in terms of n? (Solution: $j = 3n - 3 - 5$.) Again, a critical issue for mathematical expression items is scoring: there can be any number of ways to write equally correct equations. An important contribution of Bennett et al. (2000) is their scoring algorithm. They used symbolic computation principles to convert alternative answers to a simplest form, which could then be compared with the answer key. In a test of the scoring algorithm, they found it correctly scored answers with an accuracy of greater than 99.6%; moreover, most of the answers that were classified as incorrectly scored by the algorithm contained problematic subscripts (e.g. X1 rather than X_1).

Like ME items, *generating examples* (GE) items set constraints within the problem and then ask the examinee to give an equation or value that meets these constraints (Bennett et al., 2000). For example, if a and b are positive integers and $5a - 3b = 1$, what are two possible sets of value for a and b? (Solution: $a = 2, b = 3; a = 5, b = 8$.) By assessing mathematical ability with constructed response items, the construct of mathematical ability is broadened to incorporate and assess skills not feasible with a traditional multiple-choice format.

Like the previous three item formats, *multiple numerical responses* require the examinee to provide a numerical response. However, these types of question ask the examinees to insert more than one answer to complete a problem such as filling out a spreadsheet or tax form (Zenisky & Sireci, 2002). As a result, multiple numerical response questions are more complex than a traditional math problem because the examinee is required to answer multiple parts or complete several stages before arriving at a complete answer. Furthermore, the examinee must generate the responses, not merely choose from a list of options. For example, in the new computerized version of the AICPA licensing exam, the examinees must complete simulations as well as the standard multiple-choice questions. In part of the simulation, examinees are required to fill out spreadsheets, which could be classified as a multiple numerical response item.

Another example of a novel item format is *passage editing*, which requires examinees to locate errors within a passage (Davey et al., 1997; Zenisky & Sireci, 2002). After locating an error, the examinee clicks on the problematic prose. A list containing alternative ways to revise the prose appears and the examinee chooses the one he/she believes is the correct edit. Traditional items that assess verbal ability through editing direct the examinee to the error by underlining it. However, with this new format, the examinee must first locate the error him/herself before selecting a way to edit the text. As a result, this format seems to provide an improved format for measuring verbal ability: an individual low on verbal ability is likely to have a lower probability of detecting an error than an individual high on verbal ability, and therefore has a lower probability of a correct answer. When the error is underlined, examinees do not have to detect the error because that information is provided. In sum, this new format seems to provide a more stringent test of verbal ability.

Finally, *problem-solving vignettes* are questions that present a problem-solving situation, requiring the examinees to respond with solutions. These items are graded on the features of the product/solution (Zenisky & Sireci, 2002). Like the NBME and the AICPA, the National Council of Architect Registration Boards (NCARB) realized that constructed response items were a necessity in their licensing examination, which is evident in its long history of incorporating open-ended architectural site test problems in its examination. However, in an attempt to computerize the examination, NCARB incorporated problem-solving vignettes along with an innovative scoring methodology as a solution to the inefficiency of human graders (Bejar & Braun, 1999).

As a measure of site-design proficiency, the NCARB site-design test requires candidates to create architectural designs, or blueprints, which satisfy various requirements. A design problem may measure spatial arrangement proficiency, which assesses how a candidate arranges design elements according to the objectives and constraints imposed by the question (Bejar, 1991). For example, where a parking lot is sited in relation to the entrance of a store might be evaluated. The functionality of the design is also important. For example, candidates may need to alter the terrain of a site to solve water drainage problems (Bejar, 1991). Bejar's innovative scoring algorithm enables the computer to automatically score a candidate's design.

Computerization to Improve Scoring

NCARB joined with the Educational Testing Service (ETS) to develop and implement a computerized version of their site-design test (Bejar & Braun, 1999). The traditional architectural licensing test was composed of open-ended questions, which required human graders for scoring. NCARB not only changed the administrative test media but also adopted a new methodology for scoring. The computerized algorithm grades designs based on features, such as object–site relations and object–object relations (Bejar, 1991). In order to validate this new scoring methodology, two human graders and the computer scored 119 solutions to a spatial arrangement problem. Using Cohen's kappa agreement index, Bejar (1991) assessed the similarity between the computer and the two graders' ratings. He found that the agreement index for two jurors (0.77) was only slightly higher than for the computer and grader 1 (0.75) and for the computer and grader 2 (0.70). These findings show that utilizing the computational capabilities of the computer can reduce the amount of time required to score the test with little effect on the validity of scores.

There has been substantial research on automated scoring of another type of constructed response, namely the essay. Clearly, the most direct approach to assessing an individual's writing ability is to have that person provide a sample of his/her writing. However, the time consuming and expensive scoring methods of the past, which required at least two trained graders to read and score each essay, have greatly restricted the use of essays in standardized testing. As a result, test developers have used item formats such as sentence correction, which has led to criticisms that their tests do not adequately assess critical aspects of writing ability.

Test developers have realized the limitations of alternative formats and much work has been done to computerize grading of essays. Zenisky and Sireci (2002) list several methods, including project essay grade, *e-rater*, latent semantic analysis, text categorization, constructed free response scoring tool, expert systems, and mental modeling. One concern with using automated scoring systems is that examinees may try to 'trick' the program into assigning scores that are too high. This leads to the topic of the next section: the potential risks of using computerized formats for testing.

RISKS

Despite the numerous benefits derived from computerizing tests, the system is not perfect. There are in fact risks and costs associated with computerization. First, converting a traditional paper-and-pencil test to a computerized version is no easy task; it is a long and costly procedure, and data for the new administrative medium may be needed to demonstrate the validity and reliability of the new test (e.g., in a meta-analysis, Mead & Drasgow, 1993, found that speeded computerized tests were not equivalent to their paper-and-pencil counterparts). It is even more problematic to develop a brand new computerized test. This process can take years and, in the end, the test may be found wanting. Even if a computerized measure using a new format is found to be valid, questions about whether computerization improves measurement efficiency still remain (e.g., Jodoin, 2003, found that innovative items provided less information per unit of time than multiple-choice items). Additionally, tests that implement computerized scoring have been carefully scrutinized and questions still exist concerning the extent to which their scoring procedures are reliable and valid (e.g., Powers et al., 2002, found that *e-rater*, a computerized scorer, could be tricked into assigning a higher score than the essay deserved). Finally, issues about test security have become a major concern of test developers.

The Difficulties Associated with Developing and Implementing Innovative Items and Tests

Unless a test developer desires simply to convert a traditional paper-and-pencil test to an electronic page-turner format, he/she must be willing to devote much time and energy to successfully develop and implement a new test. In fact, this process should be expected to take a number of years. For example, the US Department of Defense test developers began working on the CAT version of the Armed Services Vocational Aptitude Battery in 1979 and it was not implemented until 1993. AICPA began working on the computerized version of their licensing exam in 1999 and it became operational in 2004. Even after such tests are operational, careful monitoring and further research are needed to ensure that they function as expected (e.g., the computerized GRE testing program was eventually terminated in some Asian countries because test security could not be guaranteed).

Although procedures for developing multiple-choice tests are well known and have been described in numerous textbooks, such standard procedures are not yet available for innovative computerized assessments. Instead, creativity, psychometric expertise, and hard work are required to develop innovative measures. For example, Drasgow, Olson-Buchanan, and Moberg (1999) describe the 'trials and tribulations' they experienced as they developed an interactive video assessment (IVA). These difficulties include, first, finding financing and other resources required to develop an IVA. Even if financing and psychometric expertise are available, additional difficulties may arise. In their description of the Conflict Resolution Skills Assessment, Drasgow et al. (1999) note that each stage of the development process, from writing scripts for video clips through scoring and software development, provided novel challenges. Therefore, when constructing an innovative test, test developers must realize that they will need to put forth more effort than is required for the development of a traditional paper-and-pencil test. Is all the time and effort worth the trouble? Do innovative items actually improve measurement?

The shift from administering multiple-choice items, which assess declarative knowledge, to innovative items, which are designed to assess skills and performance abilities, resulted from a desire to improve measurement. That is, test developers have wanted tests that more adequately tapped the construct of interest. However, Jodoin (2003) argues that measurement efficiency is not increased, but actually decreased, when innovative items are administered in place of traditional multiple-choice items. Data from the Microsoft Certified Systems Engineer Certification Program were used to compare the two formats. Examinees were presented with scenarios and then asked traditional multiple-choice items; in addition, drop-and-connect and create-a-tree items were administered. The results showed that the innovative items provided more information, regardless of the ability level; however, multiple-choice items provided more information per unit time than the innovative items because the innovative items required much more time to complete. In fact, the amount of information per unit time provided by the multiple-choice items was more than double the amount provided by the innovative items. Of course, this study used only two of the many innovative item types (see Zenisky & Sireci, 2002, for a comprehensive description of innovative item types), and Jodoin (2003) notes that his results should be interpreted with caution.

Bennett et al. (1999) argue that innovative items should broaden the assessment of the construct under question. They created a test consisting entirely of a new type of item they were studying, and computed its disattenuated correlation with a traditional test of the same construct. Bennett et al. found that the disattenuated correlation was only approximately 0.70, which demonstrates that this innovative item is not simply redundant with the traditional test; instead, including the innovative item format in the overall examination will broaden and enrich measurement of the trait assessed. Is this sufficient reason to sacrifice the measurement efficiency of multiple-choice items? That is an issue that the test developer must consider and decide for himself/herself.

Validity of Scoring Procedures

As previously mentioned, many concerns have been raised about the validity of using a computer to score constructed response items, especially essays (i.e. Powers et al., 2002). In fact, Powers et al. (2002) conducted an experiment where they explicitly asked their participants to try to trick *e-rater* into assigning their essay a score that was either too high or too low. *E-rater* is the computerized essay grader developed by ETS for use in grading the essay portion of the GRE, which utilizes scoring algorithms based on the rules of natural language processing. Therefore, if examinees know how the examination is scored, there may be ways in which examinees can write essays that would result in high scores from *e-rater* but low scores from a human grader.

Participants in the Powers et al. study (2002) varied in their ability to trick *e-rater*. One participant—a professor of computational linguistics—wrote a few paragraphs and then repeated them 37 times, which fooled *e-rater* into giving the highest score possible, whereas the two human graders gave it the lowest score possible. Across the 63 essays in the study, the two human graders agreed within one point (on a six point scale) 92% of the time whereas *e-rater* agreed with a human grader within one point 65% of the time. *E-rater* has been improved as a result of this study, and Powers et al. note that *e-rater* would now be able to correctly score most of these essays that had previously tricked it. Furthermore, the sample of participants in this study was not typical of the applicable population, GRE test-takers. Specifically, participants were recruited based on their expert knowledge; the sample included ETS employees involved in developing the writing assessment section of the GRE, researchers with backgrounds in computational linguistics and cognition, and specialists in artificial intelligence. Therefore, the Powers et al. study constituted a stern test of computerized essay scoring.

Test Security

Even if a test provides superb assessment of the latent trait it is designed to measure, examinees' pre-knowledge of the test items can compromise its integrity. CATs such as the ASVAB and GRE use the same item bank for a set period of time. As a result, a conspirator could take the test at the beginning of the administration cycle and memorize as many questions as possible. Then, that individual could post those questions on a web-based bulletin board for co-conspirators, who will take the test later in the administration cycle. Clearly, the item bank has been compromised and the co-conspirators (who, in turn, may also memorize and post items) have an unfair advantage over honest test-takers.

Something akin to this scenario occurred with the GRE. Apparently, thousands of Asian students collaborated via the Internet to increase their GRE scores. Students who tested at the beginning of the administration cycle would post information about the test on a web bulletin board. As a result, an abnormally high number of very high scores were obtained by students from, for example, China, which served as a red flag for the GRE Board that something had gone amiss (Ewing, 2002).

After a thorough investigation covering over 40 countries, the GRE Board uncovered web sites in China and Korea, also accessible to residents of Hong Kong and Taiwan, that provided item pre-knowledge. The computerized version of the GRE was suspended on 6 August 2002 in China, Hong Kong, Taiwan, and Korea, and the paper-and-pencil GRE was reinstated on 1 October 2002.

In sum, test developers need item banks with large numbers of items to discourage potential cheaters. In a CAT program, the item bank should be changed frequently and probably on an irregular basis (changing the item pool on, say, the second Monday of each month would appear to facilitate test compromise). Item statistics should be carefully monitored, probably on a daily or weekly basis, to look for suspicious improvements in examinee performance. Clearly, substantial vigilance is required to assure the integrity of any continuous testing program.

FUTURE DIRECTIONS

The changes and improvements in test development over the past 40 years have been monumental. By utilizing the computer and it capabilities, many limitations that test developers once faced have now disappeared. However, issues regarding the quality of traditional paper-and-pencil tests are still applicable to these new innovative items and tests. That is, the psychometric properties of newly developed tests such as the computerized version of the AICPA's licensing examination need to be assessed. For example, in addition to adequate validity and reliability, the new simulations of the AICPA's licensing examination should broaden the skills assessed over and above those measured by the traditional paper-and-pencil version.

What are the future directions of computerized assessment? Clearly, improved measurement of skills and performance abilities is high on the agenda of test developers. The flexibility of computerized assessment should allow high fidelity simulations of actual performance tasks, which will lead to more authentic assessment. Greater use of multimedia, more interactivity, and a greater reliance on constructed responses are likely to be required in these simulations. Thus, improved user interfaces, more flexible algorithms for selecting items and/or tasks to present to the examinee, and new approaches to scoring examinees' responses will be required.

The next decade should be an exciting time for test developers. Hardware and software limitations prevented test developers from creating the assessments they envisioned in the 1960s and 1970s. Now, however, improvements in hardware and software, with concomitant reductions in cost, enable test developers to create the tests and assessments they have long desired. Challenges of course remain in transforming psychometric dreams into realities, but we are in a time and place where we can go far beyond the paper-and-pencil multiple-choice item.

REFERENCES

Ackerman, T. A., Evans, J., Park, K. S., Tasmassia, C., & Turner, R. (1999). Computer assessment using visual stimuli: A test of dermatological skin disorders. In F. Drasgow & J. B. Olson-Buchanan (Eds.), *Innovations in computerized assessment* (pp. 137–150). Mahwah, NJ: Erlbaum.

Bartram, D., & Bayliss, R. (1984). Automated testing: Past, present and future. *Journal of Occupational Psychology*, **57**:221–237.

Bejar, I. I. (1991). A methodology for scoring open-ended architectural design problems. *Journal of Applied Psychology*, **76**:522–532.

Bejar, I. I., & Braun, H. I. (1999). *Architectural simulations: From research to implementation* (Research Memorandum 99-2). Princeton, NJ: Educational Testing Service.

Bennett, R. E., Morely, M., & Quardt, D. (2000). Three response types for broadening the conception of mathematical problem solving in computerized tests. *Applied Psychological Measurement*, **24**:294–309.

Bennett, R. E., et al. (1999). Psychometric and cognitive functioning of an under-determined computer-based response type for quantitative reasoning. *Journal of Educational Measurement*, **36**:233–252.

Bennett, R. E., Steffen, M., Singley, M. K., Morley, M., & Jacquemin, D. (1997). Evaluating an automatically scorable, open-ended response type for measuring mathematical reasoning in computer-adaptive tests. *Journal of Educational Measurement*, **34**:162–176.

Chan, D., & Schmitt, N. (1997). Video-based versus paper-and-pencil method of assessment in situational judgment tests: Subgroup differences in test performance and face validity perceptions. *Journal of Applied Psychology*, **82**:143–159.

Clyman, S. G., Melnick, D. E., & Clauser, B. E. (1999). Computer-based case simulations from medicine: Assessing skills in patient management. In A. Tekian, C. H. McGuire, & W. C. McGahie (Eds.), *Innovative simulations for assessing professional competence* (pp. 29–41). Chicago, IL: University of Illinois, Department of Medical Education.

Davey, T., Godwin, J., & Mittelholtz, D. (1997). Developing and scoring an innovative computerized writing assessment. *Journal of Educational Measurement*, **34**:21–41.

Drasgow, F., & Olson-Buchanan, J. B. (Eds.) (1999). *Innovations in computerized assessment*. Mahwah, NJ: Erlbaum.

Drasgow, F., Olson-Buchanan, J. B., & Moberg, P. J. (1999). Interactive video assessment of interpersonal skills. In F. Drasgow & J. B. Olson-Buchanan (Eds.), *Innovations in computerized assessment* (pp. 177–196). Hillsdale, NJ: Erlbaum.

Ewing, T. (2002, August 6). Paper-based GRE general test returning to parts of Asia. *ETS News and Media: Communication and Public Affairs*. Retrieved December 3, 2003, from http://www.ets.org/news/02072301.html

Jodoin, M. G. (2003). Measurement efficiency of innovative item formats in computer-based testing. *Journal of Educational Measurement*, **40**:1–15.

Luecht, R. M., & Nungester, R. J. (1998). Some practical examples of computer-adaptive sequential testing. *Journal of Educational Measurement*, **35**:229–249.

Luecht, R. M., & Nungester, R. J. (2000). Computer-adaptive sequential testing. In W. J. van der Linden & C. A. W. Glas (Eds.), *Computerized adaptive testing: Theory and practice* (pp. 117–128). Boston, MA: Kluwer.

McBride, J. R. (1997). The Marine Corps Exploratory Development Project: 1977–1982. In W. A. Sands, B. K. Waters, & J. R. McBride (Eds.), *Computerized adaptive testing: From inquiry to operation* (pp. 59–67). Washington, DC: American Psychological Association.

Mead, A. D., & Drasgow, F. (1993). Equivalence of computerized and paper-and-pencil cognitive ability tests: A meta-analysis. *Psychological Bulletin*, **114**:449–458.

Olson-Buchanan, J. B., Drasgow, F., Moberg, P. J., Mead, A. D., Keenan, P. A., & Donovan, M. A. (1998). Interactive video assessment of conflict resolution skills. *Personnel Psychology*, **51**:1–24.

Parshall, C. G., Davey, T., & Pashley, P. J. (2002). Innovative item types for computerized testing. In W. J. van der Linder & C. A. W. Glas (Eds.), *Computerized adaptive testing: Theory and practice* (pp. 129–148). Dordrecht: Kluwer.

Powers, D. E., Burstein, J. C., Chodorow, M., Fowles, M. E., & Kukich, K. (2002). Stumping *e-rater*: Challenging the validity of automated essay scoring. *Computers in Human Behavior*, **18**:103–134.

Vispoel, W. P. (1999). Creating computerized adaptive tests of musical aptitude: Problems, solutions, and future directions. In F. Drasgow & J. B. Olson-Buchanan (Eds.), *Innovations in computerized assessment* (pp. 151–176). Mahwah, NJ: Erlbaum.

Wainer, H., Bradlow, E. T., & Du, Z. (2001). Testlet response theory: An analog for the 3PL model useful in testlet-based adaptive testing. In W. J. van der Linden & C. A. W. Glas (Eds.), *Computerized adaptive testing: Theory and practice* (pp. 245–269). Dordrecht: Kluwer.

Wolfe, J. H., McBride, J. R., & Sympson, J. B. (1997). Development of the experimental CAT-ASVAB system. In W. A. Sands, B. K. Waters, & J. R. McBride (Eds.), *Computerized adaptive testing: From inquiry to operation* (pp. 97–101). Washington, DC: American Psychological Association.

Zenisky, A. L., & Sireci, S. G. (2002). Technological innovations in large-scale assessment. *Applied Measurement in Education*, **15**:337–362.

CHAPTER 4

Psychometric Models, Test Designs and Item Types for the Next Generation of Educational and Psychological Tests

Ronald K. Hambleton
University of Massachusetts at Amherst, USA

Of course it is difficult to predict future directions in educational and psychological test theory and practices. I can think back to 1966 when I began work on my advanced degree in psychometric methods and statistics at the University of Toronto in Canada. Multiple choice tests were popular and being touted as the answer to the messy problems associated with the scoring of essays and other performance tasks. Regression analysis, analysis of variance, and factor analysis were popular statistical methods. SPSS and SAS had not come on the scene and we trudged along with our computer cards (often they would bend and not be readable, or the card readers would mangle our cards and render them useless) and made frequent trips to the university computer center to debug our home-made computer programs. A little later, computer tapes replaced cards but they were still a pain to work with. I remember, too, using big clunky calculators to carry out hand calculations. We learned the statistical methods, and then we learned about computational shortcuts to simplify the time spent in doing hand calculations.

In 1966 it was possible to publish what today would be considered routine content validity and reliability studies. I was reminded of this when I looked through some 1966 issues of the *Journal of Educational Measurement*. Classical test theory provided the theoretical underpinnings for approaches to test design, development, and evaluation. However, classical test theory was not going to be able to handle the changes that were coming in the assessment field—for example, administering tests tailored or matched to examinee ability levels (Lord, 1980). Classical test theory was also principally focused on the

---

Computer-Based Testing and the Internet: Issues and Advances.
Edited by D. Bartram and R. K. Hambleton. © 2006 John Wiley & Sons, Ltd.

developed of norm-referenced tests (Gulliksen, 1950; Lord & Novick, 1968), and in the late 1960s tests with a different purpose were being introduced: criterion-referenced tests, which required new approaches for defining content, selecting items, evaluating tests, and using test scores, and new challenges such as setting performance standards (i.e. passing scores) and reporting test score information (see, for example, Hambleton & Novick, 1973), began to appear.

Of course, today, 38 years after I began my doctoral studies, the world of testing looks very different. In Chapter 2, Professor Drasgow and Ms Mattern write about many of the new item types that are being introduced, in part because of the need and interest in measuring higher level cognitive skills, but also because more options have become available with tests administered at computers. In Chapter 3, Professor van der Linden addresses new test designs—computer based test designs, and the power of psychometric modeling. Professor Luecht addresses multi-stage test designs in his chapter, another computer-based test design that is being implemented widely. Testing today is no longer the administration of a fixed form of a multiple-choice test that every examinee sees at the same time. For 80 years the accountants in the US did just about that by providing examinees with two opportunities a year to pass a two-day licensure exam (the Uniform CPA Exam). Today, these same examinees could take the examination on any of 240 days a year, at a computer, and when they feel they are ready, and the examination itself consists of both multiple-choice items and simulations that require examinees to work through accounting problems that mimic real job situations with scoring that incorporates patterns of responses across component parts of the simulations (see the last chapter by Breithaupt, Mills, and Melican for more details). It is a different world for examinees in accounting and nearly all other assessment fields today because of the testing innovations taking place.

Widely used statistics today are much more sophisticated than those used in 1966. Today, a good psychometrician needs to be familiar with item response theory (IRT), both binary and polytomous IRT response models, and how they are applied (Hambleton, Swaminathan, & Rogers, 1991). This topic alone would take a newcomer to the field of educational assessment at least a year to learn well. Item response theory, in principle, provides a way to build tests that are content and statistically optimal for examinees, and provides a straightforward basis for comparing examinees to each other and to performance standards even though examinees may have taken tests that differ widely in difficulty and length. Of course too, now psychometricians must learn generalizability theory (Brennan, 2001), extensions of factor analysis known as structural equation modeling (Byrne, 1998), and other multivariate statistical procedures. Criterion-referenced testing methods today are widely used, and provide a basis for constructing tests that are intended to provide content-referenced score interpretations. Finally, laptops and desk top computers have replaced punch cards and computer tapes, and the internet opens up the world for effective communications and a wide range of improvements in assessment.

The extent of the changes in test theory and testing practices today could not have been predicted 38 years ago. I know too that it is impossible to accurately predict the status of educational and psychological testing 38 years from now. But Professor Drasgow, Ms Mattern, and Professor van der Linden have clearly pointed to directions in which testing theory and testing practices will be moving. Three important topics are clear from their presentations at the conference: (1) the impact of item response theory, (2) the impact of the computer on test designs, and (3) the emerging impact of new item types on assessment practices. In the remainder of my remarks, I would like to touch on each topic, and suggest a few important areas for future research. Also, in view of the changes that are taking place in test theory and practice, I shall conclude with several remarks about the nature of training for psychometricians in the future.

TRANSITION FROM CLASSICAL TO MODERN TEST THEORY

Until recently, classical test theory has provided the statistical underpinnings for both educational and psychological tests (Gulliksen, 1950). Many of the basic formulas are well known and appear in introductory textbooks on educational and psychological testing: the Spearman–Brown formula, standard error of measurement, corrections to correlations for score range restrictions, correction formulas for correlations due to the unreliability of the measurements, formula linking test length and validity, approaches to reliability estimation, and more.

Despite the usefulness of classical test theory and models in psychometric methods, and I expect that usefulness to continue, there are definite shortcomings and they were recognized as early as Gulliksen (1950). Basically, what he and other psychometricians of the time valued were item statistics that were not dependent on the samples from which they came. If high performing examinees were used in the analyses, items appeared easier than if they were administered to lower performing examinees. Item discrimination indices such as the popular point biserial correlation are also influenced by the characteristics of examinee samples, especially score variability. However, what was valued by these early psychometricians proved to be elusive—item statistics that were independent of the particular characteristics of examinee samples. Obviously this 'sample independence' would eliminate problems associated with having details about the particular samples prior to using them in test development work. Of course, in practice, samples should be drawn that are representative of the population in which the test will be used, but this is often not possible, so the problem of sample dependent item statistics remains. Note too that test statistics such as reliability estimates are also examinee sample dependent and therefore generalizations to examinee populations may be limited in some instances.

An even bigger shortcoming of classical test theory, given today's interest in matching test difficulty to the examinee's ability level that was described by van der Linden in his chapter, is the dependence of examinee scores on test difficulty. Quite simply, examinees obtain lower scores on difficult tests, and higher scores on easy tests. Needed is a psychometric model that adjusts scores for test difficulty and makes scores 'invariant' or 'independent' of the choice of test items. Within the framework of classical test theory is the well developed topic of score equating (see Gulliksen, 1950; Kolen & Brennan, 1995) but it is not feasible to use classical test score equating when each examinee receives a unique set of items, as is the case in computer-adaptive testing.

There are many testing situations where the use of non-equivalent tests to examinees may be of interest. For example, more effective administration of aptitude tests, personality tests, and quality of life tests is possible with 'computer-adaptive tests' described in the van der Linden chapter. Testing time can be cut at least in half by adapting a test to the examinee (see, for example, Mills, Potenza, Fremer, & Ward, 2002; van der Linden & Glas, 2000; Wainer et al., 2000). Assessment begins at a level of difficulty based on the average examinee, or perhaps based on prior information about the examinee (such as might come from a previous test, or a counselor's assessment). All of these situations, and many more, are problematic with classical test theory as the measurement framework because examinee test scores are dependent on the particular sample of items and their level of difficulty.

What is needed, if the goal is to tailor or adapt the administration of tests to examinees, is an approach to ability estimation that is *not* test dependent. The influence of the particular items on the test administered to the examinee needs to be accounted for. Frederic Lord and Harold Gulliksen from the Educational Testing Service in Princeton, NJ, and many other psychometricians in the 1940s and 1950s, were interested in producing a psychometric theory that assessed examinees in a way that did not depend directly on the *particular* items that were included in a test. The idea was that an examinee may score high on an easy test or lower on a hard test, but there was a more fundamental ability that the examinee brings to any given testing situation that does not change as a function of the sample of items administered. It is this more fundamental characteristic of the examinee that is usually of interest to the assessment specialist and it is this more fundamental characteristic, referred to as a 'latent variable', that is of interest in modern test theory, often called item response theory. The construct of interest, or ability measured by the test, is more fundamental than test score because ability scores do not change with the particular choice of items in a test. Of course they can change over time due to learning, life changes, experiences, etc. If this capability were not present, the new psychometric models would have very limited utility.

The purpose of item response theory (IRT) is to overcome the shortcomings of classical test theory by providing a reporting scale on which examinee ability (the construct measured by the test) is independent of the particular choice of test items that are administered, and item statistics defined over the same reporting scale are independent of the particular examinee sample used in item calibration. What began in the 1940s and 1950s as a goal of psychometricians such as Richardson, Tucker, Gulliksen, Lawley, and others, became reality with the important publications of Lord (1952, 1980), Rasch (1960), and Lord and Novick (1968). By the early 1970s, the theory was very much in place, some computer software was available, and applications of IRT were beginning to appear.

As we begin the 21st century, IRT is being used by test publishers, large testing agencies, test developers, and agencies conducting the international comparative studies of educational achievement such as TIMSS and OECD/PISA, and assessment specialists around the world are addressing technical problems such as the automated design of tests, the study of item bias, equating test scores, computer-adaptive testing, and score reporting (Hambleton & Pitoniak, 2002; Hambleton et al., 1991). Van der Linden describes, in his chapter, the next generation of technical problems that are associated with the use of new test designs and automated test assembly (van der Linden, 2005)—building computer-adaptive tests with large numbers of specifications, controlling the exposure of items, detecting cheating, and cloning test items. He addresses each of these technical problems with IRT models.

IRT, in its basic form, postulates that (1) underlying examinee performance on a test is a single ability or trait, and (2) the relationship between the probability that an examinee will provide a correct answer (or agree with a statement, in the case of a personality or attitude survey) and the examinee's ability can be described by a monotonically increasing curve or function. We would expect examinees with more ability to have a higher probability of providing a correct answer than those with less ability, or, in the case of an instrument measuring attitudes towards a topic, we would expect those persons with very positive attitudes to agree with a statement more frequently than those persons with less positive attitudes. The estimation problem then is to place examinees and items on a reporting scale to maximize the agreement between the chosen model and the data itself (see Hambleton et al., 1991).

It may suffice to simply say that within an IRT measurement system ability estimates for an examinee obtained from tests that vary in difficulty will be the same, except for the expected measurement errors. Some samples of items are more useful for assessing ability (those that are targeted to the ability level of the examinee), and therefore the corresponding errors associated with ability estimation will be smaller than item samples that are less optimal, but the ability parameter being estimated is the same across item sets, unlike the case in classical test theory where the person parameter of interest, true score, is test dependent. Sample invariant ability parameters are of immense value in testing because tests can be matched to the ability level of examinees to minimize errors of measurement and maximize test appropriateness, while at the same time comparisons in ability scores can be made because the ability estimates are *not* test dependent.

The concepts that ability and item parameters do not change as a result of different samples of items and persons are known as *ability parameter invariance and item parameter invariance*, respectively. In theory, this is because when the item parameters are estimated, ability estimates are used in the item parameter estimation process (which is not the case in classical test theory). Also, when examinees' abilities are estimated, item parameter estimates are incorporated in that process (again, this is not the case in classical test theory). Both ability estimates and item statistics are reported on the same scale, so they look different from classical test scores and item statistics. Finally, IRT provides a direct way to estimate measurement error at each ability estimate (score level). In classical test theory, it is common to report a single estimate of error, known as the standard error of measurement, and apply that error to all examinees. Clearly, such an approach is less satisfactory than producing an error estimate at each ability score level.

Item and ability parameter invariance are of considerable value to test developers because they create new directions for assessment such as adaptively administered tests and item banking. Also, test development becomes easier with new IRT concepts such as item and test information and efficiency. Of course, the feature of *invariance* will not always be present. Item and ability parameter invariance will be obtained when there is (at least) a reasonable fit between the chosen IRT model and the test data. Not surprisingly then, considerable importance is attached to determining the fit of an IRT model to test data (see, for example, Hambleton et al., 1991).

Today, there are IRT models to handle nominal, ordinal, and equal-interval educational and psychological data: one-, two-, and three-parameter normal ogive and logistic models; partial credit and graded response models; cognitive component models; a rating scale model; a nominal response model, and many more. Multidimensional normal ogive and logistic models are available too. There are at least 100 IRT models in the measurement literature, and at least 10 are receiving fairly extensive use (van der Linden & Hambleton, 1997).

Challenges

Professor van der Linden lays out many highly technical challenges, all of which are associated with computer-based testing. My own favorite IRT research topic is associated with the all important question of model fit and how that fit should be judged in relation to a particular application. Statistical tests of model fit are of limited value because with a sufficiently large sample size (which is highly desirable for item calibration) the suitability of a model, any model and regardless of the number of parameters, will always be rejected. This means that other ways must be found to judge model fit. It is most likely that the solution will depend on judging the consequences of model misfit. When the consequences are tolerable for an intended application such as equating or test development, the model can be safely used, but such research is not common in practice, and emphasis persists in using statistical tests. More research is definitely needed for judging the suitability of IRT model fit for particular applications.

Another factor that hinders more widespread applications is the required sample size for good item calibrations. While those of us working on state testing programs in the United States or working for testing companies such as ETS or ACT have access to huge databases for IRT applications (samples of from 5,000 to 50,000 are commonly available), those less fortunate often have difficulty finding a couple of hundred examinees. Needed is more research to obtain good item calibration ('good' is defined here as model parameter estimates with low standard errors) with smaller and more realistic samples sizes that are available to many researchers. IRT Bayesian estimation appears promising with smaller examinee samples, but the suitability of these Bayesian estimates will depend on the success in generating appropriate 'priors'. (Priors are a researcher's beliefs about the actual values of item parameters.) Failure to specify priors properly could introduce substantial bias in the item calibration process, and lead to flawed ability estimates (see, for example, Swaminathan et al., 2004).

PAPER AND PENCIL TESTING TO COMPUTER-BASED TESTING

The biggest change in the next decade will likely be the administration of more tests at a computer (see, for example, Luecht, 1998; Luecht & Clauser, 2002; Wainer et al., 2000; van der Linden & Glas, 2000). Already, we are seeing hundreds of credentialing agencies in the US delivering their tests at a computer, and many more are coming on board. Admissions tests such as the Graduate Record Exam (GRE), the Test of English as a Foreign Language, better known as TOEFL, and the Graduate Management Admissions Test (GMAT) are now on-line. So, expanded testing at computers is a safe prediction.

As they shift to computer test administrations, testing agencies are moving from simply producing a fixed form or parallel forms of a test to various new test designs at a computer. Testing agencies have either moved to some form of linear test (parallel forms, or 'linear on the fly' tests with each examinee receiving a unique set of items subject to content and statistical specifications) or they have moved to computer adaptive testing (CAT). Both extremes of computer-based tests, in principle, allow for flexible scheduling of tests for examinees and immediate score reporting, and both are attractive features for examinees. CBTs also permit, in principle, the use of new item types for assessing higher level thinking skills (Irvine & Kyllonen, 2002; Zenisky & Sireci, 2002).

Our own research at the University of Massachusetts has focused on new computer-based test designs (for example, Hambleton & Xing, in press; Hambleton, Jodoin, & Zenisky, in press; Xing & Hambleton, 2004), especially multi-stage test designs. (They are not new in concept because Frederic Lord carried out research on these designs in the early 1970s, but they are fairly new in terms of being used in practice.) Instead of individualizing the test by optimal selection of *each* test item as is done in CAT, optimal selection in MST involves selecting a block of items called a 'testlet' (perhaps 15–20 test items). This is a very useful design because it allows for individualizing or adapting the test to examinee ability, while permitting examinees to omit questions within a testlet or change answers until the time the examinee decides to move to the next testlet. These two features—omitting items, and changing answers—may not seem important, but they are the two biggest criticisms examinees make of computer-adaptive tests such as the Graduate Record Exam (GRE) used in admissions decisions to graduate schools in the United States.

Test administration at a computer often involves test development via computer software. Software is needed that can mimic test design committees and can handle complex content and statistical specifications. There are a number of software packages that can now handle test development based on principles from operations research and linear programming—see, for example, the research by van der Linden, Luecht, Stocking, Jones, and others—but this software is based on statistical models and estimates of item parameters that contain error, and to date the software has not been able to completely serve as an expert system that mimics the test development work of committees. Therefore, they cannot be completed depended on to do what test developers might actually do in practice. At the same time, van der Linden has made substantial progress to that end, and his new text (van der Linden, 2005) organizes much of this important research.

Challenges

One of the most important areas for research with computer-based test designs concerns the handling of item exposure, and van der Linden addresses this topic in his chapter. With computer-based testing comes the need to expand the number of test items that are needed to maintain a valid testing program. In years gone by, examinees would all take the test at the same time, and then the test might be discarded. Today, test items are being exposed to examinees each time a test is administered, and those items must be reused or quickly the item bank would be exhausted. There is considerable fear that examinees, if they wanted, could work together to steal several test items and share them with examinees who are about to take the test, perhaps for a fee, or simply to disrupt the testing program or render the testing invalid. The answer seems to be to generate enough test items that examinees would be unlikely to have seen many of the test items that they are administered from an item bank, or, if they have, there are so many items that the only way to succeed would be to know the content! However, large banks of items cost large amounts of money and so research to produce large item banks in cost effective ways is needed.

Given the cost of producing test items, and the difficulty that testing agencies have in building up their item banks, I am surprised that some good ideas for expanding item banks are not being tried or implemented—for example, item cloning and item algorithms (see, for example, Pitoniak, 2002). I expect more research will be carried out in the coming years because computer-based testing of examinees on a flexible time schedule requires expanded item banks, or test score validity is likely to be adversely affected. The use of algorithmic item writing appears to be especially promising. For example, one could imagine algorithms built into a computer for preparing hundreds of test items involving variations on the various competencies described in the content specifications for a test. A simple example might be drawing a sample of numbers from a pool of numbers (say, 0 to 100) and asking examinees to calculate basic descriptive statistics. The only way to answer these items would be to know the formulas and have the computational skills. Even superficial changes to items might be a way to disguise items to examinees but then research would be needed to determine the suitability of the original item calibrations. There is another item calibration problem. With lots more items in an item bank, how can item calibrations be handled efficiently, since it is already the case that examinee samples for item calibration are typically limited (see, for example, Glas & van der Linden, 2003)?

Also, it has been suggested that an item bank might be divided into smaller subsets for use with computer-based tests, and then periodically the subsets could be rotated. But how many items are needed in a subset? How often should the subsets be rotated? What statistical signs might be used to determine when examinees are aware of the test items to such an extent that the test has been compromised? These are additional questions for research.

Another promising line of research involves setting conditional exposure controls on item use—a topic discussed by van der Linden. For example, we might restrict the use of an item to being seen by 20% of the examinees in a particular region of the ability continuum. However, what would be a reasonable level of item exposure? How exactly would these exposure controls work? In sum, substantial research will be needed to insure that new computer-based test designs can be implemented successfully.

MULTIPLE-CHOICE AND ESSAY ITEM TYPES TO NEW COMPUTER-BASED ITEM TYPES

More than 50 new item types have been counted (Hambleton & Pitoniak, 2002; Zenisky & Sireci, 2002), with many more variations on the way. Drasgow and Mattern offer many item type variations: they may involve complex item stems, sorting tasks, interactive graphics, the use of both audio and visual stimuli, job aids (such as access to dictionaries), joy sticks, touch screens, sequential problem-solving, pattern scoring, and more. Clearly, many new item types can be expected in the future since there is little point to assessing examinees at a computer and not taking advantage of all of the valid options that are available with computer-based testing. A consideration of computer-based tests in accounting, architecture, and medicine highlight what is possible if substantial funds and time are available (see, for example, van der

Linden & Glas, 2000; Irvine & Kyllonen, 2002; Pitoniak, 2002). However, even without substantial funds, improvements in assessment practices are possible with new item types involving sorting, classifying, and ranking tasks, and with automated scoring software, more frequent use of sentence completion, short answer, and extended answers. A review of the new item types described by Drasgow and Mattern in their chapter, and by Zenisky and Sireci (2002), clearly points to new item types that can be implemented relatively easily, with little cost, and with potential for increasing test validity.

Challenges

However, while new item types holds great promise for expanding what it is we can assess, I have five cautions for testing specialists who want to consider new item types in their tests: (1) be clear about the constructs you want to measure, and determine, via research, that the new types are necessary, and lead to the assessment of the construct of interest (I believe we are going to find that we are not always measuring what we think with these new item types), (2) be on the watch for new types, which may introduce bias into the assessment because of their novelty (for example, a new type may place members of international groups, minority groups, handicapped groups, etc. at a disadvantage), (3) all changes must be judged in terms of their contributions to score reliability and validity (newness and face validity are important but not the basis for judging the technical merits of innovations in assessment), (4) address practical considerations such as gains in test validity against the added costs of development and administration and scoring complexities, and test validity gains versus test time trade-offs (for example, often constructed response type items take more time for examinees to complete, but is the extra time leading to better measurement or better construct coverage?), and (5) consider the possibility of coachability (Are any test changes going to be coachable, and hence influence test validity negatively?). All of my cautions are about test validity, and I would not endorse the use of any new item types without research evidence to support them. These cautions serve as the basis for research regarding new item types. At the same time, I remain, like Drasgow and Mattern, very optimistic about the potential advantages of these new item types, and many more that can be expected in the coming years.

TRAINING OF MEASUREMENT SPECIALISTS

In the United States we have seen the growing demand for well trained psychometricians to work with testing agencies such as ETS, ACT, AIR, the National Board of Medical Examiners, and more, state departments of education, hundreds of credentialing agencies, and of course universities need young professors. However, the flow of graduates has been slow. Not only are the numbers low in the United States to meet current demands, but perhaps half of our current students are international; many are from Korea, China, Australia, Indonesia, and South Africa. Some of these graduates do stay in the United States, but many return home.

There are several encouraging signs, however, about the numbers of American students studying psychometric methods. First, graduate programs are being more aggressive about recruiting students. Our psychometric methods and statistics program for two years now has conducted seminars to introduce undergraduates to the field. We have already seen some results of our efforts. Other universities are implementing their own recruitment programs. Second, many testing agencies have added summer internship programs that provide financial support and most importantly, practical experiences for students working in the field. These summer internships are another incentive for graduate students to enter the field.

Of course, increasing the number of graduate students is only part of the problem. What should they be taught once they arrive? Were we to continue using our old lecture notes from the 1960s and 1970s, our students would not be prepared to meet the measurement challenges for this century. Presumably today graduate students need a balance of theory and practice in areas such as item response theory, generalizability theory, classical test theory, structural equation modeling, validity theory and practices, standard-setting, test development, performance assessment, test adaptation (or test translation), assessments for special need populations, item and test bias, score reporting, computer technology, and cognitive science. A good challenge for one of the national or international organizations such as the International Test Commission might be to form a working group to develop a three to four year program of study for measurement specialists. What should be the goals, major courses, content of these courses, and practical experiences, to produce graduates who can meet the assessment demands today? A one-year program too might be described with mainly a practical focus.

CONCLUSIONS

As highlighted by Drasgow, Mattern, and van der Linden, the next 10–20 years hold great promise for testing and assessment: expanded use of highly worthwhile IRT models for solving assessment problems, considerably more use of computer-based test designs, and the introduction of substantially more item types for assessing new skills. The potential for an increase in the validity of assessments is high, but so is the potential for a reduction in the amount of testing time, albeit with higher costs to testing agencies and examinees. However, any changes in test theory and testing practices should be based on careful and systematic research of the kind described by Drasgow, Mattern, and van der Linden, and not based on the salesmanship of computer software developers or the hopes of assessment specialists who substitute good ideas and potential for solid research evidence. With the demand for reliable and valid measures of a wide range of educational and psychological constructs and sound measurement practices to guide decision making, the need has never been greater for better tests and testing practices. However, never have the criticisms been louder of our current tests and practices. At the same time, because of research presented by Drasgow, Mattern, and van der Linden, the potential for successful theoretical and practical advances is very high!

REFERENCES

Brennan, R. L. (2001). *Generalizability theory*. New York: Springer.

Byrne, B. M. (1998). *Structural equation modeling with LISREL, PRELIS, and SIMPLIS*. Hillsdale, NJ: Erlbaum.

Glas, C. A. W., & van der Linden, W. J. (2003). Computerized adaptive testing with item clones. *Applied Psychological Measurement*, **27**:247–261.

Gulliksen, H. (1950). *Theory of mental tests*. New York: Wiley.

Hambleton, R. K., Jodoin, M., & Zenisky, A. (in press). Computer-based test designs and item types for the next generation of assessments. *International Journal of Testing*.

Hambleton, R. K., & Novick, M. R. (1973). Toward an integration of theory and method for criterion-referenced testing. *Journal of Educational Measurement*, **10**:159–170.

Hambleton, R. K., & Pitoniak, M. J. (2002). Testing and measurement: Advances in item response theory and selected testing practices. In J. Wixted (Ed.), *Stevens' handbook of experimental psychology* (3rd ed., Vol. 4, pp. 517–561). New York: Wiley.

Hambleton, R. K., Swaminathan, H., & Rogers, H. J. (1991). *Fundamentals of item response theory*. Newbury Park, CA: Sage.

Hambleton, R. K., & Xing, D. (in press). Computer-based test designs with optimal and non-optimal tests for making pass-fail decisions. *Applied Measurement in Education*.

Irvine, S. H., & Kyllonen, P. C. (Eds.). (2002). *Item generation for test development*. Hillsdale, NJ: Erlbaum.

Kolen, M. J., & Brennan, R. L. (1995). *Test equating: Methods and practices*. New York: Springer.

Lord, F. M. (1952). A theory of test scores. *Psychometric Monograph No. 7*. Psychometric Society.

Lord, F. M. (1980). *Applications of item response theory to practical testing problems*. Hillsdale, NJ: Erlbaum.

Lord, F. M., & Novick, M. R. (1968). *Statistical theories of mental test scores*. Reading, MA: Addison-Wesley.

Luecht, R. M. (1998). Computer-assisted test assembly using optimization heuristics. *Applied Psychological Measurement*, **22**:224–236.

Luecht, R. M., & Clauser, B. E. (2002). Test models for complex computer-based testing. In C. N. Mills, M. T. Potenza, J. J. Fremer, & W. C. Ward (Eds.), *Computer-based testing: Building the foundation for future assessments* (pp. 67–88). Hillsdale, NJ: Erlbaum.

Mills, C. N., Potenza, M. T., Fremer, J. J., & Ward, W. C. (Eds.). (2002). *Computer-based testing: Building the foundation for future assessments*. Hillsdale, NJ: Erlbaum.

Pitoniak, M. (2002). *Automatic item generation methodology in theory and practice* (Center for Educational Assessment Research Report No. 444). Amherst, MA: University of Massachusetts, Center for Educational Assessment.

Rasch, G. (1960). *Probabilistic models for some intelligence and attainment tests*. Copenhagen: Denmarks Paedagogiske Institut.

Swaminathan, H., Hambleton, R. K., Sireci, S., Xing, D., & Rizavi, S. (2004). Small sample estimation in dichotomous item response models: Effect of priors based on judgmental information on the accuracy of item parameter estimates. *Applied Psychological Measurement*, **27**:27–51.

van der Linden, W. J. (2005). *Linear models for optimal test design*. New York: Springer.

van der Linden, W. J., & Glas, C. A. W. (Eds.). (2000). *Computer adaptive testing: Theory and practice*. Boston, MA: Kluwer.

van der Linden, W. J., & Hambleton, R. K. (Eds.). (1997). *Handbook of modern item response theory*. New York: Springer.

Wainer, H., et al. (Eds.). (2000). *Computerized adaptive testing: A primer* (2nd ed.). Hillsdale, NJ: Erlbaum.

Xing, D., & Hambleton, R. K. (2004). Impact of test design, item quality, and item bank size on the psychometric properties of computer-based credentialing exams. *Educational and Psychological Measurement*, **64**:5–21.

Zenisky, A. L., & Sireci, S. G. (2002). Technological innovations in large-scale assessment. *Applied Measurement in Education*, **15**(4):337–362.

CHAPTER 5

Operational Issues in Computer-Based Testing[1]

Richard M. Luecht
University of North Carolina at Greensboro, USA

Computer-based testing (CBT) has enabled many new measurement technologies such as rapid item authoring, automated test assembly, new item type interfaces (e.g. computer-assisted performance-based simulations), use of adaptive-testing algorithms, testing in multiple languages, and prompt distribution of score results and reports to examinees, employers, teachers, etc. The Internet has further provided the capability to more widely distribute test materials in both secure and non-secure assessment settings throughout the world on 24/7 basis. The implication is that CBT has evolved into a highly convenient, cost-effective, efficient, and state-of-the-art mode of assessment. However, the reality is that implementing CBT tends to dramatically increase costs and raises many new operational challenges and concerns, especially for high-stake examination programs.

Computerization of an examination program requires testing organizations to design from scratch or re-engineer numerous functional procedures and systems that comprise the full testing enterprise. This can be a complex and expensive undertaking (see, for example, Sands, Waters, & McBride, 1997). CBT also introduces numerous new challenges for testing organizations such as developing efficient ways to mass produce high-quality items and test forms, dealing with test center capacity limitations, designing convenient systems for high-volume test scheduling, managing item theft and other forms of cheating under continuous modes of testing, securely transmitting high volumes of data, preventing denial-of-service attacks on web servers, designing effective accounting, quality control, and quality assurance procedures for managing and reconciling massive amounts of test data, and finally carrying out

---

[1] This book chapter is based on a presentation, Luecht, R. M. (June, 2002). *Operational issues in computer-based testing.* Invited keynote address at the International Test Commission Conference on Computer-Based Testing and the Internet, Winchester, UK.

Computer-Based Testing and the Internet: Issues and Advances.
Edited by D. Bartram and R. K. Hambleton. © 2006 John Wiley & Sons, Ltd.

ongoing psychometric analyses for calibration, scoring, and equating with sparse data.

This chapter addresses some of these challenges within the context of the various systems and procedures that make up an operational CBT enterprise. It emphasizes the need to recognize that a CBT enterprise is actually an integrated *system of systems*. Accordingly, a solid architecture may need to be engineered for CBT from the ground up—an architecture that is fully integrated, robust, efficient, extensible, and change friendly in terms of emerging new technologies.

TEST DESIGN AND DELIVERY MODELS AND FUNCTIONAL MIGRATION

One of the fundamental challenges in moving to CBT involves dealing with a variety of test design and delivery models. Available CBT test design and delivery models include fixed-item test forms, linear on-the-fly tests, computer mastery tests, adaptive multistage tests, and fully computerized adaptive tests. Each of these models serves a prescribed psychometric purpose. Some are adaptive; others are not. The challenge stems from the fact that different test design and delivery models require different systems and operational procedures to support their implementation and maintenance.

Almost any existing CBT design and delivery model can placed into one of two broad categories: (1) pre-constructed CBTs and (2) CBTs constructed online, in real time. Preconstructed tests are assembled offline and transmitted to the testing facility as needed. The simplest example is a fixed-item test form. The test delivery driver merely needs to administer the intact fixed-item test form to examinees. In contrast, CBTs that are constructed online, in real time, typically require the test delivery driver—a key component in one of the software systems discussed in this chapter—to provide extensive functionality with respect to data management, test assembly, composition, test administration, and scoring. That is, every test taker may potentially receive a unique test form, requiring the systems to manage huge numbers of possible test forms. To further complicate matters, a particular test form is not known until the CBT is completed by the examinee.

A suggestion offered in this chapter is to carefully consider the legitimate costs and benefits of online test construction. Online CBT construction places some rather heavy burdens on the operational software systems, especially when it comes to system performance, data management, and test form quality control. From a test development perspective, alone, one could argue that there are some quality assurance aspects of test development and assembly that are still best controlled—or at least carefully monitored—by human beings. This viewpoint does not preclude the capability to use computerized adaptive testing (CAT). A test can be adaptive and still be pre-constructed in a way that provides for some degree of quality assurance review. For example, a test design and delivery model like the computer-adaptive sequential testing (CAST) of Luecht and Nungester (1998) employs adaptively administered multistage tests, using a fully pre-constructed configuration that allows test developers to implement strong quality controls on the test forms before they are released. The distinction between pre-constructed CBTs and CBTs constructed in real time is relevant at many points throughout this chapter.

This chapter organizes the large array of operational CBT functional requirements into five 'systems', each with several embedded subsystems. In most cases, the system functionality is described within the context of pre-constructed test forms. For tests constructed in real time, the implied functionality does *not* change—it migrates to another system. This need for functional migration will be most evident between the test assembly and test delivery systems. This type of functional migration is highlighted, where relevant, for CAT and other types of test constructed in real time.

OPERATIONAL TESTING SYSTEMS

This chapter describes five systems that comprise a large-scale operational testing system: (1) item development and banking; (2) test assembly and composition; (3) examinee registration and scheduling; (4) test delivery; and (5) post-examination processing. Each of these systems also has several subsystems that perform specialized functions. Obviously, the individual systems and subsystems must work together in an integrated fashion. They must also be designed to allow for future changes and minimize the potential for any 'ripple effects' often associated with small system modifications that have unpredictable consequences elsewhere in the overall system. It all starts with recognizing the functional requirements of the individual systems within the integrated enterprise-level testing system. In that sense, this chapter is a high-level system design requirement document that may prove useful to organizations considering the move to CBT.

Figure 5.1 provides a conceptual architecture that shows the five systems and subsystems discussed in this chapter. Although these systems are discussed primarily from the perspective of software design, keep in mind that there are numerous implicit procedures and operations that are likewise performed or managed by humans. That is, many human activities and decisions are integral to successfully implementing and maintaining an operational CBT enterprise.

Item Development and Banking System

The item development and banking system contains three subsystems that need to work together and with other systems to generate, store, and maintain the supply of items needed to build tests. The subsystems are (1) the item

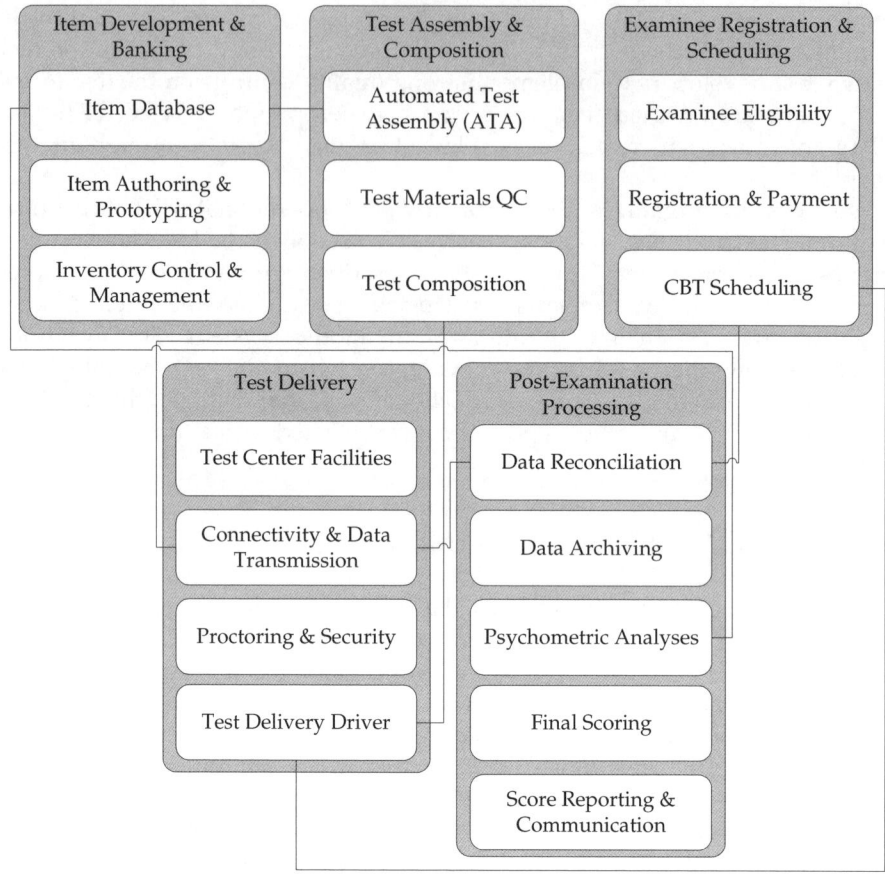

Figure 5.1   High-level conceptual architecture of a CBT enterprise

database, (2) the item authoring and prototyping subsystem, and (3) the item inventory control and management subsystem.

Item Database

An *item database* is what most people probably think of when they hear the phrase 'item bank'. Although some item databases have relatively simple file structures, an item database for CBT needs to be a complex data *repository* capable of storing sets of a variety of data objects, their relations, and associated functions—sometimes distributed across multiple sites and platforms. Fortunately, database technology has evolved from simple relational database schemes with structure query language (SQL) interfaces and basic online transaction processing (OLTP) capabilities to using data-centric models that work on distributed Internet platforms. It is even possible to have database clusters than are physically located at multiple sites, providing capabilities for massive, fully integrated data storage, retrieval, and manipulation.

An item database is a repository for storing a variety of data including text, pictorial images, exhibit references, and application data, content codes, skill codes, and other categorical attributes associated with the items, numerical item attributes such as word counts and readability indices, and statistical data such as p-values (item proportion-correct statistics), calibration-based statistics and estimation errors for various IRT models, aggregated item-set statistics, and DIF statistics. In addition, the database system needs to deal with potentially complex hierarchical relations among the data objects in the repository (e.g. managing item sets or testlets) and scripts associated with complex item types such as computer-based performance simulations.

The basic functional requirements for an item database include user-definable fields, flexible data structures based capable of supporting hierarchical data object models, capabilities to store embedded scripting and application-specific data (e.g. look-up tables or reference materials), multilingual capabilities, importing and exporting capabilities for XML and other standard database formats, robust error correction, portability across platforms, and computation support for statistical item banking.[2]

Some CBT item database subsystems are custom applications that use proprietary file formats and provide specialized data manipulation and reporting functions for particular testing applications. Other item databases are based on commercial database products such as Oracle™ (Oracle Corporation), SQL Server™ (Microsoft Corporation), or DB2 (IBM). These latter, commercial products tend to be more portable across platforms, are scalable in terms of size and scope of the database and associated applications, and typically provide very flexible and robust capabilities. For example, changing the database structure in a custom database application (e.g. adding or modifying data fields) can be tedious in terms of the required amount of design and computer programming needed. 'Ripple effects' associated with changing data structures also need to be considered in other parts of the system and may require even more extensive re-programming to be done. Making those same changes in a commercial database product, such as Oracle, SQL Server, or DB2, is relatively simple since these modern database systems can essentially self-modify the entire system-level application to take advantage of the changes.

Item Authoring and Prototyping

A second important requirement of an item development and banking system is support for *item authoring and prototyping*. Because of the unavoidable large

---

[2] Item banking refers to procedures for updating the stored statistics, such as IRT statistics, that are subsequently used for test assembly and possibly for scoring. Since each item may contain multiple statistics from different time frames or calibrations, the item banking process should provide ways to flexibly select and combine specific item statistics.

demands for items, the item authoring procedures and edit-support system components need to be efficient and extensible (i.e. capable of adding new features). There are four ways to achieve efficiency and extensibility in terms of designing an item authoring and prototyping subsystem. First, it is essential to standardize the inputs from item authors. That is, the subsystem should employ 'templates' or 'style sheets' that allow the item writers to provide the content to specific data fields within the template.[3] Item designers initially prepare the template. The item authors subsequently supply the content for each template. The item is rendered on a computer by merging the template features with the item content data. The use of templates provides a way to strictly control item production. Second, the item authoring subsystem should provide user-friendly editing tools that allow the item designers to easily generate templates and the item authors to add the requisite content for the templates. It is also important for the authoring subsystem to provide WYSIWYG[4] rendering capabilities, support the use of complex embedded scripts, and simulate test-taker functionality in real time. Third, the authoring and prototyping subsystem should provide component-based, rapid prototyping capabilities to allow item designers to create new item types. The prototyping subsystem should also enforce principled task design procedures that require the designers to justify the measurement information being gathered for a particular [valid] purpose. That is, the prototyping tools should force the designers to consider ways to *maximize* the measurement opportunities with respect to the valid knowledge, skills, and abilities being assessed. Conversely, the use of costly components or actions that lead to unintended or invalid off-task behaviors should be avoided. Finally, the prototyping tools should automatically generate templates to allow item writers to start creating content as quickly as possible. Fourth, the item authoring and prototyping subsystem should have a way of computing costs associated with using various stimuli or response capturing mechanisms. These may be direct production costs (e.g. using video clips) or indirect costs that restrict the opportunity to gather valid measurement information.

Inventory Control and Management

The third subsystem needed as part of an item development and banking system is the *inventory control and management* subsystem. Under CBT, item production must be viewed as a *manufacturing process*, where inventory management is a crucial function to ensure that supplies (the items on hand) meet current and future demands (test forms). This implies the need

---

[3] Mark-up item authoring tools that use 'data tags' to indicate the structure and format of free-form item text (stems, distractors, and other components) are usually not efficient and can even lead to the creation of nonstandard item types. It is better to provide the 'tags' as data fields in a template and allow the authors to fill in the content for each tagged field.
[4] What you see is what you get.

to develop a subsystem for tracking item inventory. A well designed item inventory control and management subsystem should work with the item database to provide five key functions. First, the inventory subsystem needs to identify and generate reports and flagging mechanisms related to critical content needs derived from the test specifications (i.e. project current and future demands). Second, the subsystem needs to track the availability of top quality items (i.e. monitor the supply). Third, the item banking subsystem must flag and develop new demands to replenish exposed or 'dated' items. Fourth, where item cloning and similar methods of generating item variants from a 'parent' or 'shell' are used,[5] the system must consistently and accurately track clones and variants on themes leading to 'item enemies' that cannot appear on the same test form. Finally, the subsystem needs to identify and quantify salient cost factors associated with item production. For example, using particular stimulus materials such as audio–video clips has production as well as performance costs. These costs need to be tracked across items and time. They may be incorporated in test assembly or used in developing future item writing templates and production specifications.

Test Assembly and Composition System

The test assembly and composition system is a critical part of the enterprise that is all too often overlooked. Test assembly is actually a three-step process. The first step involves selecting items from an item bank for specific test forms or test units such as test modules or testlets. The second step involves quality control checks on the test forms. The third step involves bringing together the selected items and composing the acceptable test forms in a format that can be rendered by the test delivery software. Some CBT vendors refer to this final step as 'publishing'.

As noted earlier, some or all of these test assembly steps may be performed 'offline' before the test materials are released to the field, or 'online' while the test is running. The issue of *where* and *when* the test assembly takes place is important in terms of *how* the test assembly system is designed and deployed—i.e., the test assembly system may be designed as a stand-alone system for offline test production or some or all of its components may be integrated with the real-time test delivery driver. This latter type of online test assembly system design is required for various types of computerized adaptive test (CAT) that select, administer, and score the test items in real time. As discussed below, the 'where/when' issue of test assembly also has quality control implications. However, the distinctions between 'offline' and 'online' test assembly do not dramatically change *what* the test assembly system does.

---

[5] Many testing organizations are recognizing the imperative to employ efficient item generation mechanisms to meet the huge demands under continuous CBT for high-stake tests that cannot risk over-exposing the test items.

Item Selection

Item selection subsystems can vary greatly. Some testing organizations prefer to use simple item database queries, random item selection strategies, or stratified random item sampling of content categories within statistically determined 'bins' to select the test items for each test form. Other organizations are transitioning toward using more sophisticated automated test assembly (ATA) software.

ATA involves the use of formal mathematical optimization procedures that include linear programming algorithms, network flow algorithms, and various deviation-based heuristics (Armstrong, Jones, & Kunce, 1998; Luecht, 1998a, 2000; Stocking & Swanson, 1998; Timminga, 1998; van der Linden, 1998). Using these types of algorithm or heuristic, ATA seeks to satisfy a particular mathematical goal, called the 'objective function', subject to any number of 'constraints' on content and other test item attributes. For example, ATA algorithms can build a test form to achieve a particular level of test difficulty or to achieve a prescribed amount of precision in some region of the score scale, subject to also meeting almost any number of content requirements or other test specifications such as minimum test length, word counts, reading levels, statistical impact on minority and majority groups, DIF, enemy items that cannot appear on the same test form, etc. These latter specifications are the ATA 'constraints'.

There are three functional requirements for an item selection subsystem—especially if ATA is employed. First, the subsystem needs to provide a means of extracting eligible item data from the item database. This extraction process requires using a database query to pull down the relevant statistical and content-related data fields for a subset of the entire item database. Second, the item selection subsystem needs a second, interactive database application to store and manipulate the various ATA statistical targets and constraints (i.e. the test specifications) used during item selection. Each ATA build becomes a 'project' that may be stored, modified, and re-run in the future. Finally, the subsystem requires a computer program—sometimes called an 'ATA engine'—to actually select the items for the test forms. Depending on the type of ATA engine used, the extracted item data, the statistical targets, and the test assembly constraints may need to be further reformatted in some type of mathematical programming syntax.

Unfortunately, despite the growing popularity of ATA for CBT, user-friendly ATA software engines are still not widely available.[6] There are ATA software systems in operational use that incorporate all three of the functions noted above. However, these systems either use proprietary corporate-owned software or rely on public-domain software developed for research rather than large-scale operational uses (see, for example, Luecht,

---

[6] Some CBT vendors currently claim to use sophisticated computerized adaptive testing (CAT) heuristics. Those claims should always be substantiated by potential clients as regards the extent of content balancing supported, choices of IRT models, and exposure control capabilities.

1998a, 2000; Luecht & Nungester, 1998; Swanson & Stocking, 1993). Despite the current, limited number of ATA software products available, there is a growing demand for ATA services. That demand is likely to lead to more software development in the near future.

Test Form Quality Control

Quality control (QC) procedures are also an essential aspect of the test assembly process. A *QC subsystem* is usually employed after the ATA procedures have assigned items to test forms as a means of 'acceptance testing' of the final test forms prior to activation. QC procedures can range from reviewing computer-generated statistical reports and outlier flagging mechanisms to identify potentially problematic test forms to having test committees conduct a formal audit or full item-level review of every test form.[7] Obviously, extensive human involvement in the QC process can be expensive (e.g. having test committees come together to manually review test forms for content validity). Also, as the number of test forms grows, the capability to physically carry out human QC reviews becomes less feasible.

Test Composition

The third test assembly and composition subsystem handles the actual publication of the test forms. That is, the *test composition subsystem* takes the item selection results from the ATA builds, pulls from the item database all of the item data needed to render the selected items for each test form or unit (text, pictorial materials, etc.), adds any relevant test administration data (splash screens, timing data, instructions, etc.), and finally reformats all of that data and saves it in a file that can be deployed for use by the computerized test driver. This composed test data is stored in what many companies call a 'resource file'. The resource file is essentially a stand-alone database file that may be structured in a proprietary test definition language (TDL), or in standard mark-up formats such as HTML or XML.

The test administration software accesses the composed test data in the resource file, rather than working directly with the item database. The reason is simple. A resource file is more compact than the item database and is typically easier to process. A resource can also be encrypted or obfuscated to prevent outside attempts to steal the item bank. External data sources such as large image files, reference databases for look-ups by the examinee, and audio files may be embedded in the resource file, referenced on a CD, or downloaded from a specific web or storage location. CAT and other methods of computer-based testing that employ real-time ATA and scoring may require additional

---

[7] CAT and other 'real-time' test assembly models typically use carefully designed computer simulations (i.e. model-generated item responses) as a type of indirect QC procedure meant to check on the integrity of the ATA algorithms and the quality of individual test forms produced.

data in the resource files including item answer keys, IRT statistical parameter estimates, exposure control parameters, and a variety of categorical content and other test assembly data.

It was noted earlier that the issue of where/when the test assembly steps take place has direct implications for quality control. Quality control steps can be readily applied when the test assembly process is performed offline (i.e. anytime before the resource file is released). It is theoretically possible to have test development staff review every test screen in the resource file. It is also possible to run real or simulated examinees through every test form in the active resource file using prescribed response patterns. This latter method is sometimes called 'master testing' and is used to verify answer keys, scoring protocols, and test routing rules. However, when some or all of the test assembly steps are moved online (in real time), quality control becomes far more difficult to guarantee with any certainty.

Examinee Registration and Scheduling System

The registration and scheduling system is often the first point of contact between the examinees and the testing system. This system allows an eligible test taker to register for the examination, pay any applicable fees, and schedule an examination date, time, and location. This system also needs to be multi-modal, providing direct access via the Internet and telephone access via toll-free 'call centers', and possibly even offering mail-order access. A discussion of the advantages and disadvantages of these three modalities is beyond the scope of this chapter. However, a well designed registration and scheduling system should ideally work for any combination of Internet, telephone, or mail-order services offered.

The registration and scheduling process requires support for three business functions: (1) handling restricted-eligibility testing; (2) providing registration and fee-payment services; and (3) offering scheduling/CBT seat reservation services.

Test-Taker Eligibility

The *eligibility subsystem* is essential for high-stake examinations and needs to restrict who sits for a test as well as where and when they can take the test. The eligibility subsystem can be viewed as a type of 'filtering' system that works with data transactions initiated by the registration and scheduling subsystems to restrict the list of individuals eligible to test, the dates/times available for testing, and access to particular test sites. The eligibility subsystem can be implemented in two ways. One way is to generate database tables containing the listings of all authorized test takers. The registration and scheduling subsystems then merely need to look-up new registrants as 'authorized' in the eligibility database table. The second approach is to establish eligibility policy rules that must be satisfied by the registration and scheduling subsystems. These policy rules could specify characteristics or attributes of authorized test takers, eligibility dates and times, and other potential screening information (e.g. retake restrictions). For many high-stake credentialing examinations, the testing organization, a state or federal licensing board, or a professional certification agency usually determines the precise eligibility policies. Regardless of who sets the policy, the policy information must then be converted to data that can be used to determine the eligibility for a specific examinee attempting access to the examination. Low-stake, on-demand examinations (e.g. IT certification tests) typically have no eligibility restrictions.

Registration and Payment Services

The *registration and payment subsystem* is often designed as a transaction based fee-for-service application. One option is to register by telephone. This option presumes that call center services are provided. If the Internet is used for online transactions, the registration and payment subsystem may use a secure socket layer (SSL) or a similar protocol to establish an authenticated connection and encrypt the transaction data exchanged between the test taker and the web server.[8] Regardless of how money is exchanged, once the candidate provides payment, the registration and payment subsystem typically provides a certificate, access token, or identification code that authorizes the user to take the test. This certificate or identification code is the test taker's 'key' to the test.

CBT Scheduling Services

The CBT *scheduling subsystem* may be designed to work jointly with the registration and payment subsystem or may be a separate service application. Having separate systems provides more flexibility. For example, a potential test taker might prefer to pay by telephone—not trusting the Internet for financial transactions—but want to schedule his or her examination date, time, and location on the web. The basic functions of the scheduling subsystem are (a) to maintain a database that has current open CBT seats,[9] arranged by testing sites, dates, and times (subject to restrictions established by the eligibility subsystem), (b) testing site selection assistance (e.g. search for sites close to a zip code or key landmark such as an airport), (c) to provide scheduling options to meet special testing needs for authorized accommodations and equipment, and (d) to create a relational link between the test takers'

---

[8] There are numerous security issues associated with web-based or even telephone transactions involving currency exchange. Schneier (2000) provides a nice overview of many of these issues.
[9] Some examinations require high-end computer equipment that may not be installed in every testing center. In addition, centers may have limited or high demands for seating where 'special accommodations' are required to test examinees with recognized disabilities.

data in the eligibility subsystem, the registration and payment subsystem and the *site.seat.date.time* records in the scheduling subsystem. This latter set of relational linkages is essential to be able to audit and reconcile the eligibility database with the registration and test scheduling databases.

Test Delivery System

The test delivery system has four basic functions. First, the system needs to transmit the examinee registration and test materials to a CBT workstation. This data can be manually copied onto a PC hard disk, downloaded from a local area network (LAN) file server, or transmitted from a central repository, via the Internet. Second, the examinee must be authenticated and logged into the system. Third, the delivery system needs to select and administer a test to the examinee. Finally, the examinee's stored test results must be safely transmitted to an appropriate data repository. The test driver may also provide capabilities for real-time score reporting.[10] In fact, there are multiple computer software and hardware components, people-based procedures, and facility configurations that make up the test delivery system. Four aspects of test delivery are outlined here: (1) the type of CBT center; (2) connectivity and data transmission; (3) proctoring and other security measures in place at the test center; and (4) the test delivery driver.

CBT Centers

There are two options for *CBT centers*. One option is to use *dedicated test centers*. These dedicated test centers may be corporate-owned centers or franchised centers. A dedicated test center often occupies a small suite of offices in a metropolitan area, employs full-time test administration staff, and has 10–30 testing stations running on a local area network (LAN). Data communications with the central test processing facility may be handled by any variety of channels, ranging from telephone modems to high-speed leased communication lines, broadband connections, or even satellite links. This type of dedicated facility has the advantage of standardized, secure control over the testing environment and all of the computer equipment. Some commercial testing vendors claim that these dedicated test centers also offer many ergonomic and access conveniences to test takers. However, using dedicated test centers comes at a price. That is, any dedicated business facility with revenue tied to service time—in this case, testing seat time—will tend to have high fixed operating costs and those costs will get passed on to test takers.

---

[10] Few, if any, high-stake testing programs use real-time score reporting. Rather, results are typically sent to a central test processing facility and checked for anomalies, prior to releasing the scores.

A second option is to take advantage of existing *multi-purpose distributed testing sites*.[11] These multi-purpose distributed testing sites can be set up in computer laboratories on college and university campuses, by using clusters of private networks at businesses, or in almost any setting that has locally networked computers that meet technical specifications and that have access to the Internet. In principle, an enormous number of secure testing seats can be activated on a single day of testing—similar to how large-scale paper-and-pencil testing is currently done. The transmission and test delivery software subsystems need to be extremely robust to allow these multi-purpose distributed testing sites to have 'plug-and-play' capabilities. That is, it should be possible to rapidly convert to a secure test center when needed. The remainder of the time, the site may serve other purposes (e.g. serving as a computer laboratory for college students).

One of the primary advantages of using multi-purpose distributed testing sites is that a testing program can offer a very high-volume testing event at multiple, convenient locations on a limited number of days, without carrying the overhead of dedicated centers. In terms of disadvantages, there are certainly nontrivial logistical and engineering challenges associated with establishing a robust, wide area network of multi-purpose distributed testing sites. However, the engineering technology currently exists to make this happen. In fact, a number of testing organizations have successfully carried out large-scale field studies using multi-purpose distributed testing sites. In any case, this appears to be the only way to legitimately add the needed capacity to accommodate large-scale testing events on particular dates.

Connectivity and Data Transmission

The *connectivity and data transmission* subsystem impacts a CBT enterprise system in two ways. First, it directly affects the extent of interactivity that is possible within various channels. Second, the type of connectivity employed can directly or indirectly affect the efficiency, accuracy, and security of the test data within particular channels.

Two fundamental characteristics of any transmission medium are channel capacity (bandwidth) and transmission speed. These two characteristics are essential since large-scale CBT inevitably requires remote testing, further implying that testing organizations must deal with potentially *different* comunication channels between various system layers. For example, local area networks (LANs) that connect the individual testing workstations to a local file server may be capable of relatively fast transmissions (100Base-T or better lines and network interface cards). These types of LAN can usually support dedicated channel, synchronous communications for transmitting blocks of

---

[11] A mutually exclusive decision is not necessary. That is, it is possible use a combined model that includes dedicated test centers *and* multi-purpose distributed testing sites. In fact, dedicated test centers could function as part of a wide-area, multi-purpose distributed testing site network.

data between the LAN server and workstations. Because bandwidth and speed are usually not serious considerations on a LAN, the connections can be highly interactive, efficient, accurate, and secure, usually with minimal administrative overhead.

However, the transmission medium used to move data between remote testing sites and a central processing facility usually lacks adequate bandwidth and speed to support highly interactive connections. Furthermore, gaining the necessary bandwidth can be very expensive. Therefore, most CBT organizations use a less expensive transmission medium that employs semi-synchronous or asynchronous communication between the remote LANs at their test centers and the central processing facility. An exception would be an organization operating its test centers as a wide-area network (WAN) using high-level data link (HDLC). Unfortunately, the more common types of lower bandwidth, slower communication medium may preclude highly interactive test delivery models such as computerized adaptive testing or the use of multi-part, interactive item types, such as computer-based performance simulations. Furthermore, a slower and lower bandwidth transmission medium tends to be less efficient and less accurate than a faster, higher-bandwidth medium, due to delay propagation, the administrative overhead of asynchronous communications, etc. In some cases, very slow 56K modem communications are still used to transmit data to and from CBT centers. Digital subscriber lines (DSLs) and digital cable service (DCS) certainly offer higher bandwidth and faster transmission rates than modem technology. However, it remains to be seen whether these broadband media can reliably establish robust and highly interactive communications. Satellite transmissions are sometimes suggested as an alternative to broadband; however, satellite transmissions typically suffer from detectable delay propagation, limiting the capability to carry out interactive communication between workstations at a center and a central processing facility.

Intermittent or delayed transmissions are clearly undesirable for interactive real-time communication activities (i.e. activities that occur while the test taker is taking his or her examination). High-resolution graphics or large sound files can also generate extremely high demands for bandwidth. Modern data compression and streaming technologies can help, but may still be affected by uncontrollable factors (e.g. sporadic traffic on the web). Physically distributing CDs or DVDs containing large graphics and sound files to the test centers seems a reasonable solution; however, this solution lacks efficiency and introduces potential system capability problems and data synchronization problems, as well as possible security breaches if the CDs or DVDs are lost or stolen.

A similar problem arises with respect to large item banks (i.e. the 'resource files' described earlier). That is, some of the connectivity issues discussed above may make it difficult to have a single-source resource file at every testing location. Instead, various versions of the resource file must be broadcast to remote test centers in anticipation of testing that will take place in the near future. In addition to the potential security risks associated with having an entire test item bank 'out there', it is also difficult to ensure that changes to test items and/or test driver components are completely up to date and synchronized across the entire testing enterprise. For example, consider the possibility that two examinees in separate locations get the same test question— except that one of the items is correct while the second is incorrect. This is a very plausible event, if the item data presented to each of these two examinees is stored locally at their respective test centers and updates are not properly synchronized. The inability to ensure simultaneous, fully synchronous updating of all active test materials is a special case of what is called 'propagation delay'. Barring the capability to ensure continuous updates (e.g. using HDLC-WAN technology), one solution is to move toward distributed systems that move smaller packets of data more often over the Internet, with embedded code similar to asynchronous communication.

The extent of interactivity relates directly to the types of data communication associated with various system-wide connections, that is, central processor to local server(s), central processor to workstations, and local server(s)–workstations. The choice of testing model and the degree to which the software uses 'distributed processing technology' or 'middleware' may also impact the system interactivity. For example, computerized adaptive tests (CATs) tend to be far more interactive—that is, more demanding in terms of channel resources—than fixed tests, since a rather sophisticated scoring procedure and a possibly even more sophisticated an item selection heuristic must be called after each item is administered. When these operations are resident on each local workstation, performance is usually excellent. When those scoring and item selection operations are moved to a middleware, distributed processing layer—either the local server or off-loaded to a processor farm, grid, or cluster—performance will probably not be degraded. However, if a central processor handles every exchange, item by item, the performance hit can be significant. In addition, the likelihood of propagation delays and intermittent transmission failures will increase by an order of magnitude, simply because there are more 'events' that can be affected.

Some of the newer distributed-processing cluster-based and grid-computing technologies (e.g. using server farms or 'metro networks') can actually reallocate and balance processing demands across a wide-area network as needed. Storage caching, compression and data-streaming technologies can also be used to reduce some real-time processing loads.

Proctoring and Test Security

The *proctoring and test security subsystem* can be comprised of a combination of software programs, hardware, and human activities. If there are any stakes associated with a test (e.g. salary increase, promotion, certification, licensure, grades, admissions), some examinees will inevitably try to cheat. Honor codes, signed attestation statements, and other types of passive security measure notwithstanding, those examinees intent on cheating will find creative ways to try to game the CBT system. They may use surrogate test takers, attempt to buy answers to questions, launch large-scale, coordinated efforts to memorize items to share with or sell to other test takers, or photograph/record test questions.

Proctoring and test center security needs to contend with as many of these potential risks as possible. In addition, there are other detection measures that testing organizations employ that are beyond the scope of the present discussion. It does seem relevant, however, to discuss four areas of test security relevant to the test center: (1) identification and authentication; (2) digital security; (3) preventing on-site cheating; and (4) reducing risks associated with collaborative theft of item banks.

Identification and authentication of the test takers is crucial for high-stake examinations. Surrogate examinees that show up and attempt to take somebody else's test can pose a serious threat to the integrity of an examination. Many testing organizations require two forms of identification, including a valid photo ID at check-in. Requiring the examinees physically sign a log or attestation statement provides a signature for the test taker's file and may discourage risk-adverse individuals from using surrogates. Many testing vendors also offer the option of taking on-site digital photos or employing some other means of biometric identification to authenticate the test takers. Finally, the access token or registration code provided to the examinee during the registration process can be used as a secondary authentication check. However, examinees can give their access token or registration code to somebody else. These identification verification and authentication steps primarily serve as 'gate-keeper' functions meant to prevent unauthorized access to the test; however, they can also provide a record of evidence that may be useful for detecting or reacting to suspected cheating after the test is completed.

A second aspect of test security relates to the prevention and detection of digital data security breaches. Digital data security breaches can range from outright data theft or eavesdropping to dealing with denial-of-service attacks (Schneier, 2000). Using network firewalls or virtual private networks, employing encryption technology, and monitoring secure transmissions between web and network routers can help to avoid some of these security breaches. Denial of service is a somewhat different security problem where the attacker attempts to slow down or stop service by overwhelming the system. These types of attack have not been reported as a serious problem in CBT to date; however, as more high-stake testing programs migrate to sending and receiving data over the Internet, test centers and servers could become vulnerable.

Outright cheating is still a major problem on a computer-based test. Having multiple test forms, using random item scrambling strategies, and exposure control mechanisms make it unlikely that two examinees sitting together will have the same test items in the same order. Testing programs can sometimes be lulled into a false sense of security by assuming that such preventative measures completely solve the cheating problem. Cheating behaviors also include attempts at copying from notes, taking notes or using small scanners or cameras to photograph test materials to share with future examinees, or using a cell phone or some other communication device to call others during a secure test.[12] One of the best prevention mechanisms for these types of security problem is to use test proctors. Proctoring can be done using human proctors and/or by using video and audio surveillance equipment to monitor the examinees while they are testing. Highly sophisticated surveillance, however, tends to be expensive and may add to the already high fixed costs of testing.

A final type of CBT security problem has to do with collaboration on the part of two or more examinees to memorize and share/sell large portions of the active item bank. This problem is actually exacerbated by having continuous testing and limited-capacity testing facilities for high-stake tests. That is, the limited seating capacity of most dedicated test center networks has forced many testing organizations to spread their testing out over multiple testing dates. Given the ongoing competition for seats between different testing organizations using the same test delivery vendor, testing often becomes a continuous or near-continuous event. Yet, continuous or near-continuous testing is very risky for *any* high-stake examination. From the moment that an item bank is 'exposed', examinee collaboration networks (ECNs) will attempt to collect as much information about the items as possible to share/sell to future examinees (Luecht, 1998b). These types of item-theft security risk/breach can have a devastating effect on the integrity of a testing program. There is an obvious solution: to increase the size and number of item banks. Large banks, frequently rotated, will help to prevent most collaboration efforts by test takers. Conservative estimates have suggested that item banks needed to be 8–10 times as large as the average test length (Mills & Stocking, 1996). Less is known about the number of banks needed per year, but three or four banks is not unreasonable.

Unfortunately, large item banks can only be constructed by *increased* item production. In turn, increased production costs will add substantially to the total cost of testing. For example, consider a testing program with the per-item costs estimated at $500. (This includes the costs to write, edit, try out, and integrate each item into a test form.) Assume that, under paper-and-pencil testing, the program generated two 100-item test forms per year, using 80% of the item bank, on average. The item production demand was for 250 items per year at a total cost of $125,000. Under continuous CBT, assume that item production needs to be ramped up to generate ten times as many items to prevent the ECNs from successfully benefiting from memorizing and sharing test items. This new demand increases cost of the item production to $1,250,000. If the number of testing days is decreased, by increasing testing seat capacity, the added production costs needed to maintain secure item banks can be proportionally reduced.

---

[12] There have been anecdotes of test takers caught hiding cell phones in the ceiling tiles of a restroom and using a restroom break as an opportunity to call somebody for assistance during an examination.

Test Delivery Software (Drivers)

A *test delivery driver* is a fairly complicated software application that typically does more than simply present items to examinees and collect their responses. The driver is partly an elaborate software user interface, combined with numerous behind-the-scenes data management capabilities and computational algorithms. As noted previously, some drivers may even employ various real-time test assembly capabilities.

This test delivery driver software needs to perform as many as seven functions: (1) test initialization; (2) test navigation for the test taker; (3) item/task presentation; (4) response capturing; (5) real-time scoring; (6) timing; and (7) selection of subsequent test units. To better understand these functions, it is important to first introduce the concept of 'test units'.

Most tests are comprised of up to four standard test units. A test item or individual performance exercise is the smallest unit of presentation. Second, items can also be grouped into sets or groups. In some cases, the items in a set or group may share a common stimulus. In other cases, the items may be grouped by a common content theme or for timing/security reasons (e.g., each set must be submitted as it is completed, preventing examinees from subsequently changing answers). Third, any combination of discrete items and item sets/groups can be combined into a section, module, or testlet.[13] The fourth and most general test unit is the test form. A test form can be a preconstructed collection of items or it can be constructed in real-time by the test delivery software. For example, a CAT may generate a test form one item at a time by moving some of the ATA functionality into the test delivery driver (see the 'Test assembly and composition system' section). At the end of a CAT, each test taker will have been administered his or her unique test form.

The test initialization process logs in the test taker and starts the test. If an intact test form, section, or set is administered; the test delivery driver typically loads the items into a navigation list control, which orders the items according to a random or some prescribed scheme. The primary function of the navigation control is to allow the test taker to move between items (or between test units). Some navigation controls only provide navigation between adjacent units (forward/backward, next/prior). Navigation controls may have an annotated listing of the items, including completion status of all of the available items in the current unit. This type of 'explorer-based' navigation allows the examinee to click on a particular item and jump directly to that item. Under CAT, items can be added to the navigation control as they are selected. The test developer decides whether backward navigation and the capability to change previous answers is allowed.

---

[13] The term 'testlets' is used in many contexts. The original introduction of the term (Wainer & Kiely, 1987) suggested that testlets were a special case of item sets that required some type of sequential problem solving, with possible dependencies between the items. The most recent use of the term in the context of 'multistage testing' implies that each testlet is an intact test section that may be adaptively administered.

The item/task presentation is handled by pulling together the item content from the resource file, adding relevant functionality from the template, and finally calling the appropriate test driver display and interactive software components to render the 'item' that the examinee sees on his or her computer screen. For example, a multiple-choice question (MCQ) links the content of the question stem, which is pulled from the resource file, to a text attribute associate with the software multi-line text display control. The content of each MCQ option (distractor) can be likewise linked to the label or caption attribute of a 'radio button'. The MCQ template positions the multi-line text display control and the radio buttons on the screen page. The test driver then renders the formatted item.

The test driver interfaces software for many modern test delivery drivers are based on reconfigured web browsers, using Netscape (Netscape Corporation) or Internet Explorer (Microsoft Corporation). Use of a web browser allows the same driver to be used across stand-alone PC, network, and Internet platforms. A combination of standard and customized plug-in components, server-side application software, and embedded programmed scripts are used to provide the necessary software functionality and security for these types of browser-based test delivery driver. The web browser platform also allows developers to use standardized rendering with hypertext mark-up language (HTML) and portable data structures via the extensible mark-up language (XML). Many of the existing test delivery drivers also use built-in templates or style sheets for composing and presenting various standard item types (multiple choice items, 'hot-spot' selection items, drag-and-drop items, etc.). Computer-based work simulations and performance exercises, or items comprised of rather complicated interfaces, are usually launched as external applications. This capability to launch an external application eliminates the need for the test delivery driver itself to provide customized functionality that is specific to a particular examination.

Response capturing involves recording the appropriate actions by the examinee as well as converting these actions to a particular data format, storing the data and then transmitting it. Response capturing mechanisms can vary from simple selections to complex actions. Consider that a multiple-choice question (MCQ) translates the examinee's selection (a mouse click) to a data record that denotes which of the MCQ distractors was chosen. In contrast, an extended response item or essay may use a text input box or word processor and require the test delivery driver to store a large block of formatted text. Interactive computerized performance simulations may require the test driver to store complex sequences of actions involving 'nodes' and 'relations' (among the nodes) or customized data structures such as data and formula entries in a spreadsheet.

Real-time scoring implies that the test delivery driver must implement some type of scoring rule and may further need to aggregate the item-level scores to produce a test-level score. A scoring rule is usually implemented as a type of pattern match between the examinee's response or actions and some idealized rule that allocates points. For example, matching the test taker's response choice against a stored answer key scores an MCQ. More complex scoring rules can evaluate complex patterns or relationships among choices of actions (e.g. scoring not only the correct actions, but also the sequence in which they were chosen). Artificial intelligence algorithms and neural nets can also be used to score constrained segments of written and spoken text. Obviously, these more complicated scoring mechanisms add complexity to the test delivery driver and tend to exponentially increase the real-time system performance demands. It is here that some of the connectivity and data transmission issues (discussed earlier) become highly relevant.

Aggregate scoring is essential for most types of computerized adaptive test (CAT). That is, a score is needed in order to sequentially tailor the test to the examinee. Many commercial test delivery drivers provide the capability to score a test using number-correct scoring or scoring based on the one-, two-, or three-parameter IRT models. (See Hambleton and Swaminathan, 1985, for a description of IRT scoring under these models.) The test delivery driver needs access to scored responses and the IRT item statistics for the items adminis-tered. These latter data are typically stored in the 'resource file' noted earlier. When called, the scoring algorithm then uses number-correct scoring, max-imum likelihood estimation or Bayesian estimation to calculate the test taker's score.

Most computer-based tests are timed. Although timing introduces potential speededness effects, the need for timing controls is usually unavoidable as a way to standardize the conditions of testing and as a means of controlling computer seat time. In a well designed test delivery driver, the test timer can be applied to any test unit. That is, the total test may have a global time limit. However, sections or even testlets may also have time limits imposed. There is limited empirical evidence that segmenting a longer test into shorter time blocks actually facilitates pacing for some examinees (Hadadi and Luecht, 1998).

The last standard function for the test delivery driver is test unit selection. It is important to keep in mind that test unit selection may apply to an item, an item set, a testlet/module, or a full test. There are actually three general ways that a test delivery driver can select the next test unit. One way is to simply select the next unit in an ordered list. The second method is to select randomly from a list of two or more test units. The final method is rule-based selection. A CAT uses a particular item selection rule that computes the precision (statistical information) for each unselected item at the current provisional score for the test taker and chooses the item with the maximum precision. More elaborate selection rules are possible, including the possibility of implementing formal ATA algorithms that incorporate content balancing heuristics and exposure control mechanisms (Stocking and Swanson, 1993; van der Linden, 2000). It is important to realize that increasingly more complex test unit selection rules tend to (a) require more data to be stored in the resource file, (b) add to the programming complexity of the test delivery driver, and (c) lead to system performance degradation or QC problems under less-than-optimal connectivity configurations (e.g. low-bandwidth transmis-sion channels).

Special Test Delivery Accommodations and Functions

In addition to the above seven standard test administration functions, the test delivery subsystem must also be capable of implementing special procedures such as workstation and/or server restarts (in the case of power failures, freeze-ups, or system crashes), and special accommodations such as extended time, software aids for visually impaired test takers, audio or reader support, or 'quiet' environments for individuals with attention deficit disorders.

Post-Examination Processing System

Once a test is completed, the test taker's data are typically transmitted back to a central processing facility. In most cases, the same data transmission channel as used to send the test materials and registration data to the test center will serve for transmitting the examination results data. When the data arrives at the central processing facility, five basic functions are needed: (1) reconciliation; (2) archiving; (3) psychometric analyses; (4) final scoring; and (5) score reporting and communication.

Data Reconciliation

Reconciliation is an essential accounting function that ensures the receipt of an uncorrupted test record for every eligible examinee scheduled to test in every test center. The *reconciliation subsystem* must provide up-to-date counts and details of discrepancies regarding the multitude of examinee records being processed through the system. Some examples of reconciliation include matching the test records received from the test centers with test-taker eligibility records, accounting for duplicate records and identifying 'no shows'. The reconciliation process also needs to verify the data integrity of each test record (e.g. identifying incomplete, partial, or corrupted test records for resolution).

Data Archiving

The *archival subsystem* places the test records into long-term database storage. This process typically stores all the examinee identification information, item identifiers, raw responses, scored response values, and cumulative time per item or performance task. Efficient relational database designs for archiving the data are relatively common. In principle, a test taker's entire examination sequence should be retrievable from the archive, regardless of how or where the data is actually stored.

Psychometric Analyses

The *psychometric analysis* subsystem is an omnibus collection of software tools and psychometric expertise that underlies scoring and item banking activities.

Item analysis and key validation are two common types of analysis that must be performed before scoring can take place. Other psychometric analyses may include IRT calibrations, equating analyses, differential item functioning analyses, dimensionality analyses, and item banking operations used to generate aggregated item statistics for subsequent scoring or for future test assembly (see the 'Item development and banking system' section). Most of the applications that carry out these types of analysis are separate software utilities. An important requirement of the post-examination processing system is therefore the capability to export item response and scored examinee data to the formats needed by various psychometric analysis software tools. For example, many item analysis and IRT calibration software programs use fixed-column, ASCII (text) response records as inputs. The need to flexibly select the intersection of a set of items with a set of test takers—usually derived by a database query that produces either normalized or rectangular person-by-item flat files—is a fundamental requirement for subsequently analysing most data, using existing psychometric analysis software tools.

Final Test Scoring

Final test scoring represents a special class of psychometric analyses. A separate subsystem for final scoring provides greater flexibility in terms of adding new scoring functions as well as migrating these same software-scoring components from post-examination processing to the test delivery driver, if needed for real-time scoring. However, it is important to realize that, for high-stake tests, there are distinct benefits associated with moving the final scoring process out of the test delivery system (e.g. being able to check for cheating problems, miskeys, etc. before scores are released).

There are three basic levels to final scoring. The first level of scoring converts the test taker's raw responses to some type of item or unit score. For example, a correct answer choice on a multiple-choice question is typically converted to a one; an incorrect choice is converted to a zero. A constructed response item might be subjected to a pattern-matching algorithm or some type of semi-intelligent scoring algorithm (see, e.g. Bejar, 1991; Luecht & Clauser, 2002). The test delivery driver may also need to support this first level of scoring functionality (i.e. raw response conversion), especially for adaptive testing. However, viewing this conversion function as part of a separate subsystem may lead to a more open-ended design that facilitates adding new scoring protocols (e.g. intelligent scoring for new item types) as well as providing easy rescore operations. The second level of scoring is aggregated scoring over items or test units. Number-correct scoring, weighted number-correct scoring, and IRT maximum likelihood or Bayesian scoring are common aggregate scoring functions. The details of these scoring algorithms are beyond the scope of this chapter. Suffice it to say that a data vector of scored raw responses and a corresponding vector or array of weights or item statistics are the required data for most aggregate scoring functions. The final scoring function is a transformation of the aggregate scoring function. These functions can range from linear scale transformations to test characteristic function transformations to tabular score look-ups. The outcome data table or file typically contains one or more score records for each examinee. These score records can then be to a database for final processing and reporting.

Score Reporting and Communication

The final functional subsystem within the post-examination processing system handles *score reporting and communication*. Once the scores are produced and loaded into a database, score reporting and communication can be managed as a rather straightforward database reporting function, using 'report forms'. A database report form is a type of template for printing reports, invoices, or correspondence in a designated format. A form letter is actually a type of report form. The common text and field formatting information are reapplied for each record. The unique information on each record such as name, examinee identification, address information, scores, etc. is added to the printed report in designated field locations. Most modern database utilities include sophisticated report design utilities and can even integrate graphics into the reports. Report outputs can be printed or generated in electronic formats (e.g. as HTML pages or XML files). Interactive score reporting applications are also possible, for examinations that provide the test takers with online access to their results. For example, diagnostic score reporting might also direct the test takers to relevant educational sources.

CONCLUSIONS

The fundamental message of this chapter should be clear. Implementing an operational CBT program requires the development of a complex enterprise involving many systems and procedures. There are two options for handling this complexity. One option is to purchase, lease, or contract with somebody else to develop and/or manage the enterprise. The other option is to develop an internally controlled enterprise. The former approach is usually more cost effective—especially if 'off-the-shelf' software solutions are readily available and prove useful. Unfortunately, 'off-the-shelf' systems rarely provide *all* of the capabilities needed by a particular testing organization. Organizations opt for a combination of internal development and contracting for some specific services and software products from external CBT vendors, professional testing organizations, and technical consultants. Obviously, the complication then becomes integration across the enterprise. In any event, organizations considering the move to CBT need to accept the high costs and extensive time needed to build a robust, operational CBT enterprise.

A final suggestion is to remember the important roles of human decision-making and processing activities and throughout the enterprise. Test development specialists, item writers, editors, psychometricians, statisticians, systems analysts, database administrators, operations specialists, and a multitude of clerical and other support staff members are all essential to the smooth functioning of the testing enterprise. Training, productivity incentives, work-load analysis, and attention to the human-factor side of systems design cannot be ignored.

REFERENCES

Armstrong, R. D., Jones, D. H., & Kunce, C. S. (1998). IRT test assembly using network-flow programming. *Applied Psychological Measurement, 22*:237–247.

Bejar, I. I. (1991). A methodology for scoring open-ended architectural design problems. *Journal of Applied Psychology, 76*:522–532.

Hadadi, A., & Luecht, R. M. (1998). Some methods for detecting and understanding test speededness on timed multiple-choice tests. *Academic Medicine, 73*:S47–50.

Hambleton, R. K., & Swaminathan, H. R. (1985). *Item response theory: Principles and applications.* Hingham, MA: Kluwer.

Luecht, R. M. (1998a). Computer assisted test assembly using optimization heuristics. *Applied Psychological Measurement, 22*:224–236.

Luecht, R. M. (1998b, April). *A framework for exploring and controlling risks associated with test item exposure over time.* Symposium conducted at the National Council on Measurement in Education Annual Meeting, San Diego.

Luecht, R. M. (2000, April). *Implementing the computer-adaptive sequential testing (CAST) framework to mass produce high quality computer-adaptive and mastery tests.* Paper presented at the annual meeting of the National Council on Measurement in Education, New Orleans, LA.

Luecht, R. M., & Clauser, B. E. (2002). Test models for complex CBT. In C. Mills, M. Potenza, J. Fremer, & W. Ward (Eds.), *Computer-based testing: Building the foundation for future assessments* (pp. 67–88). Mahwah, NJ: Erlbaum.

Luecht, R. M., & Nungester, R. J. (1998). Some practical examples of computer-adaptive sequential testing. *Journal of Educational Measurement, 35*:229–249.

Mills, C. N., & Stocking, M. L. (1996). Practical issues in large-scale computerized adaptive testing. *Applied Measurement in Education, 9*:287–304.

Sands, W. A., Waters, B. K., & McBride, J. R. (Eds.). (1997). *Computerized Adaptive Testing: From inquiry to operation.* Washington, DC: American Psychological Association.

Schneier, I. P. (2000). *Secrets and lies: Digital security in a networked world.* New York: Wiley.

Stocking, M. L., & Swanson, L. (1993). A method for severely constrained item selection in adaptive testing. *Applied Psychological Measurement, 17*:277–292.

Stocking, M. L., & Swanson, L. (1998). Optimal design of item banks for computerized adaptive tests. *Applied Psychological Measurement, 22*:271–279.

Swanson, L., & Stocking, M. L. (1993). A model and heuristic for solving very large item selection problems. *Applied Psychological Measurement, 17*:177–186.

Timminga, E. (1998). Solving infeasibility problems in computerized test assembly. *Applied Psychological Measurement, 22*:280–291.

van der Linden, W. J. (1998). Optimal assembly of psychological and educational tests. *Applied Psychological Measurement, 22*:195–211.

van der Linden, W. J. (2000). Constrained adaptive testing with shadow tests. In W. J. van der Linden & C. A. W. Glas (Eds.), *Computer-adaptive testing: Theory and practice* (pp. 27–52). Boston, MA: Kluwer.

Wainer, H., & Kiely, G. L. (1987). Item clusters and computerized adaptive testing: A case for testlets. *Journal of Educational Measurement, 24*:185–201.

CHAPTER 6

Internet Testing: The Examinee Perspective

Michael M. Harris, Ph.D.
University of Missouri—St. Louis, USA

Although testing for employment, educational, and certification purposes has been conducted for many years, Internet-based testing is a relatively new area that has only recently become quite popular. Much of the current research has focused on the test *user's* perspective, with an emphasis on psychometric differences between traditional (i.e. paper-and-pencil) testing and Internet-based testing. So far, results have *generally* supported the equivalence of these two administration modalities. Mead and Coussons-Read (2002) used a within-subjects design to assess the equivalence of the 16PF Questionnaire. Sixty-four students were recruited from classes for extra credit and first completed the paper-and-pencil version and about two weeks later the Internet version. Cross-mode correlations ranged between. 0.74 to 0.93 with a mean of 0.85, indicating relatively strong support for equivalence. Reynolds, Sinar, and McClough (2000) examined the equivalence of a biodata-type instrument using 10,000 candidates who applied for an entry-level sales position. Similar to Mead and Coussons-Read (2002), congruence coefficients among the various groups were very high. However, another study (Ployhart, Weekley, Holtz, & Kemp, 2003) reported somewhat less positive results for a large group of actual applicants for a service job. Specifically, Ployhart et al. found mean differences, as well as differences in test reliability, between Internet-based tests and paper-and-pencil tests. Two critical questions, namely whether test validities or adverse impact ratios differ depending on whether the test is administered over the Internet or using paper-and-pencil materials, have yet to be addressed in the employment context (Harris, 2002). One published study, conducted in the educational domain, found that although validity coefficients were about the same for both computer-based and paper-and-pencil based versions of a speeded reading comprehension test the average test scores were higher for the computer-based version (Pomplun, Frey, & Becker, 2002).

Computer-Based Testing and the Internet: Issues and Advances.
Edited by D. Bartram and R. K. Hambleton. © 2006 John Wiley & Sons, Ltd.

This chapter takes a different focus, addressing *examinee reactions* to internet-based testing. Interest in test-taker reactions is a relatively new phenomenon. Landy and Shankster (1994) went so far as to argue that interest in test-taker reactions heralded a major paradigmatic shift in the field of I/O psychology. Regardless, there is a growing literature that indicates test-taker reactions is an important variable for both practical and theoretical reasons. While there has been relatively little work investigating examinee reactions to Internet-based testing programs, Anderson (2003) provides a critical review of this area and presents a broad theoretical framework for understanding job applicant and recruiter reactions to new technology. This chapter takes a more narrow approach, highlighting three important antecedents to test-taker reactions and suggesting some potentially important moderators.

The remainder of this chapter is divided into five sections. First, I discuss several consequences of test-taker reactions. I then review three determinants of test-taker reactions: procedural justice perceptions, organizational privacy perceptions, and test-taking motivation (and in particular, computer anxiety), in the next three sections respectively. Finally, I offer some practical suggestions for organizations concerned with maintaining positive test-taker reactions.

Before I begin to discuss test-taker reactions, however, it is important to define Internet-based testing. The simplest definition is that Internet-based testing is a procedure that uses the Internet or Intranet for administering a test. Beyond this simple definition, Lievens and Harris (2003) observed that Internet-based testing may vary in terms of several aspects. I will address only two of these: the type of test and the test administration conditions.

The type of test that is being administered has rarely been made the focus of discussions of Internet testing. I believe, however, that the type of test being used may have an important effect on examinee reactions to an Internet-based administration. For example, if very personal questions are asked over the Internet, test-takers may be more concerned with privacy issues than if the same questions are asked in a paper-and-pencil format. Conversely, a cognitive ability test administered through the Internet may be more affected by computer anxiety than the same test administered via a paper-pencil mode. Thus, I would expect that the type of test at issue will affect the importance of each of the antecedents in the model.

Test administration can vary along several dimensions, including whether an actual live test administrator is present, the type of user interface (e.g., can the test-taker return to an earlier item?), and the technology used (e.g. the speed of the connection). It is therefore important to bear in mind that different approaches to Internet-based testing may elicit different test-taker reactions (Reynolds & Lin, 2003) and therefore results using one approach to Internet-based testing (e.g. a proctored examination) will not necessarily generalize to a different approach to Internet-based testing (e.g. a non-proctored examination).

Figure 6.1 provides an overview of this chapter. As shown in Figure 6.1, there are three determinants of test-taker reactions (i.e. organizational justice

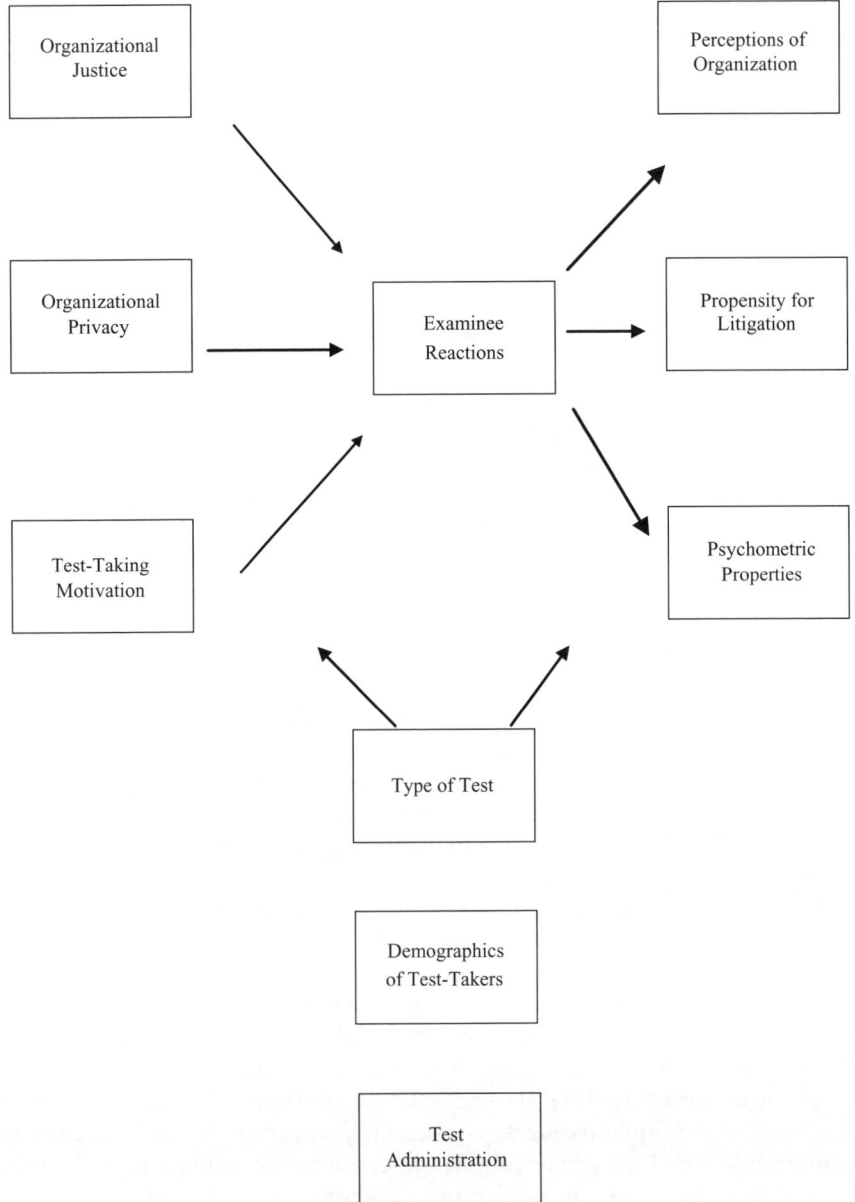

Figure 6.1 Model of test-taker reactions to Internet-based testing

perceptions, organizational privacy perceptions, and test-motivation theory). In turn, test-taker reactions are assumed to affect three variables: perceptions of the organization, propensity to engage in litigation, and psychometric properties of the test. Three variables are shown in Figure 6.1 as potential moderators of these relationships: the type of test at issue, the test administration used, and demographic characteristics of the test-taker. In terms of the latter variable, I suggest that age, as well as gender and ethnicity of the examinee, may affect their reactions. Reasons for this are addressed throughout the paper.

It should be noted here that some of the research discussed in this chapter is based on computerized versions of a particular test, not an Internet-based version of a test. The degree to which the results of these studies generalize to Internet-based tests has yet to be determined. Caution is needed, then, in generalizing from studies of computer-based testing to Internet-based testing.

CONSEQUENCES OF TEST-TAKER REACTIONS

The industrial/organizational (I/O) psychology literature has offered three important outcomes of test-taker reactions (Borman, Hanson, & Hedge, 1997):

(1) testing processes might be viewed as a reflection of the organization's characteristics, which may in turn affect job applicants' willingness to join the organization;
(2) testing procedures that elicit negative examinee reactions might encourage lawsuits to be filed; and
(3) reactions might affect psychometric properties of the test.

While there has been discussion elsewhere as to why examinee reactions may affect variables such as perceptions of the organization, I would assert that Internet-based testing has some unique properties. While these outcomes have been studied in traditional (i.e. paper-and-pencil) test situations, I believe that Internet-based testing may be even more strongly linked to these outcomes, as explained in more detail next.

While it is often said that test-taker reactions are causally linked to perceptions of the organization, there has been little discussion as to exactly which aspects of the organization might be affected. Recently, Lievens and Highhouse (2003) distinguished between instrumental perceptions and symbolic perceptions of an organization. The former construct refers to a candidate's judgments regarding such as aspects as the pay, benefits, and kind of work that might be performed, while symbolic perceptions refer to the organization's reputation (innovativeness, prestige, and sincerity). Indeed, Lievens and Highhouse found that the symbolic perceptions accounted for additional variance in organizational attractiveness above and beyond instrumental perceptions in a hierarchical regression analysis.

I would predict that Internet-based testing processes are particularly influential in determining symbolic perceptions of the organization. To the degree to which these processes are perceived to be fair and protective of privacy, I believe that Internet-based testing systems will *positively* contribute to symbolic judgments. To the degree to which these processes are perceived to be unfair and invasive of privacy, they may *negatively* contribute to symbolic judgments of the organization.

There are a number of reasons to believe that perceptions of an organization's Internet-based testing processes may have a stronger link to discrimination claims than other testing processes. First, use of the Internet may introduce additional sources of error variance including system malfunctions and slow processing speed, which are obvious sources of perceived unfairness that could cause great dissatisfaction on the part of candidates. Second, depending on how the test is administered (e.g. proctored facility or at any facility the applicant desires), differential access by minorities may create unique barriers to taking the test (Lievens & Harris, 2003). Even with the wide availability of Internet access, lack of standardization and claims of cheating are likely to arise, particularly as more companies switch to online systems.

Finally, just as simulation exercise scores may be affected by the degree of cognitive loading (Goldstein, Yusko, Braverman, Smith, and Chung, 1998), scores on tests administered over the Internet may be affected by the degree to which one is comfortable with this technology. As discussed later in this chapter, individual differences in computer anxiety may affect test scores. Different technologies over the Internet, such as Instant Messenger and pop-up menus, may be perceived differently, depending on the examinee's age. Ultimately, computer anxiety may affect the validity of a test that is administered over the Internet.

The reader should note that despite the fact that organizational justice theory, organizational privacy theory, and test-taking motivation models have generally developed separately, they are probably not completely independent. From a conceptual standpoint, Bies (1993) argued that privacy may be one component of organizational justice. Eddy, Stone, and Stone-Romero (1999) reported a large factor correlation (-0.77) between privacy and fairness perceptions of a human resource information system (HRIS), indicating that privacy and fairness are interrelated concepts. Thus, there is likely to be conceptual and empirical overlap between organizational justice and organizational privacy constructs. I suspect that test-taker motivation may also be related to these constructs; test-takers who feel that the process is not fair may also not be motivated to do well.

ORGANIZATIONAL JUSTICE THEORY

Organizational justice theory has advanced rapidly in the last two decades. Organizational justice theory assumes that there are at least two major determinants of fairness: procedural fairness and distributive fairness. The former refers to the procedures used in making decisions; in the present context, this would concern the fairness of the testing procedures. Distributive fairness refers to the outcomes received and whether one considers the outcomes (e.g. the test scores) received to be fair. A judgment as to whether the outcomes received were fair is usually based on a comparison either with what one expected to receive or with what others have received (van den Bos, Lind, Vermunt, & Wilke, 1997). While procedural fairness and distributive fairness are frequently studied in tandem, I focus exclusively here on procedural fairness, as I believe it is in this regard that Internet-based testing involves some different considerations compared with traditional testing processes. Thus, the fact that I do not discuss distributive justice here is *not* a reflection on its theoretical or practical importance; it is equally important that it be included in empirical investigations.

In one of the few empirical investigations that examined examinee reactions to an internet-based test, Sinar and Reynolds (unpublished paper) investigated a setting in which job applicants were tested in 'proctored, centralized environments (e.g. state-run employment centers) under the guidance of trained administrators' (p. 8). Among their other variables, Sinar and Reynolds examined test-takers' answers to an open-ended question ('Do you have any additional comments about this assessment process?'). Just over 10% of the sample responded to the administration process. Of those, about 25% addressed the speed/efficiency of the testing, with negative comments outweighing positive comments about two to one. Twenty percent of the comments concerned the novelty of the testing process, of which nearly all were positive and none were negative (a few were neutral). General comments and user-friendliness comprised the next two categories, with the overwhelming number being positive. Of perhaps greater interest was that 6.4% of the comments addressed 'testing environment' (sample item: everyone was nice at the staffing office). Of these comments, about four-fifths were positive. Finally, concerns about fairness/security were raised by 4% of the respondents, and of these the vast majority were positive.

Sinar and Reynolds (unpublished paper) categorized respondents into highly satisfied and dissatisfied groups (based on their comments) and examined the relationship with withdrawal from the job application process and rejecting/accepting a job offer. None of these relationships was statistically significant. As noted by the authors, however, the Internet-based testing system was carefully designed to ensure a highly effective process. The highly positive nature of the reactions was therefore not surprising. Speed/efficiency was the only area that received a significant number of negative responses; testing environment received predominantly positive comments. Fairness/security was mentioned by few respondents and most of these comments were positive. Clearly, fairness/security was not a major issue here. On the other hand, recall that the authors used a proctored, centralized setting that included trained administrators. Thus, this setting may represent the 'best of worlds' for testing. Also, this was a novelty for test-takers and they may not have considered all the possible implications.

In building on the study by Sinar and Reynolds, it is important to consider Gilliland (1993), who was the first to develop a model of procedural fairness in the context of employment testing. Gilliland hypothesized a number of relevant dimensions, including consistency, reconsideration opportunity, and feedback. A list of these dimensions is provided in Table 6.1. Bauer et al. (2001) created an empirical measure of these dimensions and concluded that a three-factor higher-order model—social, structural, and job-relatedness

Table 6.1 Procedural justice dimensions from
Bauer et al. (2001)

---

1. Job-relatedness of the test
2. Chance to perform on the test
3. Reconsideration of test results
4. Consistency of administration
5. Feedback on test results
6. Information known about the test process
7. Openness of communication about the test
8. Treatment during the test
9. Two-way communication regarding the test
10. Propriety of the questions

---

content—provided a reasonably parsimonious representation of these dimensions. The social higher-order factor included such dimensions as consistency of the test administration, two-way communication, and treatment during the test process. The structural higher-order factor covered such dimensions as reconsideration opportunity and feedback (job-relatedness content was defined by a single dimension). Even when actual test outcome and demographic variables were included as predictors, Bauer et al. (2001) found that the procedural justice factors explained additional variance in their criteria. Particularly noteworthy is that, of the three higher-order factors, the social higher-order factor was generally more important than the other two higher-order factors (structural and job-relatedness content). Clearly, then, procedural justice is likely to affect test-takers, and the social dimension appears to be one of the most important.

Lievens and Harris (2003) described how Gilliland's framework might be helpful in understanding test-taker reactions in an Internet-based context as well. In light of the social higher-order factor, they noted that having an internet-based test may change the meaning of this construct. While speculative, they argued that lack of a 'live' test administrator may be seen as a positive factor (e.g. because a computer is more neutral) or may be seen as a negative factor, because there is no two-way communication (e.g. because a computer cannot talk; however, there may be an interactive component). I believe that in most cases, however, the lack of a 'live' test administrator will be viewed as a shortcoming, rather than a positive factor. My expectation is that a 'live' administrator adds a personable, 'human touch' that most people value (unless of course the 'live' administrator is rude or unpleasant). A brief glance at some of the items in the scales of Bauer et al. (2001) suggests just how important that 'human touch' may be in the testing process. Consider, for example, that their 'treatment' scale contains items such as 'The testing staff put me at ease when I took the test'. Similarly, the 'openness' dimension includes items such as 'Test administrators did not try to hide anything from me during the testing process'. Whether a 'live' administrator can somehow be replaced by an effective Internet experience remains to be seen.

In contrast to a paper-and-pencil test process, understanding procedural fairness when an Internet-based test is used probably calls for an additional variable, namely, perceived technical problems. As is widely known, use of the Internet is fraught with a myriad of technical problems, such as crashes, slow speeds, and links that no longer exist. Such technical problems are probably best categorized as procedural issues, as they affect test administration processes, but not necessarily the outcomes. The only study that I am aware of that considered this variable is that by Harris, Van Hoye, and Lievens (2003; discussed below in greater deal), in which the item most highly correlated with reluctance to submit employment-related information over the Internet was the belief that taking a test over the Internet could put one at a disadvantage due to technical problems (e.g. crashes). I urge researchers to develop and include measures of perceived technical problems, along with other procedural justice measures, to better understand examinee reactions to Internet-based testing systems.

Another important consideration may be feedback on test results. While everyone knows that it takes a while to mark paper-and-pencil tests, it is widely assumed that tests can be quickly, if not instantly, scored over the Internet. There may therefore be an *expectation* that results should be known much quicker over the Internet.

Finally, there are a number of additional features of Internet-based testing that might be best included under procedural issues, particularly in comparison with traditional (i.e. paper-and-pencil) systems. First, Bringsjord (2001) discussed how the type of item on the GRE encouraged working out problems on scrap paper. The fact that the computer-based version made this type of problem-solving more complicated may account for the negative perceptions that examinees had of this process. Thus, if there is a need for paper-and-pencil problem-solving tactics, the use of Internet-based testing may complicate these efforts and produce negative reactions.

Second, an internet-based test may incorporate a computerized-adaptive model, in which case there are likely to be far fewer items presented to each candidate. As a result, above average test-takers will quickly be led to items that they have difficulty completing. Thus, compared with traditional systems where average or above average test-takers were able to correctly answer many more items, the same examinees may perceive they have done much less well and express negative reactions.

Third, reading information from a computer screen may make it more difficult to take an examination and may lead to negative reactions (Pomplun et al., 2002). This explanation might be particularly true for test-takers who are not familiar and comfortable with computer screens.

Fourth, use of a mouse click to record one's answer may be faster than marking correct answers with a pencil on a computer-scan sheet (Pomplun et al., 2002). Again, however, examinees who are not accustomed to using a mouse may find it more awkward and difficult to record answers this way.

Fifth, if the Internet-based testing system does not allow one to return, or change answers, to previous items, some examinees may become frustrated by their inability to make modifications. In turn, this may elicit negative reactions. It is particularly important to note that the impact of such differences is most likely to be perceived by test-takers who are accustomed to paper-and-pencil procedures. For examinees who have never taken paper-and-pencil versions, Internet-based testing may be the norm, rather than the exception, and they will not be bothered by these issues.

Finally, psychometricians tend to believe that standardization equals fairness. Because Internet-based testing should increase standardization, one might assume that it will increase perceptions of fairness. I, however, believe that test-takers may not view fairness in exactly the same way. I think the results from Bauer et al. (2001), as well as from other areas, support the notion that interpersonal treatment is at least as important as standardization during test administration. Similar notions have been argued by Gilliland and Steiner (1999), who state that use of a highly standardized interview may actually *reduce* perceptions of procedural fairness. As tests are increasingly delivered over the Internet, new constructs and measures may need to be developed to fully understand procedural fairness.

ORGANIZATIONAL PRIVACY

Unlike organizational justice, organizational privacy is a less coherent theory. However, the organizational privacy construct provides some potentially useful concepts that we would do well to pay heed to. I begin first with a definition and description of the dimensions of privacy, and then provide an overview of the model of Stone and Stone (1990).

Stone and Stone (1990) defined privacy as the condition under which individuals have control over the release and dissemination of personal information, the ability to act autonomously, the capacity to isolate themselves from observation, and the ability to act freely. Similarly, Lee and LaRose (1994) described four dimensions of privacy, including physical privacy, informational privacy, psychological privacy, and interactional privacy. Physical privacy refers to freedom from undesired observation or intrusion. In the Internet context, this might involve freedom from having one's surfing behavior being monitored. Informational privacy is defined as control over when and to whom personal information is released. In the Internet context, this might refer to whether test-scores are released to a third party. Psychological privacy is defined as control over the release of information that would inform the recipient of one's internal (e.g. personality) state. Finally, interactional privacy refers to maintaining the secrecy of communication between individuals. In the Internet context, this may refer to interception of emails that an employee sends or has received from friends.

In the context of Internet-based testing, I believe that informational privacy is likely to be of particular concern. More generally, informational privacy is best understood as the 'perceived control over the conditions of release, use, retention, and disposal of personal data' (Cho & LaRose, 1999). While acknowledging that such concerns are also possible in the 'paper-and-pencil' testing environment, it may be argued that information privacy is of even greater concern in the Internet environment, owing to the potential for others to very easily obtain large amounts of data and efficiently combine these data with other data to lead to more insidious invasions of privacy.

Although not designed with the Internet in mind, Smith, Milberg, and Burke (1996) developed a broad empirical measure to assess informational privacy concerns. Based on a review of the literature, they measured five major dimensions.

1. Collection of data: concern that there is too much data available in databases.
2. Unauthorized, secondary (internal) use: concern that information collected by the organization for one purpose will be used by the same organization for a different, unauthorized, purpose.
3. Unauthorized, secondary (external) use: concern that information collected by the organization will be given to another party for another purpose (this dimension was subsequently combined with the above dimension).
4. Improper access: concern that data are readily available to parties not authorized to use them.
5. Errors: concern that protection against both deliberate and accidental errors in the data is not adequate.

In addition, they offered two 'tangential' dimensions, which were subsequently dropped.

1. Combining data, which they described as concern that information from different databases might be combined to form larger, more invasive, databases.
2. Reduced judgment: concern that important decisions are increasingly made in an impersonal, ineffective way.

In terms of results, it is noteworthy that while Smith et al. (1996) found differences from sample to sample, the dimensions that were generally of greatest concern (i.e. had the highest means) were improper access and unauthorized secondary use.

Turning now to the model of organizational privacy of Stone and Stone (1990), it should be observed that while their framework was intended to cover a wide range of organizational privacy issues it predates the Internet. They included a relatively large number of variables that affect perceptions of the degree to which there is concern with organizational privacy, including information factors (e.g. procedures used), the physical environment (e.g. degree of crowding), and a host of social, cultural, organizational (e.g. privacy norms), and individual factors (e.g. personality). I will focus here on their information factors, which appear to have the greatest applicability to Internet-based testing.

In terms of information factors, Stone and Stone suggested that the *purpose* of information collection was likely to affect concerns about privacy. Information that was seen as more relevant was expected to raise fewer concerns about privacy. Thus, the greater the fit between the type of information being collected and the stated purpose of the data collection, the less the concern over privacy. They also suggested that certain types of information (e.g. sexual orientation information) were perceived to be more invasive of privacy than others (e.g. previous job history). In the present context, some tests (e.g. biodata) may be perceived as presenting greater privacy concerns than other tests (e.g. cognitive ability).

Authorization of information was viewed as another important determinant of privacy perceptions. In cases where individuals have control over the release of information, they have fewer privacy concerns. In support of this component of the model, Eddy et al. (1999) employed a field study of a human resource management information system. They found empirical evidence that having control over the release of information reduced privacy concerns. The identity of the recipient of the information was also deemed an important determinant of privacy perceptions. Stone, Gueutal, Gardner, and McClure (1983) found the respondents had more positive attitudes towards their ability to control information held by *employers* than towards other institutions, such as insurance companies and law enforcement agencies. Eddy et al. (1999) reported that restriction of information to internal use (i.e. within the organization) reduced privacy concerns.

Another determinant of privacy in the model of Stone and Stone (1990) was the collection procedure. Because this model was developed prior to the widespread popularity of the Internet, this method was not considered. Nevertheless, a number of considerations offered by Stone and Stone logically apply to Internet-based testing. An individual's understanding of what is being measured and the degree to which the process appears to intrude upon the individual were hypothesized to serve as mediating factors linking collection procedure to privacy concerns. Hence, as suggested in the model provided in Figure 6.1, administration processes are likely to moderate the relationship between privacy concerns and test-taker reactions.

A recent study by Harris et al. (2003) provides the only empirical evidence in regard to Internet-based testing and privacy concerns that we located. Harris et al. obtained privacy ratings from a US and Belgian sample of college students. Sample predictor items included 'Companies sell employment-related information (e.g. answers to a test) that they collect from unsuspecting applicants over the Internet' and 'There are strict laws protecting the confidentiality of employment-related information submitted over the Internet'. The criterion item was 'I would avoid submitting employment-related information over the Internet'. In partial support of their hypothesis, Harris et al. found that some of the predictor items significantly correlated with the criterion for the US sample. Only one of the seven predictor items was significantly correlated with the criterion for the Belgian sample. Even for the U.S. sample, the correlations were fairly modest (0.20s and 0.30s). As noted earlier in this chapter, concern with technical problems correlated more highly ($r = 0.50$) with reluctance to submit information over the Internet. Moreover, on average, respondents were rather neutral about privacy, indicating modest concern with regard to misuse of employment-related information they submitted over the Internet. As expected, Harris et al. found some significant relationships between self-rated knowledge of the Internet and concern for privacy. The direction of these relationships, however, differed for the US and Belgian sample. In the US sample, respondents with more knowledge of the Internet were less likely to indicate that companies needed to get approval from applicants to release information. For the Belgian sample, the reverse was true; the more knowledge of the Internet the respondent had, the more likely he or she felt that a company needed approval. For the US sample only, more knowledge of the Internet was associated with less concern about using the Internet to submit employment-related information.

There are a number of issues here for future investigators to consider. First, we need much more research on the effects of privacy concern on test-taker responses. In other words, does concern over privacy affect how examinees answer test questions? I suspect that when there are privacy concerns some kinds of test may be more susceptible to distortion than other tests. For example, it seems likely that inquiries regarding sensitive topics, such as political beliefs, may be answered differently if a candidate has concerns as to whether other organizations may view the results. In turn, this may affect test validity. Second, future research should investigate the role of culture on privacy notions. Based on the work of Harris et al. (2003), the next step would be to measure culture to determine whether this explains differences in privacy perceptions (Milberg, Smith, & Burke, 2000). Third, more research is needed regarding the antecedents (e.g. organizational reputation) and correlates (e.g. belief in the just world hypothesis) of privacy concerns. Finally, there is an opportunity here for researchers to refine and update the Stone–Stone (1990) model to fit the more specific context of Internet-based testing in the workplace.

TEST-TAKING MOTIVATION

Arvey, Strickland, Drauden, and Martin (1990) developed a framework addressing examinee motivation towards tests, which included dimensions such as lack of concentration, belief in tests, and comparative anxiety. Schmit and Ryan (1992) found strong support for the hypothesis that test-taking motivation moderated the validity of two employment tests, though the effect was in the opposite direction for a personality and ability test. While all of these scales may be relevant, I will focus on one in particular for Internet-based testing: computer anxiety. Given that some people feel less comfortable on computers, computer anxiety may be particularly important here. This is likely to be particularly true if a speeded test is used.

There has been a reasonable amount of research regarding computer anxiety in general. As defined by Chua, Chen, and Wong (1999), computer anxiety refers to the apprehension felt by individuals towards computers. A meta-analysis by Chua et al. indicated that women displayed more computer anxiety than men and there was an inverse relationship between computer anxiety and computer experience. This suggests that demographic variables (e.g. gender) might well affect the relationship between test-taking motivation and examinee reactions.

There has also been debate as to the dimensionality of computer anxiety. Research by Beckers and Schmidt (2001) supports the argument that computer anxiety is a multidimentional construct, suggesting that different components of computer anxiety may have different effects on criteria of interest.

Despite the fact that there has been research on computer anxiety, there has been limited application of this construct to test-taking. O'Connell, Doverspike, Gillikin, and Meloun (2001) examined the relationship between computer anxiety, test anxiety, and test scores for a sample of 405 candidates for an entry-level production position. The test, which was computer administered, was a composite based on six competency areas, including personality, situational judgment, and reasoning skills. Both test anxiety and computer anxiety ($r = -0.23$ and -0.43, respectively) were negatively associated with a composite test score. Using a hierarchical regression analysis, even when test anxiety and negative affectivity were first entered, computer anxiety explained additional variance in test scores.

Frericks, Ehrhart, and O'Connell (2003) examined the relationship between computer anxiety, test anxiety, and test scores (i.e. cognitive ability, process monitoring, situational judgment, and conscientiousness) for three randomly assigned samples of employees at a manufacturer of farm and construction equipment. One sample completed a paper-and-pencil version of the test, a second sample completed a computer-based version, and a third sample completed both versions, with a separation of five days. They found that computer anxiety was negatively related to test scores (particularly on a process monitoring test), even when controlling for test anxiety and negative affectivity. Interestingly, however, when demographic (i.e. gender, age, computer experience, and education level) variables were controlled for, computer anxiety was only significantly related to the process monitoring test. Contrary to expectations, computer anxiety was related to not only the computer-based versions of the tests, but the paper-and-pencil version as well. Finally, using the third sample, Frericks et al. investigated whether differences in scores between the computer-based version and the paper-and-pencil version were explained by computer anxiety. The only significant correlation ($r = 0.32$) was for the conscientiousness scale, wherein subjects with greater computer anxiety had lower computer-based scores compared to their paper-and-pencil test scores. On the basis of their results, Frericks et al. concluded that computer anxiety may simply be part of general state anxiety.

A third study was conducted using an educational test. Employing two randomly assigned samples of college students taking the GRE, Bringsjord

(2001) reported a study of computer-based testing versus paper-and-pencil testing. She measured a variety of variables, including test anxiety, state–trait anxiety, computer attitudes, and mode preferences (e.g. 'I prefer paper and pencil tests over computerized tests'). She found that while test anxiety was negatively related to GRE score for both samples, the effect was somewhat different in each. That is, while test anxiety demonstrated a fairly uniform effect across all levels for the computer-administered group, for the paper-and-pencil group scores were much lower only across high levels of anxiety. The interaction between test anxiety and sample, however, was not statistically significant. Subjects in the computer-administered group exhibited a significantly longer response time to questions, particularly those items assessing analytical reasoning and logical reasoning. Part of the explanation for response time differences was in the use of scrap paper to solve problems.

In terms of computer attitudes, while Bringsjord (2001) did not directly assess the relationship with test scores, she did report that subjects with more positive computer attitudes also reported lower test anxiety. Finally, both groups of subjects showed a preference for paper-and-pencil testing, though the computer-administered group was slightly less positive about such testing. A verbal protocol analysis following the test administration showed that few of the frustrations expressed by the paper-and-pencil group was due to the test mode, while a large proportion of the computer-based group's frustrations involved discontent with the administration mode itself. Oddly enough, despite these findings regarding reactions, on average, subjects in the computer-based administration had higher scores than subjects in the paper-and-pencil version. What is interesting about this study is that subjects were quite negative about the computer-administered version of the test, and most likely had a difficult time with the transition between figuring out answers, reading the questions, and recording their answers. These problems would be quite unlikely to occur for other types of test, such as personality measures.

Clearly, much more research is needed here to understand computer anxiety and its effects on test performance. While it seems reasonable to expect that there will be a greater effect on a timed test, Frericks et al. (2003) found that computer anxiety was also related to performance on paper-and-pencil tests. More careful research is needed to study the relationships between computer anxiety, test anxiety, state anxiety, Internet-based test performance, and job criteria of interest. Second, as noted above, computer anxiety appears to be a multidimensional construct; which dimensions are related to test scores, and whether this varies by type of test, should be examined more carefully.

It is also important to understand the relationship between computer anxiety and various demographics, such as age and gender. If computer anxiety is related to age, for example, an Internet-based test may create adverse impact against people over 40. We also need to understand whether computer anxiety moderates the validity of a test for certain groups (e.g. people over

40 years old). Given that women appear to have greater computer anxiety than men, we need to examine the effect of gender on test scores. Finally, if computer anxiety is related to test scores, researchers should determine whether there are any strategies for addressing this problem. Will a brief training and practice session, for example, help reduce anxiety and eliminate problems that interfere with maximum performance on the test? Such questions are potentially of great practical importance.

SUGGESTIONS FOR MAINTAINING POSITIVE EXAMINEE REACTIONS TO INTERNET-BASED TESTING

Based on the above research and theory, this section outlines some possible practical suggestions for improving examinee reactions to Internet-based testing.

Clarify the Purpose of the Testing Program

Test-takers should be informed of the purpose of the testing program and why the data are being gathered (e.g. to help predict job performance). Tests should be designed to have the maximum face validity (appearance of job related-ness) possible.

Provide Information About Storage of the Data, Disclosure of the Data, and the Candidate's Rights to the Data

In the US at least, many test-takers are unaware of what rights, if any, they have to the data, where it is stored, and who may be given this data. This type of information is particularly relevant for Internet-based testing and careful thought should be given to the most appropriate way to balance the rights of all stakeholders. In other parts of the world, such as the European Union, there are laws (see, e.g. European Union, 1995) that require companies to follow privacy regulations.

Provide Practice and Test-Taking Tips

It seems reasonable to expect that some practice items will help alleviate anxiety and level the playing field for test-takers. It should be made clear to all test-takers what some of the key 'tips' are in taking the test. For example, if it is not possible to return and change an answer, test-takers should be informed of this before the test begins.

Provide the Human Touch

There should always be some kind of access to a 'live' human being, even if this is nothing more than a toll-free telephone number to contact. Having a 'real' person may help calm an anxious test-taker, particularly if there is a technical problem.

Consider a Certification Program

One approach to reducing privacy concerns is to establish industry standards, which can be used to serve as a 'seal of approval'. Note that this may already be a requirement in order to meet the rules of the Data Protection Act and Safe Harbor Privacy framework. Truste (*www.truste.org*) has established a program that organizations may voluntarily adopt towards this end. Truste's focus is on developing 'a seal that would send a clear signal to consumers that they could expect companies to adhere to certain requirements about the way Web sites handled data, and that an independent, third-party would hear and respond to their complaints and resolve their disputes'. The core components of this program are the following.

Notice

Web sites displaying the TRUSTe seal must post clear notice of what personally identifiable information is gathered and with whom it is shared. This disclosure must be easy to read and accessible by one mouse click from the home page.

Choice

Users must have the ability, through opt-in or opt-out functions, to choose whether to allow secondary uses of that personal information. In effect, users must be able to prevent the Web site from selling, sharing, renting, or disseminating their personally identifiable information.

Access

Users must have reasonable access to information maintained about them by a Web site to correct any inaccuracies in the data collected.

Security

The Web site must provide reasonable security to protect the data that is collected.

SUMMARY

In my opinion, all it takes is one highly publicized problem to give Internet-based testing a poor reputation. To avoid such problems, organizations that use Internet-based testing should strive to create processes that will elicit positive examinee reactions. Taking steps to ensure procedural fairness, privacy, and test-taking motivation will help reduce examinees' concerns and instill a sense of good will and trust, which in turn should lead to desired actions (e.g. accepting job offers) on their part. Furthermore, taking such steps will help protect the testing industry from privacy-related debacles that may arise. If privacy-related problems do surface, the testing industry will be in a far better position to respond. Finally, taking such precautions will separate the highly reputable from the less reputable testing companies.

REFERENCES

Anderson, N. (2003). Applicant and recruiter reactions to new technology in selection: A critical review and agenda for future research. *International Journal of Selection and Assessment*, **11**:121–136.

Arvey, R., Strickland, W., Drauden, G., & Martin, C. (1990). Motivational components of test taking. *Personnel Psychology*, **43**:695–716.

Bauer, T., Truxillo, D., Sanchez, R., Craig, J., Ferrara, P., & Campion, M. (2001). Applicant reactions to selection: Development of the selection procedural justice scale (SPJS). *Personnel Psychology*, **54**:388–420.

Beckers, J. J., & Schmidt, H. G. (2001). The structure of computer anxiety: A six-factor model. *Computers in Human Behavior*, **17**:35–49.

Bies, R. J. (1993). Privacy and procedural justice in organizations. *Social Justice Research*, 6:69–86.

Borman, W. C., Hanson, M. A., & Hedge, J. (1997). Personnel selection. *Annual Review of Psychology*, **48**:299–337.

Bringsjord, E. (2001). *Computerized-adaptive versus paper-and-pencil testing environments: An experimental analysis of examinee experience.* Dissertation conducted at the University of Albany, State University of New York.

Cho, H., & LaRose, R. (1999). Privacy issues in Internet surveys. *Social Science Computer Review*, **17**:421–434.

Chua, S. L., Chen, D., & Wong, A. F. L. (1999). Computer anxiety and its correlates: A meta-analysis. *Computers in Human Behavior*, **15**:609–623.

Eddy, E. R., Stone, D. L., & Stone-Romero, E. F. (1999). The effects of information management policies on reactions to human resource information systems: An integration of privacy and procedural justice perspectives. *Personnel Psychology*, **52**:335–358.

European Union. (1995). Directive 95/46/EC of the European Parliament and of the Council of 24 October 1995 on the protection of individuals with regard to the processing of personal data and on the free movement of such data. *Official Journal L* **281**:0031–0050.

Frericks, L., Ehrhart, K. H., & O'Connell, M. S. (2003, April). *Computer anxiety and test performance: Comparing selection test formats.* Paper presented at the Society for Industrial and Organizational Psychologists Conference, Orlando, FL.

Gilliland, S. W. (1993). The perceived fairness of selection systems: An organizational justice perspective. *Academy of Management Review*, **18**:694–734.

Gilliland, S. W., & Steiner, D. D. (1999). Applicant reactions. In R. Eder & M. Harris (Eds.), *The employment interview handbook* (pp. 69–82). Thousand Oaks, CA: Sage.

Goldstein, H., Yusko, K., Braverman, E., Smith, D., & Chung, B. (1998). The role of cognitive ability in the subgroup differences and incremental validity of assessment center exercises. *Personnel Psychology*, **51**:357–374.

Harris, M. (2002, April). *Virtually hired? The implications of web testing for personnel selection*, discussant comments. Symposium presented at the Society of Industrial and Organizational Psychologists (SIOP) conference.

Harris, M., Van Hoye, G., & Lievens, F. (2003). Privacy and attitudes towards internet-based selection systems: A cross-cultural comparison. *International Journal of Selection and Assessment*, **11**:230–236.

Landy, F., & Shankster, L. (1994). Personnel selection and placement. *Annual Review of Psychology*, **45**:261–296.

Lee, L. T., & LaRose, R. (1994). Caller ID and the meaning of privacy. *Information Society*, **4**:247–265.

Lievens, F., & Harris, M. M. (2003). Research on Internet recruitment and testing: Current status and future directions. In I. Robertson and C. L. Cooper (Eds.), *International review of industrial and organizational psychology* (Vol. 18, pp. 131–165). Chichester: Wiley.

Lievens, F., & Highhouse, S. (2003). The relation of instrumental and symbolic attributes to a company's attractiveness as an employer. *Personnel Psychology*, **56**:75–102.

Mead, A. D., & Coussons-Read, M. (2002, April). The equivalence of paper- and web-based versions of the 16PF questionnaire. In F. L. Oswald & J. M. Stanton (Chairs), *Being virtually hired: Implications of web testing for personnel selection*. Symposium presented at the Society for Industrial and Organizational Psychology, Toronto.

Milberg, S., Smith, H. J., & Burke, S. (2000). Information privacy: Corporate management and national regulation. *Organization Science*, **11**:35–57.

O'Connell, M. S., Doverspike, D., Gillikin, S., & Meloun, J. (2001). Computer anxiety: Effects on computerized testing and implications for e.Cruiting. *Journal of e.Commerce and Psychology*, **1**:25–38.

Ployhart, R., Weekley, J., Holtz, B., & Kemp, C. (2003). Web-based and paper-and-pencil testing of applicants in a proctored setting: Are personality, biodata, and situational judgment tests comparable? *Personnel Psychology*, **56**:733–752.

Pomplun, M., Frey, S., & Becker, D. (2002). The score equivalence of paper-and-pencil and computerized versions of a speeded test of reading comprehension. *Educational and Psychological Measurement*, **62**:337–354.

Reynolds, D., & Lin, L. F. (2003, April). *An unfair platform? Subgroup reactions to Internet selection techniques*. Paper presented at the Society for Industrial and Organizational Psychologists Conference, Orlando, FL.

Reynolds, D. H., Sinar, E. F., & McClough, A. C. (2000, April). Evaluation of an Internet-based selection procedure. In N. J. Mondragon (Chair), *Beyond the demo: The empirical nature of technology-based assessments*. Symposium presented at the 15th Annual Conference of the Society for Industrial and Organizational Psychology, New Orleans, LA.

Schmit, M., Ryan, A. M. (1992). Test-taking dispositions: A missing link? *Journal of Applied Psychology*, **77**:629–637.

Sinar, E. F., & Reynolds, D. H. (2001, April). Applicant reactions to Internet-based selection techniques. In F. L. Oswald (Chair), *Computers = good? How test-user and test-taker perceptions affect technology-based employment testing*. Symposium presented at the Society for Industrial and Organizational Psychology Conference, San Diego, CA.

Smith, H. J., Milberg, S. J., & Burke, S. J. (1996). Information privacy: Measuring individuals' concerns about organizational practices. *MIS Quarterly*, **20**:167–196.

Stone, D. L., & Stone, E. F. (1990). Privacy in organizations: Theoretical issues, research findings, and protection mechanisms. *Research in Personnel and Human Resources Management*, **8**:349–411.

Stone, E. F., Gueutal, H. G., Gardner, D. G., & McClure, S. (1983). A field experiment comparing information-privacy values, beliefs, and attitudes across several types of organizations. *Journal of Applied Psychology*, **68**:459–468.

van den Bos, K., Lind, E., Vermunt, R., & Wilke, H. (1997). How do I judge my outcome when I do not know the outcome of others? The psychology of the fair process effect. *Journal of Personality and Social Psychology*, **72**:1034–1046.

CHAPTER 7

The Impact of Technology on Test Manufacture, Delivery and Use and on the Test Taker

Dave Bartram
SHL Group, UK

The chapters by Luecht (Chapter 5) and Harris (Chapter 6) address different aspects of how technology is impacting testing. Luecht considers how technology has impacted testing in the high stake world of licensing and certification examinations. Harris focuses on the impact of technology on testing in the work and organizational field. While Luecht considers system related issues associated with the whole test design, development and delivery process, Harris takes a very different perspective—that of the person on the receiving end of these systems: the test taker.

TEST MANUFACTURE AND DELIVERY

In his chapter, Luecht provides a very clear specification of the various systems that comprise a CBT system. While his chapter focuses on the design, development and delivery of examinations (such as tests for certification or licensure), most of what he says has general applicability. In outline he defines CBT systems as comprising five main systems, each with their own set of subsystems.

1. Item development and item banking.
2. Test assembly and composition.
3. Examinee registration and scheduling.
4. Test delivery.
5. Post-examination procedures.

These can be divided into two main meta-functions: test creation and test use.

Computer-Based Testing and the Internet: Issues and Advances.
Edited by D. Bartram and R. K. Hambleton. © 2006 John Wiley & Sons, Ltd.

Test Creation: Three Generations of Manufacturing

Luecht's first two systems define a 'test factory': design, development, manufacturing, warehousing and inventory control, product assembly and, finally, delivery to the customer. Item development and item banking requires an item database, item authoring and prototyping tools and interfaces and some means of managing content through item inventory control and management. Test assembly and construction requires item selection and quality control procedures and procedures for dealing with the final rendering of the test—whether for online delivery or for offline printing as a paper test. The factory analogy is a useful one as it allows us to consider a number of different ways in which CBT systems might work and how test production has evolved.

The first generation of tests was pre-industrial. In the pre-industrial world, product manufacture was a distributed craft activity. Guilds and other organisations brought produce together from manufacturers and found markets for it. Until relatively recently the development of tests has followed the craft industry approach (and still does in many areas). A test author crafts a new product and then seeks a publisher to sell it.

In the second generation of test production, we see the application of industrialisation procedures to tests. The first stage of industrialisation was to bring these resources together into factories and to 'de-skill' the craftsmen. We are seeing this happen now as the larger test producers automate the procedures needed for item design and creation, develop item banks and item warehouses and automate the quality control procedures needed to ensure that the finished products meet some pre-specified requirements and psychometric standards. However, this first stage of industrialisation still follows the traditional manufacturing model in most cases. It is a 'push' model that works on the basis of identifying a market need, creating a product that should meet that need and then pushing this out into the market. Tests are designed and developed, admittedly with far greater efficiency and control over quality, and then made available for delivery, being stored either physically or virtually in a 'warehouse' until required.

The third generation of test production involves the application of new industrialisation procedures to 'just-in-time testing'. Here the factory process is a 'pull' one rather than a 'push' one. The requirements are identified from the market; these requirements are converted into a technical specification and fed into the factory as an 'order' and the factory then delivers a test directly back into the market.

Luecht talks of the difference between pre-constructed tests and tests that are constructed online or in real time. The above concept of just-in-time test manufacture is somewhat different. Pre-constructed tests may either be created through the old 'push' process or the newer 'pull' process. 'Just in time' does not necessarily mean in real time—though it includes this. It may be necessary for just-in-time created tests to be piloted before they are used so that some item parameter estimates can be checked. Creation of tests in real time is no more complex, from a manufacturing point of view, but is much more demanding on the quality of our psychometric models and our ability to produce accurate estimate of the psychometric properties of the final test. Where items are drawn from a well calibrated bank (as, for example, in adaptive testing) this is possible. Where the test creation process involves item generation, estimates have to be made of the properties of the newly generated items (see van der Linden's chapter). The more radical the generation procedures, the more variable the 'offspring' of the prototype items, the more likely it is that the margin of error on these estimates will be so large that some piloting is required.

Nevertheless, the move from craft industry to post-industrial manufacturing processes is a major change in testing. It has impacted most the areas of high volume, high stakes testing where there is a very strong 'pull' for more tests, item renewal on a regular basis, high volumes of test takers, high risks associated with security and cheating and so on. Not surprisingly it is in the licensing and certification field and the high volume educational testing areas that we see these procedures most highly developed. Industrialisation involves costly investments, but the pay-off is higher efficiency and, in the longer term, better profitability.

The same industrialisation process is beginning to take place in the I/O field now. Initially it was confined to the large scale military testing programs (such as the US ASVAB), but increasingly these procedures are being adopted by the more traditional test designers and producers. SHL, for example, now delivers over one million online test administrations worldwide in a year, and the numbers are growing rapidly. In the past two or three years it has radically redesigned its test production procedures, developing industrialised just-in-time procedures like those discussed above. The new approach, however, has not replaced the craft industry. In clinical testing and in the lower volume testing areas, it is still common practice for a test to be developed by one person, and then to be pushed by him or her into the market.

Paradoxically, the Internet has not only provided the technology to support the technologically sophisticated third generation of industrialisation, it has also opened up new opportunities for the 'sole trader' craftsmen. Anyone can create a test and publish it on the Internet. Indeed, if you Google 'psychological tests', you are directed toward sites such as *www.queendom.com*, *www.psychtests.com*, and *www.tickle.com*. These contain hundreds of so-called 'tests', most of which provide no indication of who produced them, what they measure or what their psychometric properties are. While many are offered for 'fun', it is well known that they are also being used in high stakes situations, such as selection and recruitment, by those who want to cut costs. While the Internet has made it possible for legitimate lone craftsmen to get to market more easily, it has, unfortunately, also created a high degree of confusion and chaos in that market at the same time. Lack of regulation makes it difficult for members of the public to know when they are being tested by a genuine psychometric instrument and when they are completing something that was thrown together by someone with little or no knowledge of test design and construction.

The International Test Commission (ITC) hopes that the development of the Guidelines on Computer Based Testing and Internet-Delivered Testing (ITC, 2005) will help to differentiate the wheat from the chaff. However, it needs more than guidelines. We need to be able to educate the public about the dangers of using badly designed assessments, and to be able to provide them with some means of distinguishing proper tests from the mass of other stuff on the Internet. In the UK, the British Psychological Society (BPS) has initiated a test registration scheme. This will provide test distributors with a means of 'quality stamping' their products if they meet a set of minimum technical psychometric standards. The BPS is working closely with the test publishers to implement this scheme and to market it to the test taking public. The standards it is using to define the minimum criteria for adequacy are taken from the European Federation of Psychologists' Associations (EFPA) Test Review Criteria (Bartram, 2002; for details see *www.efpa.be*).

Test Use: the Market Place

The last three systems in Luecht's 'system of systems' all relate to issues of test use: managing the assessment process, delivering the tests, and scoring and reporting. He distinguishes between 'dedicated' test centres and 'multi-purpose distributed test sites'. In Chapter 1, the present author distinguishes four modes of administration: open, controlled, supervised and managed.

Luecht's discussion covers the latter two of these. Test centres are examples of places where test administration can take place in managed mode. The location is specified, the physical security levels are definable and known, and the nature and technical specification of the computer equipment is under control. As a consequence, test materials can be securely downloaded and item types can be used that make particular demands on the user work-station (e.g. streaming video). For high stake testing, managed mode is ideal, but in practice not always attainable. Supervised modes of administration provide for control over test taker access and behaviour, through local proctoring, but do not provide guarantees of system security or control of the test taking environment. A further difference between these two modes is that tests delivered into controlled mode (supervised) environments may encounter technical problems associated with local security measures. The barriers that organisations now put up, through fire-walls, spam filters, and other devices, to protect themselves can produce problems for the delivery of tests and test administration related messages. For example: automatically generated emails that inform test administrators of their login username and password may get filtered out as 'spam' and never reach the user; organisational IT policies may restrict use of java applets or other downloads that are necessary for the delivery of timed tests.

Outside direct system security issues, there is also the problem of tests becoming compromised through people cheating. This is a major issue for the sort of high stake examinations that Luecht discusses. Indeed, since the

Winchester ITC Conference, a specialist company has been set up by some of the leading figures in the testing field to provide security services to the testing industry (*www.caveon.com*). Caveon provide a range of services, including forensic data analysis to detect aberrant response patterns both at an individual level and geographically (Foster & Maynes, 2004), and searches of the Internet to detect rogue training or practice sites that use items from copyright tests.

High and Low Stakes

There are two ways of looking at testing from the test taker's point of view. It can be seen as a barrier to some goal (such as a job, or certification), which he or she has to overcome in order to progress his or her career as desired; or it can be seen as an opportunity for discovering more about oneself. Typically we regard the former as high stakes and the latter as low stakes. This classification reflects more what is done with the information gained from the test than the risks associated with the testing process. For so-called high stake testing, the test scores are provided for someone other than the test taker to make a decision that can have a significant impact not only on the test taker but also on others (the hiring organisation, potential clients of licensed practitioners etc). Assessment for 'self-discovery' purposes, on the other hand, though it can have a very high impact on the individual concerned, tends to have less impact on others. In developing models of impact, we need to consider a larger number of factors than are generally considered in the high versus low stake distinction.

1. What is the impact of the results of the test on the person who sponsored the assessment (e.g. the third party who is using test data to aid in the making of a decision)?
2. What is the collateral impact of the results of the test on people associated with the test taker (e.g. family and friends)?
3. What is the direct impact of the results of the test on the test taker?

   In each case, these impacts might be moderated by the following.

1. Cheating or collusion by the test taker.
2. The use of inappropriate tests or tests with poor psychometric properties.
3. Inappropriate modes of administration.
4. Poor reporting.

Score Reporting

One of the major factors affecting the impact a test has is score reporting. How the information about test performance is presented and to whom are the main determiners of impact. It is surprising, therefore, that score reporting has received such scant attention, in comparison with other aspects of testing. The ITC Guidelines for Test Use (2001) emphasise the importance of providing feedback and of reporting that is unbiased and that does not over-interpret the results of a test. The more recent Guidelines on Computer Based Testing and Internet-Delivered Testing (ITC, 2005) also place an emphasis on the need for test developers, test distributors, and test users to pay attention to the provision of feedback.

In the traditional I/O testing scenario, results (especially of personality and other self-report inventories) were often fed back to test takers in a face-to-face session that provided opportunities for the feedback provider to address issues, and the recipient of the information to ask questions. While it is still recommended that complex score reporting (such as the feedback of the results of a multi-scale personality inventory) should be supported as much as possible or practical with personal contact, the growth of Internet-based testing has tended to make feedback and reporting as 'remote' an event as the test administration. Luecht has relatively little to say about reporting, as he is dealing with the relatively simple case of an examination, which produces a single outcome, possibly with some diagnostic breakdown of subscores. The more complex issue of reporting back to non-experts (test takers, line managers, children, parents, etc.) on constructs such as personality, intelligence, or motivation needs further attention.

While as psychometricians we rightly tend to pay attention to the validity of a test, the actual impact the test has on people is mediated through reporting. Reviews of tests tend to focus on the test itself and ignore the computer-based test interpretation reports that test users may be provided with. This issue has been addressed recently by the BPS in their test review procedure. The EFPA Test Review Criteria (Bartram, 2002) also contain criteria for the description and evaluation of computer-generated reports. The latest edition of *BPS Reviews* (these reviews are published on the BPS Psychological Testing Centre website *www.psychtesting.org.uk*) is using this model and will be providing reviews of computer generated reports as well as of the tests from which they are generated.

In short, there are three distinct ways we can look at validity.

1. What is the validity of the test score? What does it correlate with? What is the convergent and divergent construct validity? What is its criterion related validity for various criteria? And so on.
2. Where the test scores are used to generate a report, what is the validity of the link between the statements made in the report and the test scores? If the report provides an interpretation for a lay user, then the consequences of the test will no longer be determined by the scores on the test, but by the words in the report.
3. Finally, while a report may faithfully represent the information contained in the test scores, those who have access to the report may not have sufficient training or knowledge to understand that information and may misapply or misuse it.

It is because test results tend to impact indirectly on outcomes and because their effects are mediated through reporting processes, assessment policies and their combination with other information that the simple psychometric concepts of validity have limited value in applied settings. The latest Standards on Psychological and Educational Testing (AERA/APA/NCME, 1999) acknowledge this in Standards 1.22 and 1.23 with the concept of consequential validity. This is an issue to which far more attention needs to be paid in the future in understanding some of the difference between the science and the practice of testing.

IMPACTS ON THE TEST TAKER

Harris, in Chapter 6, considers a range of issues relating to the impact of testing on the test taker. His focus is primarily on the test taker as a job applicant, but what he has to say applies also to certification and educational examinees. Research on applicant reactions has increased substantially over the period since the Winchester ITC conference.

Equivalence of Online and Offline Testing

It is also worth noting that further research on the comparisons between online and offline administration has continued to support their equivalence. Bartram and Brown (2004) and Bartram, Brown, and Holzhausen (2005) have shown that both the normative and ipsative versions of the Occupational Personality Questionnaire (OPQ32, SHL, 1999) are not affected by changes in administration mode. They compared presentation under supervised paper and pencil conditions with matched samples of people completing the same tests online without supervision. The data were all *in vivo* studies involving genuine job applicants or people taking tests for development purposes. No differences were found in terms of scale means, SDs, reliabilities, or scale covariance matrices. Salgado and Moscoso (2003) report similar results for a Big Five instrument, and Mylonas and Carstairs (2003) found no effects of administration mode for the Motivation Questionnaire (SHL, 2002).

Research on the computerisation of cognitive tests has tended to relate to comparisons between paper and stand-alone computer version, rather than online administration (see, e.g., Mead & Drasgow, 1993). One recent study (Kurz & Evans, 2004) has compared a number of computer generations (offline MSDOS, offline Windows and online web-based) of the same numerical and verbal reasoning tests with their paper-and-pencil forms. This reported consistently high retest correlations between different modes and no changes in means and SDs. However, the same study noted problems associated with speeded tests (such as clerical checking). As concluded in Chapter 1, it seems that transfer of tests from paper to computer, whether online or offline, is largely unproblematic so long as the computer version is carefully designed to preserve the ergonomic features of the paper version and so long as the tests involved are not particularly speeded.

Cheating

The whole issue of 'cheating' needs to be considered from a very different viewpoint for personality inventories than for cognitive ability tests. For the former there are no 'right answers' and hence there is no scoring key to be compromised. Response bias, 'faking good', and so on are invisible processes that can occur as readily in a proctored situation as an unproctored one. As Harris points out, we need to consider test administration modes in relation to the type of test being administered: self-report inventories as opposed to cognitive or knowledge tests.

The use of cognitive tests in controlled mode (i.e. restricted but unsupervised) raises interesting questions. We would generally regard cognitive tests as needing to be restricted to supervised conditions of administration, in order to ensure that cheating was not possible and the security of the items was not compromised. Supervision is also important for checking the identity of the test taker. Baron, Bartram, and Miles (2001), however, describe the use of third generation test manufacturing procedures as the basis for online ability screening instruments that are presented in controlled mode as part of a job recruitment process. The instruments are constructed using item sampling from a bank with various constraints set to control test length and difficulty. A different test is created for each test taker, thus making it difficult to cheat. The delivery software is also carefully constructed to make it impossible to interfere with timing or other aspects of the delivery and administration (any such attempts are detected and reported). The use of online screening tests such as this provide organisations with considerable cost benefits in terms of the overall average cost per hired person, as it enables them to screen out a higher proportion of applicants before they are brought into an assessment centre. It is important to note that the use of this sort of pre-screen assessment prevents people from getting others to help them complete the test—or even getting someone else to do the whole test on their behalf. However, it is also important to understand that the screening test is part of a larger process, a process that is made explicit to the test taker: Anyone who passes the screen may be reassessed under supervised conditions later, in order to detect any false positives, and all applicants are asked to 'sign up' to an honesty contract (see Chapter 1).

Test Taker Reactions

Harris reviews three key variables in relate to test taker reactions.

1. Perceptions of the organisation. The experience of test taking will have an impact on the person's image of the organization and could, of itself, affect

a job applicant's decision as to whether to continue with the application or not.

2. Propensity to engage in litigation. The experience could be one that encourages the test taker to take the organisation to court, if the process or the outcome is perceived to be overly unfair.

3. The reactions to the testing situation might affect the psychometric properties of the test.

These can all be considered within the framework of Gilliland's (1993) application of Greenberg's (1987) conceptualisation of organisational justice to assessment. Greenberg distinguished between two independent conceptual dimensions for understanding organisational justice theories: a content–process dimension that relates to outcome theories (distributive justice) and process theories (procedural justice), and a reactive–proactive dimension that relates to theories that focus on the restoration of justice and those that focus on how people seek to attain justice. While much of the research on applicant reactions has focused on procedural justice issues, it may be that it is perceived unfairness in either process or outcome that leads to people seeking to attain justice through either legitimate (e.g. appeals or litigation) or illegitimate (e.g. cheating) means.

Rugg-Gunn, Price, and Wright (2004) report an interesting study that was carried out to explore the anecdotal reports from UK graduate recruiters that female applicants were being put off by the increasing use of online recruitment methods. They received 4,352 responses (40% female) to their survey. What they found was that some companies were creating a more negative impression of themselves for female applicants, in particular, as their use of online recruitment was perceived as being uncaring and symptomatic of how they would treat their employees. They also found the following:

- Females worried more than males about completing tests online.
- They worried more about other candidates cheating, but perceived themselves as more honest when completing online questionnaires. However, neither males nor females believed that cheating was much of an issue.
- They were more concerned about the sequencing of testing in the online application process, preferring tests to come after, rather than before, an initial short listing.

Overall there were no significant gender differences in attitudes to the use of the Internet in general or to the use of online application forms. The main reasons for the gender differences in reactions to testing were dehumanisation, privacy and security concerns. The researchers followed the survey up with some focus groups to explore some of these issues in more depth. They found that while males saw tests as a challenge, females saw them as a necessary evil; males saw no difference between online and paper-based testing, females expressed a preference for paper-based because they felt more in control in this mode. Other research (e.g. Kurz & Evans, 2004) has tended to show a general preference for completing tests on computer or online rather than on paper, though this preference may be stronger for males than females.

These results are consistent with a study reported by Bank (2005), in which 815 out of 1,300 candidates responded to a questionnaire about their reactions to an online ability screening test (as described by Baron et al., 2001). Bank found that in general:

- candidates generally like to be tested online
- online testing for selection or screening enhanced the reputation of the employer
- access to online equipment was no problem
- online test administration can be delivered without (or with minimal) technical problems
- cheating was seen as being of little concern.

However, he also found similar gender differences to those reported by Rugg-Gunn et al:

- Females found it significantly more difficult to get access to a computer.
- Females perceived the navigation to the site and taking the assessment as significantly more difficult than males.

The recommendations by Rugg-Gunn et al. (2004) for recruiters centre around two issues, information provision and good design:

- give the candidates more information up front
- be explicit and transparent about the process (provide a candidate service level agreement)
- ensure that competency based questions match the role
- maintain your website—update information regularly
- keep the candidates informed of their application progress
- consider the personal touch in your online process (e.g. names and telephone numbers, status checking, and online chat rooms)
- make sure that your systems are user friendly
- take ownership of the process (e.g. not outsourcing to a call centre)
- provide constructive feedback.

Many of the potential pitfalls and adverse reactions to online testing can be mitigated through providing test takers with the information they need and the means of making direct contact when they need to. This piece of research emphasises the need for someone to provide the 'human touch' even when administration is remote. This can be achieved by providing a contact number or email support, or through other methods. Such reassurance is important for test takers.

Fairness in testing needs to be considered very broadly when considering the impact on different modes of assessment and types of test on test takers.

From the test manufacturing standpoint we tend to focus on standardisation, reliability, validity, freedom from bias, and other such technical issues. The test user is concerned about practicality—time taken, cost, training requirements, and so on. Both test users and test takers are concerned with the overall acceptability of the process. As noted above, justice models are helpful in providing a framework for exploring these issues.

We also need to re-evaluate the importance of face validity in considering applicant reactions. Face validity is generally looked upon as the poor relation of validity by psychometricians; however, it is key to acceptability. Test takers are unlikely to object to the use of a test that is transparent in its content, which asks questions that appear to relate to the type of work they have applied for. They are more likely to object to tests that are abstract or obscure in their content. The use of tests with good face validity is important in managing applicant reactions even though it needs to be remembered that face validity has no necessary relationship to construct or criterion related validity.

Personal and Organizational Privacy

Harris reviews a number of concerns regarding privacy from the Smith, Milbery and Burke (1996) study:

(1) concern that there is too much data available in databases;
(2) concern that information collected by the organization for one purpose will be used by the same organization for a different, unauthorized, purpose;
(3) concern that information collected by the organization will be given to another party for another purpose (this dimension was subsequently combined with the above dimension);
(4) concern that data are readily available to parties not authorized to use them;
(5) concern that protection against both deliberate and accidental errors in the data is not adequate.

He goes on to talk about the need for research on how differences in culture might affect these privacy concerns. Interestingly, it is in this area that one finds very marked differences of approach between the US and Europe. While Harris talks of reliance on voluntary systems such as TRUSTe, in Europe privacy has been the subject of both a European Directive and national legislation. EU Directives are mandatory instruments and override any local national legislation within the EU. Since 1998 there has been a new legislative framework relating to personal data privacy and protection in place in Europe. This legislation is important for all areas of personal data, not least the sort of data processed in the course of psychological testing and assessment over the Internet. Such data includes not only the information about an individual's scores on a test but also the reports that might be generated from these scores, either by computer or by human test interpreters. It is especially important in that it applies across borders and has implications for how the data of EU subjects may be treated when it is moved outside the EU.

The legislative framework within which this policy is set is defined by the European Union Council Directive 95/46/EC of the European Parliament and of the Council of 24 October 1995 on the protection of individuals with regard to the processing of personal data and on the free movement of such data. This directive sets the requirements for personal data management throughout Europe and has been legally binding on all member states since 24 October 1998. The countries covered by the EU Directive are the countries of the European Economic Area (EEA). In 1988 the EEA comprised the 15 member states of the European Union plus Norway, Iceland, and Liechtenstein, but excluded the Channel Islands and the Isle of Man. It now also applies to the 10 new accession states. The directive imposes legal requirements on organizations that might transfer personal data out of the EEA.

The purpose of the directive is to protect 'the fundamental rights and freedoms of natural persons, and in particular their right to privacy with respect to the processing of personal data' (Article 1). It provides a *minimum* set of requirements that all member states must legislate to meet. In the UK, the 1998 Data Protection Act (DPA) represents the national legislation that enforces the directive. This is supported by a detailed draft code of practice on 'The Employment Practices Data Protection Code: Part 1: Recruitment and Selection (2002)'.[1]

'Personal data' is defined as any information that relates to an identified or identifiable person (the data subject). A distinction is drawn between sensitive and non-sensitive personal data. Sensitive data is information relating to racial or ethnic origin, political opinions, religious beliefs, membership of organisations, physical or mental health, sexual life, or offences or alleged offences.

A distinction is also drawn between data controllers, data processors, and third parties.

1. *The controller* is the person or other authority who determines the 'purposes and means of the processing of personal data'. In job selection, this is the hiring organization.
2. *The processor*, on the other hand, is 'any person (other than an employee of the data controller) who processes the data on behalf of the data controller'. This would include an Internet application service provider.
3. *Third parties* are any other person or authority authorized by the controller or processor to process the data.

In general, the obligations under the directives and related national Acts apply to data controllers. They have to ensure, contractually, that any data processor they employ enables them to fulfill their obligations.

---

[1] Available from *http://www.informationcommissioner.gov.uk/eventual.aspx?id=446*

In relation to psychological testing, the data controller may be the test user or the test user's employer, or the party for whom the testing is being carried out. Data processors are third parties who process data on behalf of data controllers. These would include providers of Internet based assessments, bureau services, fax-back scoring and interpretation, and so on. Test publishers and suppliers who offer online assessment services for test users are data processors, not data controllers. However, they have to ensure the systems they offer their users enable them, as data controllers, to meet their obligations under the Act.

The EU approach to data protection act does much the same by law as TRUSTe does by choice. Only time will tell which is the more effective approach. As Harris argues, it may be that these different approaches reflect cultural differences and as such may reflect two ways of achieving the same ends within different cultures.

Harris summarises the main issues relating to managing applicant reactions in terms of five key areas.

1. Clarify the purpose of the testing program.
2. Provide information about storage of the data, disclosure of the data, and the candidate's rights to the data.
3. Provide practice and test-taking tips.
4. Provide the 'human touch'.
5. Consider a certification programme.

These reinforce the lessons we learn from studies such as that by Rugg-Gunn et al. (2004), that people want to be informed, to know what is going on and why; they need to have reassurance if they are anxious and need to know where to go for help if they have a problem. Finally, they want to be reassured that they are dealing with a legitimate organisation and being asked to undergo a legitimate process. While we could argue that the development we have seen in the technology of design, manufacture and delivery of tests really is 'rocket science', treating people as people is not. It is very important that we continue to listen to test users and test takers and take note of their reactions if we are to make the most of the exciting opportunities afforded by new technology for testing.

REFERENCES

American Educational Research Association, American Psychological Association & National Council on Measurement in Education (1999). Standards for Educational and Psychological Testing, Washington DC, American Educational Research Association.
Bank, J. (2005). Gender differences in the perception of ability screening online. Paper presented at the Society for Industrial and Organizational Psychology Conference, Los Angeles, CA.

Baron, H., Bartram, D., & Miles, A. (2001). *Using on line testing to reduce time-to-hire*. Paper presented at the Society for Industrial and Organizational Psychology Conference, San Diego, CA.

Bartram, D. (2002). *EFPA review model for the description and evaluation of psychological tests*, Version 3.2b. Brussels: European Federation of Psychologists Associations.

Bartram, D., & Brown, A. (2004). Online testing: Mode of administration and the stability of OPQ32i scores. *International Journal of Selection and Assessment*, **12**:278–284.

Bartram, D., Brown, A., & Holzhausen, G. (2005). Online personality testing. Is unsupervised administration an issue? In *Proceedings of the British psychological society occupational psychology conference* (pp. 199–200). Leicester: British Psychological Society.

Foster, D., & Maynes, D. (2004, February). Detecting test security problems using item response times and patterns. In D. Foster, & R. Hambleton (Eds.), *Solve testing security problems using technology and statistics*. Symposium presented at the Association of Test Publishers Conference.

Gilliland, S. W. (1993). The perceived fairness of selection systems: An organizational justice perspective. *Academy of Management Review*, **18**:694–734.

Greenberg, J. (1987). A taxonomy of organizational justice theories. *Academy of Management Review*, **12**:9–22.

International Test Commission (ITC). (2001). International Guidelines for Test Use. *International Journal of Testing*, **1**:93–114.

International Test Commission (ITC). (2005). *Guidelines on computer based testing and internet-delivered testing*. Retrieved *www.intestcom.org*

Kurz, R., & Evans, T. (2004). Three generations of on-screen aptitude tests: Equivalence of superiority? *British Psychological Society Occupational Psychology Conference Compendium of Abstracts* (p. 202). Leicester: British Psychological Society.

Mead, A. D., & Drasgow, F. (1993). Equivalence of computerized and paper-and-pencil cognitive ability tests: A meta-analysis. *Psychological Bulletin*, **114**:449–458.

Mylonas, G., & Carstairs, J. (2003). *Comparison of a computer-administered motivation questionnaire under supervised and unsupervised conditions*. Macquarie, NSW: Macquarie University.

Rugg-Gunn, M., Price, R., & Wright, A. (2004). *Gender issues in online selection*. Warwick: Association of Graduate Recruiters.

Salgado, J. F., & Moscoso, S. (2003). Paper-and-pencil and Internet-based personality testing: Equivalence of measures. *International Journal of Selection and Assessment*, **11**:194–295.

Smith, H. J., Milberg, S. J., & Burke, S. J. (1996). Information privacy: Measuring individuals' concerns about organizational practices. *MIS Quarterly*, **20**:167–196.

SHL. (1999). *OPQ32 manual and user's guide*. Thames Ditton, UK: SHL.

SHL. (2002). *Motivation questionnaire: Manual and user's guide*. Thames Ditton, UK: SHL.

CHAPTER 8

Optimizing Quality in the Use of Web-Based and Computer-Based Testing for Personnel Selection

Lutz F. Hornke and Martin Kersting
Aachen University of Technology, Germany

INTRODUCTION

This chapter traces the history and development of computer- or web-based testing. It is argued that for all kinds of testing the standards of quality and control can only be achieved by experimental approaches that guarantee objectivity, reliability and, above all, validity. A brief look at possible areas of application clearly indicates that there is a growing demand for computer- and web-based tests. Apart from traditional multiple-choice item formats, the most promising approach is seen in simulation and game test procedures. Very often they are cast in joblike scenarios so that managers and applicants find them particularly attractive for their real life perspective. However, these tests are problematic in terms of providing good psychometric measurements. Finally, we propose some ideas and criteria for quality assurance.

The introduction of computer-assisted testing (CAT) is directly connected to the prevalence of personal computers themselves. Thus, 1/1/1980, the earliest date put into the boot ROM of the first IBM PCs, may be taken as the starting point of CAT. Sands, Waters, and McBride (1997) tell this story very well. However, there had been earlier attempts, which were compiled by Suppes, Jerman, and Brian (1968), and by Suppes and Morningstar (1972) in their seminal report on computer-based training. And if one goes back even further, then Pressey's (1926) learning machine may be considered a very early attempt at 'mechanising' training and testing, although it was quite far removed from what we today understand as computerized testing.

Computer-Based Testing and the Internet: Issues and Advances.
Edited by D. Bartram and R. K. Hambleton. © 2006 John Wiley & Sons, Ltd.

Hence the advent of versatile PCs marks the beginning of the modern approaches to testing and training. PCs flourished as mass storage became available, so that nowadays they are to be found in every office and most homes. This increase of storage on hard drives and CDs and in other forms, also allows for the use of sounds and motion in training and testing. It is possible to envision a future when testing embedded in training and psychological testing will be done with PCs or with something like a general home multi-media control box, the successor of our present television set, which will be a versatile computer that, apart from radically transforming our home life, providing entertainment, tele-work and education, will also fulfil training and testing functions. Already the modern testing of today emulates a good television show and is a far cry from the electronic page turners of the early days.

In psychological measurement generally, and in computer-based testing in particular, it is considered to be crucial to keep all items concealed from participants. Only specimen items are released to participants so that they get an idea of what is going to be asked of them, what the testing session will look like, and what possible results would emerge. In many cases this information is so inadequate that it patently fails in preparing the participants for the real testing situation.

An entire literature stemming from psychological experimentation has been borrowed for computerised testing, but the fundamental emphasis is still on 'experimental control'. Testing should be organised in such a way that nothing but the underlying psychological trait or competency carries over into the results. Standardisation is another important factor besides 'experimental control'—seating arrangements, lighting, taped instructions, strict time control, and other conditions have to be the same for every participant. If any of the situational factors are considered to have a bearing on the final results, then all participants must be equally subjected to them in the same manner. Paper–pencil testing, individual testing of one person by one psychologist, and even computer-assisted testing follow the same principle of control and standardisation in order to ensure quality of results.

However, this sense of strict control becomes more difficult to implement with the notion of an entertainment box in any household where testing may also be delivered. Nevertheless, the internet makes this possible, and there is no way of stopping it. Rather, the challenge is how to assure quality of individual results and personnel decisions. Careers and pay will depend on it, as will self-esteem and social recognition. It seems that solutions at hand continue to follow the strict control paradigm and use technical devices to achieve this end, but the question remains as to how the professional development of internet-based testing programs can be taken forward.

COMPUTER- AND INTERNET-BASED TESTING

It is impossible to predict what form CAT will take in the future. New programming tools, new test designs, and new ways of measuring complex behaviours are constantly being devised. So most of the features of tests are in flux. The sections below aim simply to provide an overview of contemporary testing programmes. Computer- and web-based tests were advocated for the following reasons. They:

- make scoring and norm-based interpretation easier and assure objectivity;
- use psychometric features to estimate a person's ability efficiently;
- allow us to design items that make use of certain *multimedia* features such as simulation and *dynamic* presentation formats in order to *better* diagnose problem solving abilities;
- provide scores in order to obtain immediately a:

  - number right score, formula score, maximum likelihood score (1PL, 2PL, 3PL)
  - process scoring (as in the learning test approach)
  - person fit index (IRT based), response time index, plausibility check
  - norm or criterion referenced score
  - feedback of results (personalised, immediate, quality based on item content, behaviour oriented).

ABCNews (17 December 2000) states on its web-page that 'The biggest advantages of computer-adaptive testing are time-related. The test is offered on demand at many testing centers around the country. Students see their scores immediately. Adaptive tests are usually shorter than paper-and-pencil tests. The GRE, for example, has gone down from three hours to two hours, 15 minutes. Proponents of computerised tests say they more accurately reflect the taker's ability. The computerised GRE now includes a writing assessment. The Test of English as a Foreign Language now includes an audio component'.

This list of advantages of CATs is further supplemented by the accounts given in other chapters in this book. Some of what flows over the internet at the moment is innovative not so much in terms of constructs or psychometrics but more in terms of design features of new item types. Here, one finds not only the good old multiple choice items but also items enriched with sounds, motion pictures, and audio–video sequences. Laboratories announce that olfactory as well as tactile oriented items may be the fad of tomorrow. Some 400 smells can be produced electronically today and could be used in assessing firemen, health inspectors, perfume designers and many more. So quite new means of 'controlling' testing are being developed.

The more recent psychometric developments in item response theory (IRT) will have to deal with issues of equivalence of scales, parallel measures, repeated measurement, and psychometric properties. Furthermore, the design of a testing system has to address the problems of test faking, checking the identity of participants, personal data and item security, and response latencies due to participants or due to operating systems or hardware.

Administering tests over the web requires taking account of environmental and situational control issues, public versus in-house provision of test systems, and computer system requirements and idiosyncrasies such as different handling of shapes, colour, sound, motion, streaming formats for motion pictures, display settings, browser configuration, and stability of communication on/off line. Undeniably, reliability, validity, appeal, and user friendliness and, for most companies and managers, costs, are important. Again, this is by no means a complete list.

TESTING (FOR) THE HOMO LUDENS

Problem Solving Scenarios

While the vast majority of all current CATs and web-based tests use traditional page-turning items, it seems that the more innovative item sets built on content and psychometric criteria as in Computer Adaptive Tests and problem solving scenarios will be very well suited for the *Homo ludens* of the future. Therefore the latter test formats are given some attention here. Problem solving scenarios explore aspects such as the finer cognitive processes involved in problem solving, e.g. typical stages of problem solving, general or specific strategies, typical errors and differences in the problem solving skills of experts and novices. Research also focuses on the relation between problem solving skills and personality characteristics on the one hand, as well as the relation between problem solving ability and intelligence or knowledge, on the other. It is claimed that newly coined concepts such as 'heuristic competencies', 'operative intelligence', 'system based thinking', and 'net based decision making' can be measured through these scenarios.

According to Dörner, Kreuzig, Reither, and Stäudel (1983), complex problems can be described and simulated as systems of interconnected variables. These problems have the following characteristics:

- *Complexity.* Numerous aspects of a situation have to be taken into account simultaneously by participants.
- *Interconnectivity.* The various aspects of a situation are not independent and cannot, therefore, be independently influenced. Interconnectivity also includes the important role of feedback loops and side-effects.
- *Dynamics.* Changes in the system conditions also occur without intervention from the problem solver.
- *Intransparency.* A situation is labeled intransparent when only a part of the relevant information is made available to the problem solver.
- *Polytely.* Sometimes the problem solver must simultaneously pursue multiple and even contradictory goals.

Computer-simulated scenarios are used as a way of translating such complex problems into an assessment context. Subjects have to run a city 'transportation system' (Broadbent, 1977), or manage a small factory. Funke (1991) provides an overview of the various scenarios. Mostly one finds simulations of a 'company' competing on some market with different 'organisational units' (e.g. research policy, developing and launching new products). For example, the TAILOR SHOP scenario or equivalent derivatives asks participants to maximise benefits and stabilise the company over a period of time. The success of each participant or a small group is judged against 'cumulative gains' and 'future orientation'. Information about these performance criteria is displayed to participants continuously. The scenario as such deals with the production of shirts. However, the system is kept relatively un-transparent, being based on 24 system variables of which only 11 are modifiable by participants. Results emphasize measures such as final value of the company, relative gains with equal weights given to all periods, and relative gains with higher weights given to later periods.

Another system, FSYS (Wagener, 2001) has a different set-up: an agricultural service company dealing with tree plantation and care and marketing lumber. Profits may be maximised by taking action against insects and anti-soil pollution. Participants are evaluated according to the stock value of the company, avoidance of errors, setting priorities, early exploration of system, information retrieval before decision making, attention given to stock value, and assertiveness while controlling company.

The most prominent example is the simulation called 'Lohhausen', where the subject has to act as the mayor of a small simulated town with the name 'Lohhausen' (Dörner et al., 1983). Subjects are able to manipulate taxes, influence production and sales policies of the city factory or the housing policy and so on. They are simply told to provide for the prosperity of the town over a simulated ten-year period within eight two-hour experimental sessions.

Scenario Difficulty

Of course, it is possible to give some ideas as to what moderates a scenario's difficulty:

- *Content:* knowledge in general, knowledge of the subject matter of the scenario, product, market and so on, acceptance of content and task by participants, generality or specificity of content, and impact of lateral knowledge.
- *User interface:* methods of instruction, mode of interaction with other participants or the system, motivational character of the scenario and displays, ergonomics of the interface, mode of acquiring information, note taking system, organisation of interaction, and means of input.
- *Formal structure of system:* number of variables, manipulation of system, number of periods and interaction time, real time simulation, number of nodes between input and internal variables, and nature of interaction of variables.
- *Feedback of information:* information about trends, delayed system information, percentage of trivial rules, assisting functions; information about system status, rules, and success criteria.

- *Evaluation of results:* methods, dimensions, functional structure of systems, randomness, compatibility with prior knowledge, structural redundancy, antagonistic features, number and reducibility of rules, compensatory features, time-lagged controls, side-effects, internal dynamics, reversibility, traps, difficulty range of tasks, and needed forecasting.

These facets may be used to make a scenario easier or harder, but it is not possible to predict the overall difficulty level from the facets before the test.

Advantages and Disadvantages of Using Computer-Based Scenarios for Diagnostic Purposes

In Europe, and especially in the German-speaking countries, computer-based scenarios are used as assessment tools in both research and practice. Some of the complex problem-solving scenarios used in the context of personnel selection are presented by Funke (1995), and a discussion of the advantages and disadvantages of this form of application can be found in Funke (1998). The main advantages of using computer-based scenarios as diagnostic tools are that the tasks (1) are highly motivating and (2) involve novel demands that (3) are deemed to have higher face validity than intelligence tests, and (4) test takers enjoy working with the simulations (see Kersting, 1998).

Much attention is given to face validity in that authors advocate that the simulation scenarios are much closer to the nature and challenges of prospective jobs than ordinary tests. So incumbents are led to see simulation scenarios as representative tasks. The lay public is intrigued by the content and purported relation of the scenarios to real life challenges. This makes it hard, from time to time, to insist on empirical facts. For example, rarely is a thorough task or job analysis presented to verify the cognitive demands of both jobs and simulation tasks in regard to validity; rather, users rely on the nice mock-ups of a scenario per se. There is a strong reliance on 'faith' to demonstrate what one encounters in real life.

Candidates are more open in their responses than with traditional 'tests' (Shotland, Alliger, & Sales, 1998). Feedback and administration within organisations is easier as the meaning of the test is 'obvious', face validity increases motivation, face validity correlates with the attractiveness of the organisation, and managers 'love' face valid computer tests (Smither, Reilly, Millsap, Pearlman, & Stoffey, 1993). In relation to online assessment in general, 84% of users of an on-line procedure reported a 'positive experience' (Vlug, Furcon, Mondragon, & Mergen, 2000) and on-line assessment was rated significantly 'more fair' and 'more satisfying' than the paper–pencil version (Reynolds, Sinar, Scott, & McClough, 2000). Scenario-based tests provide more realistic job preview, require less time for follow-up interviews, and make it easier for candidates to self-select and to accumulate knowledge about job characteristics during the selection procedure. There is nothing wrong with face validity—it is just the weakest criterion in arguing for the quality of a testing instrument as a predictor of future performance.

However, the diagnostic use of computer-based scenarios also entails serious difficulties that have yet to be overcome.

(1) The central question of appropriate approaches to the operationalization of problem solving quality remains largely unanswered.
(2) The reliability of the measurements obtained with some of the computer-based scenarios is less than satisfactory (see below).
(3) The existence of a task-independent and thus generalizable problem solving ability has not yet been substantiated. This indicates that the ability to steer the system is dependent not only on the skills of the problem solver, but evidently also on the nature of the task in question.
(4) The main problem is construct validity. It is still unclear which skills are actually measured by means of the computer-based scenarios (see Süß, Kersting, & Oberauer, 1992; Süß, Oberauer, & Kersting, 1994). Either the measurement has to be interpreted as an indicator of an independent *ability construct* (as suggested by newly coined concepts such as 'net-worked thinking', 'heuristic competence', and 'operative intelligence'), or the scenarios are regarded as a new *measurement method* which, in a certain respect, is better able to measure established constructs such as intelligence than has previously been the case (e.g. in a more differentiated manner or with a higher level of acceptance). Beckmann and Guthke (1995) have summarized the European research dealing with the controversial relation between traditional measures of intelligence and problem solving skills.
(5) Evidence for the criterion validity of the measures used is also urgently needed.

Reliability

Theoretically, it is to be expected that the reliability of scenario-based control performance measures will be lower than that of other performance measurements, e.g. intelligence tests, as problem solving scenarios provide more degree of freedom for the test taker and control performance is probably determined by heterogeneous factors. Due to the dependence of each system state on the preceding ones, unintended sources of variance such as motivational fluctuations or fatigue can build up, creating sequential dependencies in processing times. The long duration of response times, as compared to intelligence tests, does not increase the reliability. As a rule, each run of the simulation merely results in 'single act' criteria (Fishbein & Ajzen, 1974).

Psychometric results from simulation games yield in some cases estimates of different kinds of reliability. To give some examples, Köller, Strauß, and Sievers (1995) used three variants, all of which are based on a 'tailorshop' scenario: Textile Production, Fuel Delivery, Coal Distribution. As dependent variable the 'number of periods with capital gains' was used. For Fuel and Coal scenarios the number of periods with capital gains correlated at $r = 0.69$, for Textile with Fuel $r = 0.41$ and for Textile with Coal $r = 0.44$. Funke (1995) used a parallel version of a video recorder production scenario and found an $r = 0.83$.

As for *internal consistency*, Müller (1993) found $r = 0.83$ to $r = 0.86$ for two independent parts of a simulation game. In contrast, the test–retest reliability, which Müller based on a repeated test after 5 months, was $r = 0.53$ and thereby clearly lower. In the investigations by Süß et al. (1992, 1994), 137 test takers repeated the 'tailorshop' after an interval of one year. The retest stability was $r = 0.46$.

According to the reviewed studies, in certain scenarios at least some specific measures satisfy the reliability requirements necessary for diagnostic use, in spite of unfavourable theoretical prerequisites (e.g. multiple performance conditionality, learning effects, and the low level of aggregation). Funke (1995, S. 189 f) states that the reliability of performance on scenario-based problem solving tasks is on the same level as the reliability of so-called 'simulation oriented' methods (such as group discussions). In general, performance on tasks such as these shows lower reliability than intelligence tests.

Criterion Validity

Thus far, only a single study (Kersting, 1999, 2001) has directly compared the predictive criterion validity of computer-based scenarios with the validity of existing procedures deemed to have overlapping coverage. A total of 104 police officers were tested. For a subgroup of 26 participants it was not possible to analyse criterion validity because they attended a police academy.

For all participants general intelligence according to the Berlin Model of Intelligence by Jäger was assessed (BIS; Jäger, 1982, 1984; see Bucik & Neubauer, 1996; Wittmann, 1988). Before or after completing the intelligence test all participants worked on two computer-based problem solving scenarios. The scenarios that were used both referred to an economic context. One was the so-called 'tailorshop' (where subjects have to manage a tailoring factory); the other was the scenario 'Disco', which required the management of a computer chip factory. In both these scenarios the goal was to manage the company in a way that maximized the company's assets at the end of the game. Control performance is – according to the instructions given – measured as 'final asset value'. Both scenarios generated similar findings. Due to restrictions of printing space, only the results of the 'tailorshop' scenario will be presented here. After having worked on the 'tailorshop' task subjects had to work, among other things, on a paper–pencil test to assess system-specific knowledge. This paper–pencil test asks, for example, about the relationship of distinct key variables in the 'tailorshop'.

For the purpose of criterion validity a series of retrograde and concurrent criterion measures were assessed. The present account focuses on predictive validation. A postal questionnaire of criterion data on participant's job performance was conducted on average one year and seven and a half months after the initial testing. For some 73 out of the 78 initial participants the questionnaires were returned; this equals a response rate of 94%. Their age ranged from 28 to 57 (median = 36). In most cases job performance ratings were obtained from their direct supervisors, who were asked to rate their subordinates on a series of job-related performance dimensions, all of which could be attributed to intelligence, problem solving ability, and cooperative ability. The latter was used for the purpose of discriminant validation.

Raters were at first requested to mark for each of the three dimensions on a four-point scale how in terms of the respective dimensions the ratee, in comparison to colleagues, belonged to different quartiles of the comparison group. After these initial questions, which assess the extent of general abilities, 15 items tapped specific behaviours considered to be relevant to everyday job performance. They were indicators of constructs such as intelligence, problem solving ability, and cooperative ability. To give an example, in one of these items related to problem solving ability the term 'sensibility and flexibility towards changes' has been explained as follows: 'The achievement to continuously confront one's own actions with reality and to adjust one's own decisions flexibly to feedback'.

However, the rating scales measuring problem-solving behaviour and intellectual behaviour on the job were highly correlated, and were thus combined into a scale called 'quality of problem solving behaviour and intellectual behaviour in daily job performance'.

Table 8.1 shows correlations of these criteria with intelligence, problem solving and knowledge. The table shows the correlations of these predictors with the supervisor assessments made about one and a half years later. Problem solving and intelligence related job performance could best be predicted by intelligence ($r = 0.39$). The problem solving scenario and the knowledge test also proved to be valid predictors.

Table 8.1 Predictive criterion validity—comparing problem solving scenarios and intelligence tests

	Quality of problem solving behaviour and intellectual behaviour in daily job performance	Partial correlations, controlling for...			Job performance: cooperative ability
		Intelligence	Problem solving	Knowledge	
Intelligence	0.39**		0.33**	0.32**	0.07
Problem solving	0.37**	0.29*		0.32**	0.19
Knowledge	0.30*	0.23	0.23		0.06

Source: From Kersting (2001). *Diagnostica*, 47, 67–76.

For all predictors the assessment of cooperative ability demonstrated discriminant validity. Additionally, partial correlations were computed. It is immediately obvious that the different variables predict similar variance to a large extent. This leads to the question of whether a combination of predictors is able to raise the validity of the prediction, i.e. incremental validity. This was tested by a hierarchical regression analysis. In the first step, based on the highest bivariate correlation, intelligence was included, yielding an R of 0.39. By also including system specific knowledge about the 'tailorshop' as a second predictor, R was raised to 0.46. This equals an incremental percentage of explained variance of 7%. Another increment in prediction was achieved by including the third predictor, control performance on the 'tailorshop', but was significant only at the 10% level. After inclusion of all predictors a multiple correlation of $R = 0.50$ was obtained.

Considering a predictor above and beyond intelligence thus provides a substantive contribution to predictive power. On purely statistical terms control performance and knowledge proved to be similarly adequate in achieving significant prediction increments. The variable that was added to intelligence on the second step led to a statistically significant increase of the multiple R. The variable that was included on the third step did not. The sequence in which the predictors were included in the hierarchical regression shown here was based on the theoretical assumption that the systematic variance in control performance on problem solving scenarios can essentially be attributed to intelligence and knowledge. Accordingly, based on these theoretical assumptions, intelligence and knowledge were given priority in the hierarchical regression analysis.

Problem solving scenarios are diagnostically interesting, because it is not only intelligence *but also knowledge* that is required for managing these scenarios. Inclusion of knowledge in job performance may yield an increment in overall validity. For practical purposes it may be worthwhile to use both intelligence and knowledge assessment. Problem solving scenarios will be helpful in this regard, because managing complex problem solving scenarios demands acquiring knowledge, which could subsequently be tested.

Significant progress in the domain of problem solving assessment cannot be expected until both the operationalization of problem solving quality and the psychometric quality of assessment instruments are improved. Above all, it is essential to classify the ability tapped by the performance measures within an existing nomological network. Studies are required in which sufficiently reliable measures are implemented by means of *different* computer-based scenarios, and differentiated measures of intelligence are administered in sufficiently large samples. At the same time, tests of additional theoretically relevant constructs such as knowledge also need to be administered. In investigations of this kind (see Wittmann & Süß, 1999) it was shown that the systematic variance captured by problem solving scenarios can mainly be attributed to intelligence and prior knowledge. There is no empirical evidence for the existence of something like a problem solving ability as an independent construct.

QUALITY ASSURANCE

Returning to the initial argument for a controlled psycho-diagnostic experiment, it seems obvious that the test environment for unsupervised web-based testing in particular is quite uncontrolled. There may be background proctors such as friends and relatives if testing is done at home. Moreover, participants may use books, information materials, or the 'internet' as an aid in responding, not to mention unobserved effects resulting from emotional and physiological states such as fatigue, boredom, and so on. Even the differences in technical equipment, browsers, operating systems, and displays may cause variations in results that are error variance. Participants may 'fake', repeat tests, or return to previous items, if no precautions are taken. This can be remedied to some degree by sophisticated software, but ultimately full control is only possible by using professional testing centres as is done by ETS and other big test delivery companies. Even in self-assessments for vocational and educational purposes, some minimal standards for controlling the testing situation must be ensured.

It should be mentioned here that simulations and games have their own drawbacks and lack of proper control too. Typical problems include misunderstanding instructions and lack of personal contact or emotional 'rapport' with assessors, which is hardly compensated by an impersonal FAQ list, wordy reports based on few items, impersonal transfer of results, no personal feedback in case of unfavourable results, lack of acceptance of the psychometric procedures, security of data transmission, anonymity, and test fairness, to name just a few.

All the various drawbacks and problems of control discussed in this chapter are nothing but a challenge to improve quality. It is essential that several qualitative and quantitative studies are carried out to identify and remove flaws. With modern IRT it is not only possible to reach an economical score estimate, but also to use statistical fit indices in order to gauge whether the participant is responding in line with a theoretical model. Whenever there is a low fit for a series of responses, it becomes imperative to find out how to improve the test administration algorithm. The same holds true for timing controls and protocols. They tell, on an item by item basis, how long a participant has been working on each task. They provide the basis for detecting aberrant response patterns. Having a cup of tea during the test may be fine, but a ten minutes interruption of a cognitive task lowers validity and reliability!

Intelligent programming of computer and web based test administration routines for the future poses a big challenge. Group testing in the past showed that participants did not always function at the level for which the test was designed, frequently leading to false decisions. To overcome such problems in the open environment of web testing is the challenge that lies ahead of us. ETS, for example, have used video cameras to monitor participants in order to safeguard against 'false test takers' and 'helpers'. Modern technology will bring further support in this respect.

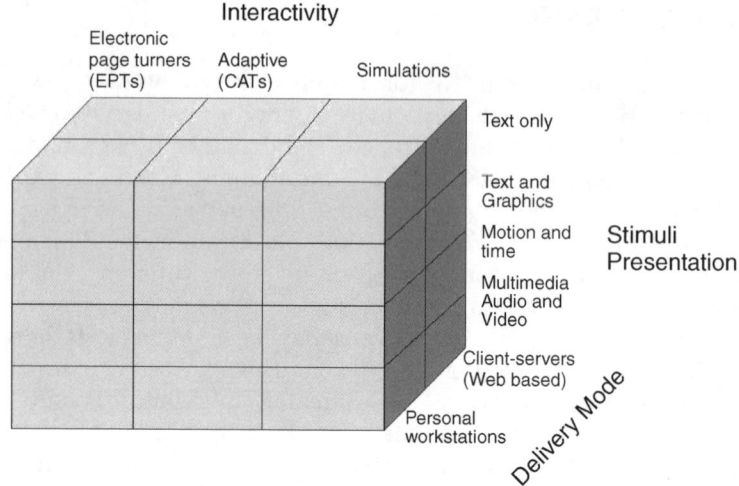

Figure 8.1   Three mode model of modern tests and their future challenges (in red)

It seems that internet-based tests lead to more self-disclosure (Locke & Gilbert, 1995), an aspect assessors are looking forward to with some excitement. The more we invest in quality assurance and personally appealing instructions, the more the people will come to value these assessments.

Web-based tests in the future will be much more than they are today (see Figure 8.1). They are communications with people who are very eager to learn about themselves and the demands of their job, a company, a university, and the like. Cheating is deplorable and exercised in order to attain a particular goal. Thus future tests need to be subjected to the best quality assurance procedures available, well marketed, and presented in an intelligent way so that everyone understands that cheating is counterproductive and works against the interests of both the individual and the organisation. Those who understand this will respond to web-based testing in the controlled manner the program and the assessors require. Participants should enrich their test taking by exercising internalised control, so that the test enables them to show their true behaviours and characteristics. In this regard web-based testing, apart from posing a challenge in terms of experimental controls, psychometric intricacies, and measurements, also opens up fresh opportunities for a gaining a wider recognition of psychological testing.

REFERENCES

Beckmann, J. F., & Guthke, J. (1995). Complex problem solving, intelligence, and learning ability. In P. A. Frensch & J. Funke (Eds.), *Complex problem solving: The European perspective* (pp. 177–200). Hillsdale, NJ: Erlbaum.
Broadbent, D. E. (1977). Levels, hierarchies, and the locus of control. *Quarterly Journal of Experimental Psychology*, **29**:181–201.

Bucik, V., & Neubauer, A. C. (1996). Bimodality in the Berlin Model of Intelligence Structure (BIS): A replication study. *Personality and Individual Differences*, **21**:987–1005.

Dörner, D., Kreuzig, H. W., Reither, F. & Stäudel, T. (1983). *Lohhausen. Vom Umgang mit Unbestimmtheit und Komplexität [Lohhausen. On dealing with uncertainty and complexity]*. Bern: Huber.

Fishbein, M., & Ajzen, I. (1974). Attitudes towards objects as predictors of single and multiple behavioral criteria. *Psychological Review*, **81**:59–74.

Funke, J. (1991). Solving complex problems: Exploration and control of complex systems. In R. J. Sternberg & P. A. Frensch (Eds.), *Complex problem solving: Principles and mechanisms* (pp. 185–222). Hillsdale, NJ: Erlbaum.

Funke, J. (1998). Computer-based testing and training with scenarios from complex problem solving research: Advantages and disadvantages. *International Journal of Selection and Assessment*, **6**:90–96.

Funke, U. (1995). Using complex problem solving tasks in personnel selection and training. In P. A. Frensch & J. Funke (eds.), *Complex problem solving: The European perspective* (pp. 219–240). Hillsdale, NJ: Erlbaum.

Jäger, A. O. (1982). Mehrmodale Klassifikation von Intelligenzleistungen: Experimentell kontrollierte Weiterentwicklung eines deskriptiven Intelligenzstrukturmodells [Multimodal classification of intelligence tests: Experimentally controlled development of a descriptive model of intelligence structure]. *Diagnostica*, **28**:195–225.

Jäger, A. O. (1984). Intelligenzstrukturforschung: Konkurrierende Modelle, neue Entwicklungen, Perspektiven [Research on intelligence structure: Competing models, new developments, perspectives.] *Psychologische Rundschau*, **35**:21–35.

Kersting, M. (1998). Differentielle Aspekte der sozialen Akzeptanz von Intelligenztests und Problemlöseszenarien als Personalauswahlverfahren [Differential-psychological aspects of applicants' acceptance of intelligence tests and problem solving scenarios as diagnostic tools for personnel selection]. *Zeitschrift für Arbeits- und Organisationspsychologie*, **42**:61–75.

Kersting, M. (1999). *Diagnostik und Personalauswahl mit computergestützten Problemlöseszenarien? [Assessment and personnel selection with computer-simulated problem solving scenarios?]* Göttingen: Hogrefe.

Kersting, M. (2001). Zur Konstrukt- und Kriteriumsvalidität von Problemlöseszenarien anhand der Vorhersage von Vorgesetztenurteilen über die berufliche Bewährung [On the construct and criterion validity of problem solving scenarios based on the prediction of supervisor assessment of job performance]. *Diagnostica*, **47**:67–76.

Köller, O., Strauß, B., & Sievers, K. (1995). Zum Zusammenhang von (selbst eingeschätzter) Kompetenz und Problemlöseleistungen in komplexen Situationen [Correlation of (self assessed) competence and performance of problem solving in complex situations]. *Sprache & Kognition*, **14**:210–220.

Locke, S. D., & Gilbert, B. O. (1995). Method of psychological assessment, self disclosure, and experiential differences: A study of computer, questionnaire, and interview assessment formats. *Journal of Social Behaviour and Personality*, **10**:187–192.

Müller, H. (1993). *Komplexes Problemlösen: Reliabilität und Wissen [Complex problem solving: Reliability and knowledge]*. Bonn: Holos.

Pressey, S. L. (1926). A simple apparatus which gives tests and scores – and teaches. *School and Society*, **23**:373–376.

Reynolds, D. H., Sinar, E. F., Scott, D. R., & McClough, A. C. (2000). Evaluation of a Web-based selection procedure. In N. Mondragon (Chair), *Beyond the demo: The empirical nature of technology-based assessments*. Symposium conducted at the 15th Annual Society for Industrial and Organizational Psychology Conference, New Orleans, LA.

Sands, W. A., Waters, B. K., & McBride, J. R. (1997). *Computerized Adaptive Testing*. Washington, DC: American Psychological Association.

Shotland, A., Alliger, G. M., & Sales, T. (1998). Face validity in the context of personnel selection: A multimedia approach. *International Journal of Selection and Assessment*, **6**:124–130.

Smither, J. W., Reilly, R. R., Millsap, R. E., Pearlman, K., & Stoffey, R. W. (1993). Applicant reactions to selection procedures. *Personnel Psychology*, **46**:49–76.

Suppes, P., & Morningstar, M. (1972). *CAI at Stanford 1966–68. Data, models, and evaluation of arithmetic programs.* New York: Academic.

Suppes, P., Jerman, M., & Brian, D. (1968). *Computer-Assisted Instruction: Stanford's 1965–66 arithmetic program.* New York: Academic.

Süß, H. M., Kersting, M., & Oberauer, K. (1992). The role of intelligence and knowledge in complex problem-solving. *The German Journal of Psychology*, **16**:269–270.

Süß, H. M., Oberauer, K., & Kersting, M. (1994). Intelligence and control performance on computer-simulated systems. *The German Journal of Psychology*, **18**:33–35.

Vlug, T., Furcon, J. E., Mondragon, N., & Mergen, C. Q. (2000). Validation and implementation of a Web-based screening system in the Netherlands. In N. Mondragon (Chair), *Beyond the demo: The empirical nature of technology-based assessments.* Symposium conducted at the 15th Annual Society for Industrial and Organizational Psychology Conference, New Orleans, LA.

Wagener, D. (2001). *Psychologische Diagnostik mit komplexen Szenarios: Taxonomie, Entwicklung, Evaluation* [*Psychological assessment with complex scenarios: Taxonomy, development, evaluation*]. Lengerich: Pabst.

Wittmann, W. W. (1988). Multivariate reliability theory: Principles of symmetry and successful validation strategies. In J. R. Nesselroade & R. B. Cattell (Eds.), *Handbook of multivariate experimental psychology* (2nd ed., pp. 505–560). New York: Plenum.

Wittmann, W. W., & Süß, H.-M. (1999). Investigating the paths between working memory, intelligence, knowledge, and complex problem solving via Brunswik Symmetry. In P. L. Ackerman, P. C. Kyllonen & R. D. Roberts (Eds.), *Learning and individual differences* (pp. 77–104). Washington, DC: APA.

CHAPTER 9

Computer-Based Testing for Professional Licensing and Certification of Health Professionals

Donald E. Melnick and Brian E. Clauser
National Board of Medical Examiners, Philadelphia, USA

Health professionals occupy a unique place among occupations. Few other professional roles provide the status that is provided to health professionals—allowing them to bypass the usual norms of personal privacy and individual autonomy. Acts performed every day by doctors and nurses in caring for patients would be considered simple or aggravated assault in any other setting. The surgeon's actions on anesthetized patients routinely circumvent the usual boundaries of individual autonomy.

As a result of the unique trust placed upon and privileges provided to practitioners of the healing arts, the health professions have long histories of regulation by local, regional, and national governments to assure that those allowed to practice can be trusted, not only to violate usual social boundaries in interacting with patients, but also to act in the best interest of the patient while making decisions with potential profound impact on the patient (Derbyshire, 1969; Shryock, 1967). In the best tradition of learned professions, many occupations in health care are committed to self-regulation, establishing voluntary systems of credentialing that exceed the requirements imposed by governmental regulatory authorities and mandating that their members cooperate fully with the established regulatory mechanisms (General Medical Council, 1998; American Medical Association, 1997; Medical Professionalism Project, 2003).

Throughout this chapter, we will describe the systems of regulation that apply to medical doctors. However, the principles described regarding

Computer-Based Testing and the Internet: Issues and Advances.
Edited by D. Bartram and R. K. Hambleton. © 2006 John Wiley & Sons, Ltd.

assessment of doctors can be generalized to other regulated health professionals. While systems of regulation differ from country to country, this chapter will draw primarily upon experience in the United States. Again, the principles described regarding assessment of doctors in the United States have considerable application in other national contexts.

OVERVIEW OF PROFESSIONAL REGULATION OF DOCTORS IN THE US

Governmental regulation of doctors is generally represented through some form of licensure. Most governments have established laws that limit the practice of medicine to those who have been granted the legal right to practice, based on an assessment by a government-sanctioned regulatory body. The licensing authority will generally document that an individual practitioner has successfully completed minimum educational requirements and meets standards of minimum proficiency in the competencies considered essential for practice. The latter documentation is often accomplished through examination programs. Sometimes the authority to conduct these examinations is delegated to recognized medical schools; in other instances, examinations developed outside the medical schools are required.

In most instances, the legal authority, or license, to practice medicine grants a broad right to practice within the profession. Licenses generally allow general, undifferentiated practice (LaDuca, Taylor, & Hill, 1984; LaDuca, 1994). Typically, the profession itself adopts additional assessment of credentials for various domains within medicine. In various specialty domains, additional training and experience prerequisites are defined and assessments of competency administered in granting voluntary certification as a specialist. While not necessary to practice legally, these certifications are often required as conditions of participation in institutional health care, such as academic settings or hospitals.

Finally, institutions that provide health care, such as hospitals and health maintenance organizations, define minimum requirements for credentialing, which must be met before an individual licensed and/or certified doctor is permitted to practice in that setting. In general, the credentialing processes verify education and experience and authenticate documentation, but do not administer additional assessment.

A number of types of organization support this process of licensure, certification, and credentialing. In the US, licenses to practice medicine (and nearly all other professions) are granted under the authority of specific state laws. These laws generally establish a board, often including both medical professionals and lay persons, to oversee administration of the law by some component of the executive branch of the state government. The state boards of medicine evaluate credentials of doctors applying for a license, oversee the periodic renewal of license registration, and respond to breaches of professional standards by licensed doctors.

Specialty certifying boards or colleges are self-governing, professional organizations that establish standards and grant credentials for specialty practice. In the US, 24 of the boards with the broadest recognition have joined together in the American Board of Medical Specialties® (ABMS®) (ABMS, 2002). The ABMS establishes standards for specialty certification programs and monitors its member boards' conformity with those standards. However, a number of specialty certifying boards exist that are not part of the ABMS. Their certifications have variable degrees of rigor.

Hospital and healthcare organizations have medical staff and credentialing committees. These groups establish criteria for granting specific privileges related to patient care and audit doctor credentials for meeting these criteria. National organizations, such as the Joint Commission on Accreditation of Healthcare Organizations (JCAHO), establish common standards for credentialing in accredited hospitals.

Related to these organizations are the national entities that accredit medical schools (the Liaison Committee on Medical Education or LCME) and graduate medical education programs (the Accreditation Council for Graduate Medical Education or ACGME). While not directly engaged in providing credentials for individuals, these organizations define minimum standards for the educational programs, with a direct impact on both the learning experiences and the mandated assessments of individuals.

Finally, several organizations specialize in the development of assessment tools for licensure and certification purposes. Many specialty certifying boards have developed expertise in assessment. The National Board of Medical Examiners®, a non-profit organization established in 1915, is a hybrid organization. Originally established to provide a voluntary certification of readiness for licensure, the NBME® now provides broad testing agency services for the health professions. It collaborates with the Federation of State Medical Boards, an association representing the individual state licensing authorities, to sponsor and create the United States Medical Licensing Examination™ (USMLE™). It also provides assessment services to many specialty certifying boards and other health professions' licensing and certifying bodies, assessment tools for use by medical schools in intramural evaluation of students, services supporting the role of state licensing authorities in identifying doctors in need of remediation, and services for medical schools and licensing bodies around the world. In aggregate, the NBME administers more than 200,000 high-stake examinations each year.

COMPUTER-BASED TESTING IN THE REGULATION OF US HEALTH PROFESSIONALS

The NBME has provided examinations used to license doctors since 1916 (Hubbard & Levit, 1985). Until the mid-1960s, the NBME's Certifying Examination program was the only national system of assessment for medical licensure. Individual state licensing boards developed their own examinations for the doctors who did not possess the NBME Certificate. In the mid-1960s, the NBME developed an alternate national examination, the Federation Licensing Examination (FLEX), for use by individual states in place of locally developed examinations. In 1992, these two licensing examination systems were merged to create USMLE.

From their inception until the early 1950s, these national licensing examinations included essay examinations and laboratory and bedside demonstrations of skills. During the 1950s, the essay examinations were supplanted with multiple-choice questions, and in the early 1960s, the bedside oral examination was eliminated because of its lack of reliability. In following years, a number of paper and pencil test formats were utilized, including sequentially answered patient management problems, sets of multiple-choice questions answered after viewing a movie of a doctor–patient encounter, and many variants of multiple-choice question (MCQ) formats. However, by the time USMLE emerged, the national examination used only MCQs administered twice each year in a paper and pencil format.

During the 1980s the NBME explored the use of computers for test administration, and by 1995 the first NBME-developed computer-based test was administered. USMLE became a computer-based test in 1999. Many NBME-supported medical specialty certifying examinations and licensing examinations in allied health professions are now computer-based tests. In 2003, the NBME will deliver about 125,000 computer-based tests. Several other computer-based testing programs are well established in the health professions. They include the US national licensing examinations for nursing and the Canadian medical licensing examinations.

Computer-based tests for high-stake licensure and certification are administered in several different configurations. Very large-scale tests, such as USMLE, are offered continuously at dedicated, secure testing sites around the world. Other tests with intermediate numbers of examinees are offered during discrete testing 'windows' lasting from days to months. Examinations with smaller numbers of test takers are administered much like paper-and-pencil tests, on a single date with a simultaneous testing at many test sites.

EXAMINATION FOR MEDICAL LICENSURE IN THE US—USMLE

USMLE was created to evaluate the readiness of physicians to enter medical practice. It is intended to provide a single, uniform measurement tool, a common yardstick, for US medical licensing authorities to use in granting an initial license to practice medicine. It attempts to provide measures that are as valid and reliable and as focused on protecting the public interest as is possible while assuring fairness to examinees (NBME, 2003).

The three Step examinations that make up the USMLE are designed to provide a cohesive, comprehensive evaluation of the knowledge and skills required for the practice of medicine. Each Step is designed to be part of the whole; no single Step can stand alone as an adequate evaluation for licensure.

Step 1 assesses biomedical scientific knowledge, emphasizing the application of knowledge in specific clinical or experimental situations. Step 2 assesses the knowledge of clinical science that underlies the safe and effective care of patients in a supervised setting. It attempts to assure that individuals in post-graduate education have and can apply the knowledge essential for carrying out the unsupervised components of their duties. Step 3 assesses knowledge and its application in clinical situations necessary for the unsupervised practice of medicine, focusing on common clinical problems and ambulatory settings characterizing medical practice in the US.

USMLE is the only examination available for doctors with the MD degree seeking initial licensure in the United States.[1] Results of the first two component Steps of USMLE are used by medical schools, both to gauge individual student progress as well as to evaluate the educational effectiveness of the school in relationship to national performance norms. Results of the first two USMLE Steps are also used by some residency program directors in screening program applicants. The Educational Commission for Foreign Medical Graduates (ECFMG), charged by the US Department of State with granting visas for non-US citizens seeking entry for advanced medical training and for assessing qualifications of applicants graduating from schools outside the US or Canada for post-graduate education positions, uses these examinations as one of several requirements to grant its certificate.

COMPUTER-BASED USMLE

In 1995, the USMLE sponsors called for the implementation of computer-based testing (CBT) in USMLE. This move to computerization of USMLE was made possible by the emergence of secure, large-scale computer-based testing networks. The NBME developed a strategic alliance with Drake Prometric, subsequently acquired by Sylvan Learning Systems and then by Thomson Learning, to meet the needs of our testing programs.

Paper and pencil USMLE examinations were administered only twice each year; CBT administration occurs 6 days each week throughout the year. Paper and pencil examinations required two forms of the test each year; CBT uses more than 100 forms for each Step during the year. Paper and pencil tests utilized about 1,500 test questions from a pool of a few thousand each year; in CBT, each Step utilizes several thousand items from a pool of 15,000 items during the year. Paper and pencil examinations were scored in large batches with each administration, and scores were not reported for about 10 weeks. With CBT, examinations are scored each week, and results are provided in 2–3 weeks from the test date. Finally, the paper and pencil tests were well understood by test takers, having been used with little change for nearly

---

[1] In most US jurisdictions, individuals holding the Doctor of Osteopathy degree may obtain licensure by successful completion of USMLE or the COMLEX, a similar examination developed by the National Board of Osteopathic Medical Examiners.

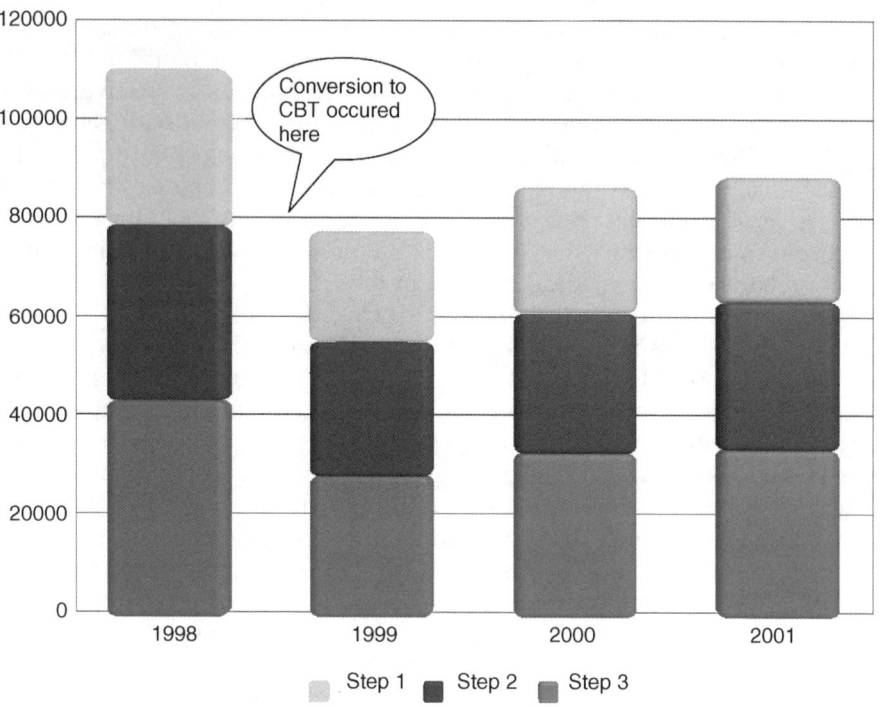

Figure 9.1   USMLE examinee numbers

50 years. Computer-based tests continue to be a novel experience for test takers, with resulting increased anxiety for already anxious examinees, at least in the early months of CBT testing.

Figure 9.1 shows one of the realities of CBT. In most high stake examinations converted to CBT, the transition results in those who can opt to delay testing doing so. Total examinee volume dropped dramatically in anticipation of CBT, although this decline certainly had many other contributing causes. However, since testing program revenues depend on examinee fees, the short-term decline in examination utilization can have a substantial impact on the financial health of the testing program. However, in high-stake, mandatory testing programs, the declines in test use will generally represent delays in testing rather than loss of examinees.

CBT ALLOWS INNOVATIVE TEST FORMATS—PRIMUM™ CLINICAL CASE SIMULATIONS

In addition to converting the paper-and-pencil-administered MCQ tests to computer administration, a new test format, not possible without computer-based testing, was introduced in Step 3. Primum Clinical Case Simulations (CCSs) recreate a virtual clinical environment, which appears to evoke authentic clinical management behaviors (Melnick, 1990a; Melnick, 1990b; Melnick & Clyman, 1988). The observed and recorded behavior is scored. This new testing format has been a component of Step 3 since 1999. It makes up ½ day of the 2 day test. Its score is combined with the MCQ score in making pass–fail decisions. The Primum CCS simulated environment has several key characteristics. Clinical realism is achieved by providing all the resources— thousands of tests and treatments, appropriate locations for care encounters, realistic cues from patients and other members of the healthcare team—that would be available in a real-life context. The simulation creates a sense of time realism. As the test taker moves the clock forward, 'patient' condition changes based on the combined effects of the disease course over time and the effects of the actions of the examinee. The test taker 'writes' orders for tests and treatments using an uncued, free-text order entry system.

The simulated patient case begins with a statement of the patient's reason for the encounter. The test taker is then free to gather several kinds of information. The patient may be queried for more information about the problem and other medically relevant history. The test taker may undertake various physical examination maneuvers. Simulated time moves forward as the test taker uses time to gather this information. The test taker may also, at any time, write orders for diagnostic studies, such as blood tests, x-rays, scans, etc. Results of these orders do not appear until a prescribed time has passed. At any point, the test taker can initiate treatments or undertake procedures such as surgical interventions. However, in order to monitor the results of these interventions, the test taker must initiate additional history-taking, physical examination, or tests. Depending on the patient's condition, the test taker may receive spontaneous cues from the patient, the patient's family, or other members of the health care team, reporting major changes in the patient's condition. At any point in time, the patient can be moved between home, office, hospital, and intensive care. Of course, the availability of tests and treatments varies across these sites of care. The system ultimately ends the simulation, and presents the next case.

The history of developing the Primum simulation system contains some lessons for those anticipating the creation of new, authentic performance assessments. The impetus for the NBME's effort to apply computer technology to its testing programs was clearly linked to the decision made by the NBME in the early 1960s to eliminate the bedside clinical component from the certifying examination. It was with great reluctance that the NBME bowed to the mounting evidence that these exams were unfair. In 1968, the NBME's Research Advisory Committee—Alexander Barry, Robert Ebel, Hale Ham, Bill Mayer, Jack Myers, Kenneth Rogers, Dael Wolfle, and Louis Welt— recommended that NBME develop a computer-based simulation system to test physician skills previously tested in bedside examinations. A prototype simulation of initial patient diagnostic evaluation was demonstrated for the American College of Physicians meeting in 1970.

From 1970 to 1975, work on the simulation system continued as a joint effort with the American Board of Internal Medicine (ABIM). During this phase, five models were developed and/or evaluated. The INDEX system allowed the physician to obtain history, physical examination, and some test results by entering numbers from a coded index list; after 10 minutes of gathering data, the physician had to provide a diagnosis. The CASE system functioned much like INDEX, except that it allowed for free text input of questions. MATRIX required the physician to make a diagnosis based on cues, and used Bayesian probability to score the accuracy of the diagnostic decision. The computerized patient management problem (PMP) was a traditional PMP without back-tracking. CRISYS was a physiologic cardiovascular simulator, with dynamic patient response to interventions. Each model was tested; student and physician reactions were collected and evaluated. None of these systems offered the promise of a reliable and valid measure of patient management skills.

From 1975 to 1982, the joint NBME/ABIM project continued at the University of Wisconsin. The focus of effort during this phase was the development of a management model, which realistically avoided cueing and simulated the movement of time. Patient care, as in real life, no longer ended with the diagnosis, but required continued care of the patient. The first bona fide scoring systems were developed, based on scoring systems for latent image PMPs. A large field trial was conducted, and it provided tantalizing indicators that the simulation measured unique competencies in a reliable and valid manner.

Concurrently with this work, the NBME was attempting to create an infrastructure that would allow computer delivery of its examinations. In 1986, it created Computer-based Testing and Learning, Inc. (CTL) as a wholly owned subsidiary for this purpose. In 1988, recognizing that the initial business plan for CTL was overly optimistic, the NBME withdrew its support and the subsidiary was closed. Clearly an idea that was ahead of its time, CTL worked with several clients who subsequently found other outlets for computer-based testing, including the National Council of State Boards of Nursing and the National Council of Architectural Review Boards. Primarily because of a lack of delivery vehicle, but also because of refinements needed in case scoring, the planned 1989 implementation of case simulations in the NBME certifying program was indefinitely deferred.

Despite indefinite postponement of implementation plans in 1989, development work continued unabated. The project focused on dissemination of the case simulation technology to medical schools. More than 90 medical schools in the US and abroad used the NBME system for instruction, self-assessment, and (in more limited numbers) for end of clerkship evaluations. The continued collection of data from thousands of student–case interactions allowed refinement in the scoring of the simulations. Scoring approaches concentrated on replicating expert global judgments of examinee case management strategies. Enhanced case authoring tools were developed that capitalized on the database of existing cases, using graphical and highly indexed computer-aided design tools to streamline case authoring. The simulation system was rewritten using state of the art techniques, including a graphical interface, the potential for integration of digital audio and video, and object-oriented database and programming.

The challenges of developing and delivering a computer-based simulation of the patient management environment were significant, but this was only part of the effort required to produce a useful assessment tool. In order for the system to be useful for licensure evaluation, it had to be possible to quantify examinee responses as an indication of proficiency: it was not only necessary to collect meaningful examinee responses; it was necessary to score them. During much of the period in which Primum was being developed, effort was also underway to create scoring procedures. The evolution of these procedures was associated with dramatic changes; four conceptually different systems were developed.

Each of these scoring procedures required that the simulation system be able to capture examinee responses and compare them to a key. The procedures differed in which information was used to calculate the scores and how that information was aggregated. The simplest and earliest procedures were based on the scoring approaches that had been applied to PMPs administered on paper. Although there were many variations on this theme, the basic approach is that examinees are given points for selecting keyed actions that were identified as beneficial for management and points are lost for ordered actions that are non-indicated and may be dangerous to the patient. The main problem with this approach was that test-wise examinees could sometimes achieve adequate scores by ordering non-intrusive procedures and avoiding potentially risky procedures. Adequate scores did not necessarily reflect adequate management.

A second scoring procedure that was examined applied the Rasch model to the response patterns based on the key (Julian and Wright, 1988). More than any of the others, this approach is purely data driven. It provided an implicit weighting for items based on the likelihood that examinees of a given proficiency level would order those actions.

Both of these approaches were limited by the fact that the resulting scores may not show a strong correspondence to the judgments that expert clinicians would make if they reviewed the associated examinee performances. The final two scoring approaches that were studied share in common the fact that they are both explicit efforts to model that expert judgment.

Again, both approaches begin with items that could be quantified based on a kind of key. Content experts reviewed case material and identified actions that would be beneficial for the given case presentation. This definition of 'beneficial' was process rather than outcomes based in that beneficial items were those that would be appropriate for patients with a given presentation. For example, diagnostic tests that would rule out reasonable differential diagnoses may be considered as 'beneficial' as those that would identify the specific problem that would ultimately prove to be the 'correct' answer. In addition to identifying those actions that would be considered beneficial, content experts categorized the non-indicated actions based on their level of potential risk to the patient (or level of invasiveness). These latter two procedures differed in terms of how the scored actions were combined to create an aggregate score. The first of these procedures used linear regression. For this approach, content experts categorized the 'beneficial' actions in terms of their importance in the context of the case. Actions were considered 'essential for adequate care', 'important for optimal care', or 'appropriate for optimal care'. Non-indicated actions were similarly placed in one of three categories defined in terms of the associated level of risk and/or intrusiveness. Finally, a variable was created that represented the time frame in which the essential actions were completed. To produce scores, counts of actions were produced for exa- minees. These counts, along with the variable associated with timing, were then used as the dependent measures in a multiple regression. The indepen- dent measure was a rating of the examinee's performance on the case. In effect, the regression procedure allowed for the estimation of optimal weights for predicting the rating of the examinee's performance based on the seven scoring variables (counts of actions in each of the three categories representing beneficial actions, counts of actions in each of the three categories representing non-indicated actions, and the timing variable). The resulting weights could then be applied to produce predicted ratings for performances that had not been reviewed by experts.

This regression-based procedure produced scores that were highly corre- lated with the actual ratings. The one potential limitation of the procedure was that although resulting scores had a high correspondence to the expert ratings the structure of the scoring procedure was at best an approximation of the logic that experts used in making their judgments. In response to this limita- tion, a procedure was developed in which an effort was made to combine the scorable items using logic statements that directly approximated the rules that experts used when rating examinee performance. These logical statements defined the combinations of diagnostic studies, therapeutic interventions and follow-up required for a given score. The logic also included requirements about timing and sequencing (e.g. 'treatment must be initiated prior to the end of the first day' or 'credit is given for treatment only if the results of a diagnostic study are seen prior to initiating treatment').

These latter two procedures were evaluated in detail during the years immediately preceding operational implementation of the simulation as part of USMLE. An obvious first step in that evaluation was to compare the correlations between the scores produced using these methods with the expert rating these scores were intended to approximate. Several published studies report correlations between one or both of these scores and ratings of the same performances (Clauser, Margolis, Clyman, & Ross, 1997a; Clauser et al., 1997b; Clauser, Subhiyah, Nungester, Ripkey, Clyman, & McKinley, 1995). The results lead to two general conclusions: (1) the resulting scores have a generally high correlation with the related ratings and (2) scores from the regression-based procedure are generally more highly correlated with the rat- ings than are those from the rule-based procedure. Table 9.1 provides one set of these correlations (taken from Clauser et al., 1997b).

Subsequent studies compared the reliability (or generalizability) of scores produced using the two methods, as well as the correlation between the observed scores produced using these methods and the proficiency measured

Table 9.1 Correlations between ratings and regression-based and rule-based scores

Case	Regression-based score	Rule-based score
1	0.81	0.77
2	0.91	0.85
3	0.89	0.87
4	0.88	0.84
5	0.84	0.69
6	0.86	0.87
7	0.79	0.79
8	0.95	0.86

by the ratings of performance (i.e. the correlation between the observed scores produced with the automated systems and the true scores based on raters) (Clauser, Swanson, & Clyman, 1999; Clauser, Harik, & Clyman, 2000). Results suggested that the regression-based scores were more reliable that the rule-based scores. The reliability analysis additionally indicated that using the regression-based procedure produced a score that was approximately as reliable as that which would have been obtained if two experts had rated each examinee performance. The scores produced using both procedures were also shown to have an essentially perfect correlation with the true score associated with the rating. These studies were important because (1) all else being equal, a more reliable score is to be preferred and (2) increasing the reliability at the expense of decreasing the correlation with the criterion may be an unwise trade-off between reliability and validity.

Based on the results of these and other related studies, a decision was made to implement the regression-based procedure for operational scoring of Primum. Since November of 1999 this procedure has been used to score approximately 100,000 examinations. The experience of the NBME has demonstrated that this type of automated scoring procedure can be psychometrically defensible and logistically feasible. Clearly, the effort can be considered a success. Nonetheless, there were lessons to learn in the process. One important lesson is that complexity has a cost. Even with the reasonably straightforward regression-based scoring approach, each case and each key require many hours of staff time not only for development but for the many important steps in the quality control process. A second, but related, lesson is that decisions about the intended interpretation of the scores should be made early on in the development process. Development of the simulation and the scoring system should then proceed in tandem. Complexity in either part of the system should be justified by its relevance to the inferences that will be made based on the scores.

After more than three years of testing, examinees express strong approval of the test format. In post-test surveys, examinees express appreciation for a test format that allows demonstration of their clinical management skills.

However, the complex, proprietary systems for delivering the simulation have posed challenges in integrating them with the vendor's test delivery systems. The software environment for simulations is much more complex resulting in various computer network performance problems and examinee problems during test administration. On the positive side, the simulation provides unique information about examinees, information that is judged to be important by content experts and is shown to be valuable in assessing the competencies considered important for licensure.

LESSONS LEARNED IN IMPLEMENTING CBT

The long journey from concept to implementation is remarkable, but the results appear to make the journey worthwhile. As Christopher Columbus said, 'Here the people could stand it no longer and complained of the long voyage; but the Admiral cheered them as best he could, holding out good hope of the advantages they would have' (Christopher Columbus: *Journal of the First Voyage*, 10 October 1492). The journey provided a number of important lessons.

First, measures are more difficult to create than methods. While the technology of computer-based testing is always the first topic of conversation, experience at the NBME has proved over and over that the technologic problems are far less daunting than the measurement problems. The most recalcitrant problems throughout the developmental history of the simulation project were the extraction of meaningful measures from the plethora of observational data.

The simulation model was conceptually complete by the late 1970s. Many refinements have been made, updating the model to take advantage of emerging technology. Virtual disks in random access memory (in 1984), analog videodisk (in 1985), digital audio and video (in 1994), object-oriented programming (in 1993)—these are examples of the changes made technologically. However, the basic logical structure of the system has been stable for many years. Appearances have changed, but the basic structure of the simulation engine has not. The dumb terminal of 1978, completely character based and requiring input of coded numbers from a printed index, has given way to the networked personal computer running under Microsoft® Windows® and exploiting its graphical interface. It can include full motion segments as part of the patient introduction, free text entry on a mock order sheet, and iconic representation of time and location.

However, scoring research has continued throughout the developmental timeline, and the research has not been just the incremental exploitation of technology, but has required repeated creative approaches to solve specific recalcitrant problems. In particular, scoring and simulation design must proceed hand in hand, each informing the other. The major approaches to scoring have built less upon one another than upon the weaknesses discovered with the predecessor scoring method. Initial scoring approaches adapted PMP scoring systems. As with PMPs, this system rewarded thoroughness rather than efficiency, and often scored good novices higher than highly competent experts. The Rasch partial credit model allowed better use of information gathered about timing and sequencing of actions and depended on item difficulty to weight the various actions. Separate categories for very risky actions were segregated from actions that were allowed to compensate for one another. The latter represented a conceptual shift toward combining quantitative data with qualitative information in scoring, the first step toward a rule-based, case-logical approach. The most significant step forward in scoring strategy was the move to capturing and replicating expert judgments about global case management. This approach has increased the precision with which the computer-generated scores can replicate the judgments of experts about the performances.

Second, test delivery is more technologically demanding than test development. Throughout the history of the NBME's CBT projects, applying technology to the task of test method development has been easy. In fact, we have had to work hard to keep up with rapidly evolving technology in selecting tools to solve our unique problems. It has always seemed that, just as we squeezed a technology to solve a problem, a new technology emerged that solved the problem without contortions.

It is very easy to forget the requirements for successful delivery of a technology-based test. Whether testing a few hundred or tens of thousands, the logistical challenge of providing a suitable testing environment with standardized test conditions is immense. It is easy to buy a few of the latest PCs or peripheral devices for a development environment, and tempting to do so to allow the latest and best tools to be applied to solving problems. However, cost becomes significant when it is scaled up to a delivery system. A home PC cost $3400 in December 1994. By October 1995, the exact same computer cost $2400, but, of course, it was no longer 'state of the art'. By 2002, it was not possible to buy the same computer, except at a junk sale. Providing state of the art and updating it frequently is likely to make a delivery system economically nonviable. NBME experience indicates that computer-based testing should target well defined, standard technology that is available economically. Only in this manner is it likely that large-scale test administration systems will be available at a defensible cost. The software for delivering this test was usable in the late 1980s, but no system for secure computer delivery of tests existed. While such systems exist today, and new approaches using Internet technology offer alternative delivery vehicles, the constraints of the capacity of available testing networks place new demands on tests that have historically been administered simultaneously to large numbers of examinees.

To make a technology-based testing program work, a test sponsor needs not only expertise in testing, but also equivalent expertise in technology, at both hardware and software system development levels. In addition, the effective design, construction, financing, marketing, and management of a technology-based delivery system is mandatory. Anyone wishing to sponsor a computer-based testing program must either develop or acquire these competencies.

Test developers should outsource those parts of the task that are beyond their competencies. Partnering with a test delivery vendor experienced in CBT will help a computer-based testing program to succeed.

Technology-based testing creates a vast menu of possible innovation. Our experience suggests that implementing computer-based testing is more likely to succeed if potential changes are adopted only incrementally and only if they add value. For example, in planning for computer delivery of the USMLE MCQ examination, we explored various adaptive testing models, including full adaptive administration and computer-adaptive sequential or multi-stage testing (CAST) (Luecht & Nungester, 2000). We ultimately decided not to implement these strategies. They proved unnecessary to reach the precision necessary for our pass/fail decisions in the context of content sampling considered essential to the test's validity.

While computer-based testing increases the security of test administration, it offers new potential for examinees to reproduce item banks by memorization. It is necessary to protect the integrity of high-stakes exams by either limited, simultaneous test administration (not possible with very large numbers of examinees) or the use of very large item banks. Costs of developing these banks may dwarf the costs of technology development.

It is essential to gain examinee buy-in by creating added value through computer-based testing. This can be accomplished by offering greater convenience, more rapid score reporting, more rapid access to repeat a failed examination, etc. Given the costs of implementing computer-based testing, it is unlikely that CBT will result in reduced costs to examinees.

OPERATIONAL CHALLENGES OF COMPUTER-BASED TESTING

Continuous testing—a mandatory feature for large-scale computer-based testing—affects every aspect of developing, producing, administering, and scoring an examination. For twice yearly paper and pencil tests, the test development cycle was driven by the production needs of two test forms per year. The authors received test item writing assignments and wrote items. Authors participated in peer review of the test items, and committees of test item authors selected items for the next test form, using both newly written items and previously used items from a relatively small pool. Test form books and answer sheets were produced and shipped to test centers. Examinees registered for a specific examination administration and took the test on the prescribed dates. Answer sheets were returned and scanned. Preliminary scoring, calibration, key validation, final scoring, and score reporting took place as batch processes for large numbers of examinees. This cycle repeated itself, in the case of USMLE, twice each year for each Step.

For CBT, an analysis of pool needs, rather than needs for a specific test form, drive item writing assignments to authors. Authors write assigned items and peer committees review the items, as in the past. However, the committee of item authors does not select items for test forms; rather, the items are entered into a pool for pretesting. Another pool containing previously used and pretested items is used to assemble draft test forms using automated test assembly (ATA). However, frequent and repeated expert review is required to assure the adequacy of the individual items in the live pool. Furthermore, experts must review at least a sample of the test forms to assure that the ATA software is performing acceptably and to tweak the test assembly rules. Only after these reviews can test resource files be released for use in the delivery system.

Like in the old system, the examinee applies, but, under CBT, the examinee receives authorization to test in a 3 month window, schedules with the vendor, and takes the test. Test responses are returned daily, and scoring is performed and score reports are released weekly. Calibrations and key validation activities take place soon after the release of a new resource file. In CBT, test item development, test form development, and test administration have no intrinsic links, and all are continuous.

Large item banks are necessary for continuous testing, placing huge demands on resources and test development capabilities. To begin CBT, a massive expansion of test item pools was required. Figure 9.2 shows the number of test items developed for USMLE from 1994, the year prior to CBT, through 2001. Ramping up test development takes time. The implementation decision for CBT in USMLE was made in 1995, but item development took 2 years to reach an adequate level. The effort in test development more than doubled for a period of 4 years, and, while declining now, is likely to remain above pre-CBT baselines indefinitely.

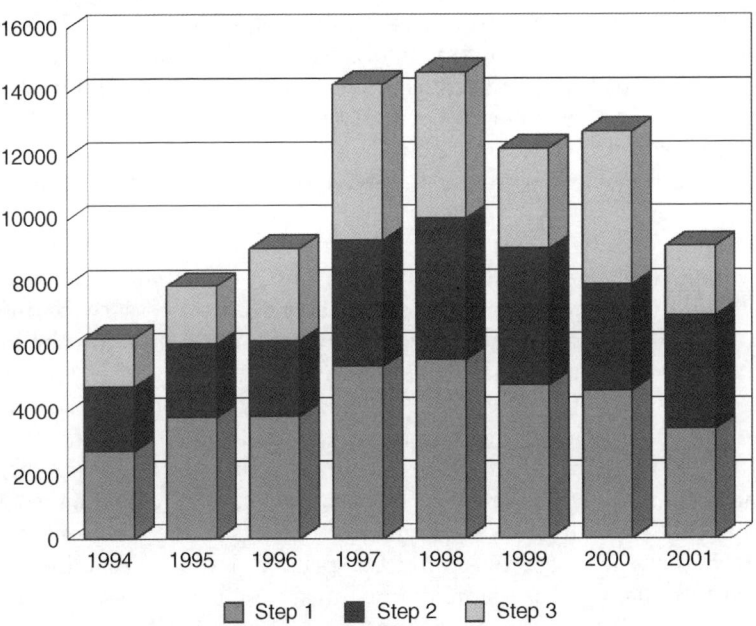

Figure 9.2   Test items developed for USMLE, by year

With continuous testing, organized efforts to memorize and expose item banks is a threat—in NBME's experience substantively magnified by the availability of the Internet as a means of communication among past and future examinees. In paper and pencil testing, the key concern was access to the exact sample of questions before they were administered. Frequent theft of examination materials occurred, and a flourishing market developed for the sale of these materials to dishonest examinees. CBT has eliminated this particular problem. Random form assignment at the time the test is initiated, coupled with the availability of many minimally overlapping forms based on the large item pools, results in little risk of an examinee knowing in advance of the test the identity of the items that will be seen.

However, continuous testing allows more opportunity for exposure of items to reproduction from memory. More items are revealed, and examinees acting in concert have extended opportunities to memorize and assemble test items. Monitoring the Internet provides good evidence that compilations of test materials are available. This increased threat to examination integrity requires careful item exposure controls limiting the number of times an item may be seen across forms.

In many high-stake paper and pencil tests, the test sponsor controls the administration of the test. While the NBME attempted this approach for CBT, it required resources that exceeded those available, even to a reasonably large and well established testing agency. Even much larger test sponsors have found it undesirable to unilaterally develop CBT delivery mechanisms. A test delivery vendor is essential, but that vendor will certainly cause headaches and heartaches. No test vendor will meet expectations for quality and consistency. The vendor is likely to require publication of test materials in unique formats, requiring the development of appropriate interfaces with the test developer's item banking and publishing systems. Quality assurance activities increase as new sources of error occur at the hand-off points in publishing to the vendor's system. Unless all examinee services will be outsourced to the vendor, a path not likely to be followed by those engaged in high-stake assessment, new systems must be developed to connect registration, eligibility verification, test scheduling, status determination, incident reporting and investigation, and test result transmission and reconciliation. Finally, even the best vendor will have human lapses in the systems necessary to control the hardware and software in the delivery network, not to mention the humans who staff the test centers, call centers, and other points of potential error. Placing the test administration task in the hands of the vendor will demand that the test sponsor invest heavily in independent quality assurance.

CBT test administration provides accurate timing information regarding examinee behavior with test items. This new data stream regarding test timing adds new challenges to test development. It brings to the forefront the question of whether the test is or should be speeded for some or all examinees. New test formats, like case simulations, raise new psychometric issues. Our experience with CBT has provided item and examinee level data on test timing that we could only dream about in the past. Assuming that the test delivery

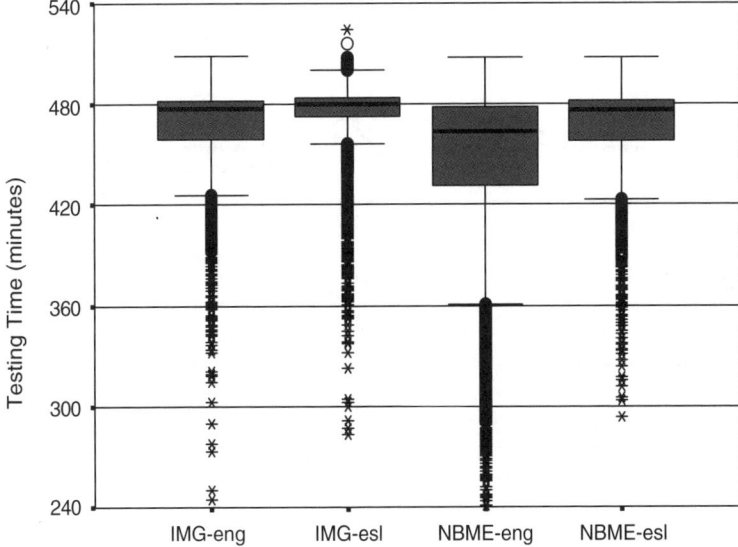

Figure 9.3 Examination time used for USMLE Step 2 by native (eng) versus non-native (esl) English speakers and US/Canadian examinees (NBME) versus international medical graduates (IMG)

software is designed to capture time information, this newly available information provides a quantitative base for making decisions about timing (Swanson, Case, Ripkey, Clauser & Holtman, 2001).

Figure 9.3 shows box plots of Step 2 examinees' total testing time used. The examinees are divided into four groups: medical students from schools outside the US and Canada with English as their first language, international students with English as a second language, US and Canadian students with English as their first language, and US and Canadian students with English as their second language. The actual testing time allowed was 480 minutes. The data points exceeding 480 minutes arise from a software design decision that allows the examinee to complete the displayed item even after the section time has expired. Accumulation of extra time on these 'last items' across many sections can lead to a total test time in excess of the upper limit for the test day. The figure demonstrates that the median time needed for the ESL groups was very close to the allowed time, while a large portion of the sample fell at or above the maximum time, even for those with English as their first language. The test appears to be speeded for substantial portions of all groups, but for ESL examinees more than native English speakers.

Figure 9.4 displays testing time as a function of total test score, again divided into the four groups. The curve for US students with English as a second language is hidden behind the international student native English speakers' curve. Again, the time provided appears to be inadequate, with the amount of inadequacy dependent both on group membership and

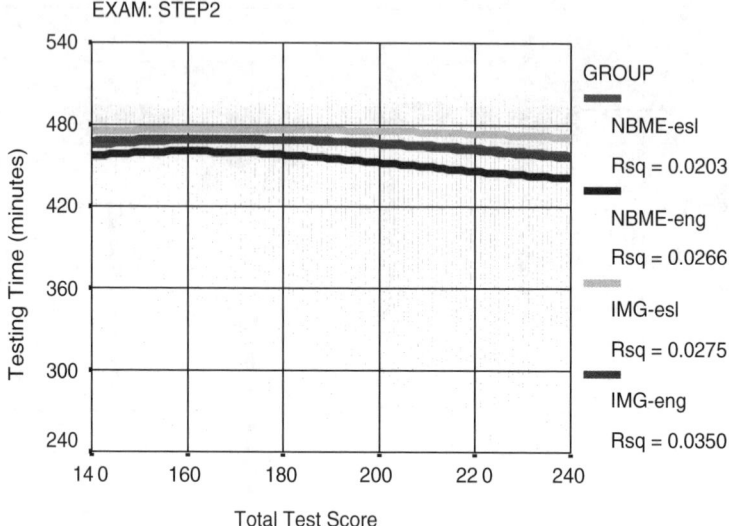

Figure 9.4 Testing time as a function of test performance, native English speaking status (eng and esl), and location of medical education (NBME = US/Canadian, IMG = international medical graduate)

proficiency. Lower-proficiency examinees are more adversely affected than high-proficiency examinees. Note that NBME's pre-CBT field tests using an adaptive sequential testing model indicated that this difference might not be the case in an adaptive testing context, where more able examinees may be time challenged because of their interaction with more difficult test material. These data have supported analyses that would have been impossible in paper and pencil testing. They have resulted in changes in item pacing for the Step 2 examination.

These timing data provide just one example of new data available from CBT that affect test form construction (to assure equivalency) and test administration standards. If this information is judiciously collected, analyzed, and acted upon, a higher-quality, fairer test will result.

The use of new formats, such as Primum CCS, force important considerations, such as their relationship to overall performance, the evidence that they provide unique information, judgments about how this information should be integrated into the overall test decision, etc. Furthermore, newer testing formats all seem to be less time efficient than MCQs, and careful consideration needs to be given to supplanting time allocated to MCQs in favor of new, more authentic assessment tools. The complex scoring approaches described for Primum CCS demand new approaches to test validation. All in all, these challenges provide full employment for future generations of measurement specialists. At this point in the history of CBT, it would be erroneous to conclude that an operational CBT program can be implemented without a significant investment on an ongoing basis in continued research and development.

FUTURE POTENTIAL FROM CBT

In licensing and certifying examination programs for medicine, testing the range of competencies necessary for safe and effective practice is essential. However, for four decades tools have not been available that allowed defensible assessment of some of these competencies. The emergence of technology-based testing, allowing innovative testing formats such as simulations, has contributed to renewed interest in developing licensing and certifying examination instruments that assess a more complete range of relevant competencies than is now the case.

What are the competencies needed to practice safely and effectively? Figure 9.5 shows a taxonomy for the competencies of doctors, proposed by

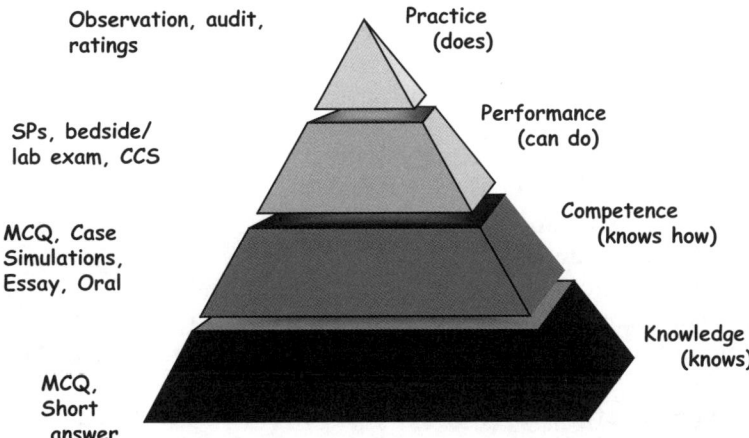

Figure 9.5 The 'Miller' pyramid: sequential stages of competency and tools for their assessment

Miller more than a decade ago (Miller, 1990). In this model, the foundation of physician effectiveness is knowledge. An effective physician knows. Built upon knowledge must be competence. The physician must not only know, he or she must know how—to be able to apply knowledge appropriately. However, this is not enough. The effective practitioner must be able to perform based on knowledge and competence. The 'can do' is at least as important as the 'knows how'. Finally, all of this must be put into daily practice. Even the physician who can perform effectively may not do so consistently. MCQ examinations do a superb job of testing knowledge, and with careful attention to test design and question writing they may test knowing how. The addition of computer-based case simulations to USMLE enhanced the examination's ability to test competence, and it begins to test performance in certain aspects of the doctor's tasks. However, other tools will be necessary to allow full testing of the performance level, and practice monitoring tools will be required to evaluate the physician who is in practice after completing a comprehensive and effective licensing examination.

Another taxonomy for the competencies of doctors was recently developed by the Accreditation Council on Graduate Medical Education and the American Board of Medical Specialties in the US. The six general competencies are proposed as relevant to all doctors. The basic competencies are:

(1) patient care
(2) medical knowledge
(3) practice-based learning and improvement
(4) interpersonal and communication skills
(5) professionalism
(6) system-based practice.

Full descriptions of these competencies can be found on the ACGME and ABMS web sites—*www.acgme.org* and *www.abms.org*.

Other efforts at reaching consensus regarding the structure of requisite competencies for doctors have arisen concurrently in many parts of the world, with very similar results. They include the Association of American Medical Colleges' Medical Schools Objectives Project, the CanMeds 2000 report (focusing on patient expectations) from the Royal College of Physicians and Surgeons of Canada, and the work of the United Kingdom's General Medical Council published in *Good Medical Practice.* All of them provide taxonomies of physician competencies that map into one another, as shown in Table 9.2. While the taxonomies have been simplified for comparison, each taxonomy captures the key elements of the others.

The emergence of these highly consistent definitions of doctor competence supports efforts to design assessment tools to match the competencies. Today,

Table 9.2 Comparison of taxonomies of medical competency

ACGME/ABMS	AAMC MSOP	CanMeds 2000	GMC
Patient care	Clinician	Clinical decision maker	Good clinical care
Medical knowledge	Researcher, educator	Medical expert	
Practice-based learning	Lifelong learner	Scholar	Keeping up to date
Interpersonal, communication skills	Communicator	Communicator	
Professionalism	Professionalism	Professional	Professional relationships with patients
System-based practice	Manager	Manager, collaborator	Working in teams

the quality of our assessment of *medical knowledge* is excellent. While efforts are being made to assess *patient care skills* (through low-fidelity, clinical vignette MCQs and case simulations) and other methods to assess *interpersonal and communication skills* using standardized patients are planned in the near future, neither of these competencies is adequately assessed today, and *practice-based learning and improvement, professionalism,* and *systems-based practice* are not assessed at all.

If the competencies are to be broadly tested, then new technology will be required to enhance our tools for assessment. Technology holds the promise to support development of tools that will allow broader assessment of the requisite competencies. Some of the areas in which this might be the case include stimulus enrichment, constructed response formats, simulation and virtual reality, observational assessment, and ratings.

Digital images provide opportunities for broadening assessment. In particular, the ready availability of high-definition three-dimensional images of human anatomy, thanks to the Visible Human Project of the National Library of Medicine, provides fully manipulable images controlled by the computer user (Senger, 1998). A new item format might instruct the examinee to locate and tag a specific anatomical structure in the virtual cadaver. Peripheral devices are now available that simulate odor (Platt, 1999), thus offering the opportunity to include this additional sensory stimulus in the assessment context.

The computer provides the opportunity to use large-scale constructed response problems. For example, concept mapping allows demonstration of sequencing and relationships among individual concepts in a physiologic, biochemical, or disease process (Novak, 2003). Assessing understanding of the relationship of isolated concepts might be accomplished by a drag-and-drop assessment tool that requires the test taker to arrange elemental concepts into a coherent pattern and to create appropriate connectors among the concepts that describe the nature of the relationships among them.

Computer-based testing would allow an adaptation of policy capture, clinical judgment analysis (LaDuca, Engle, Wigton & Blacklow, 1990; LaDuca & Leung, 2000). In this experimental assessment tool, the computer presents many case instances with randomly or systematically varied cue values. The test taker provides a judgment—prognosis, likelihood of the presence of a specific disease, etc.—based on the cue values. When this is repeated over a large sample of case instances, a model of the examinee's judgment the relative weighting of cues in making a clinical judgment, can be compared with a model based on evidence or expert consensus. While the assessment utility of this testing format, made possible by computers, is unclear, field testing has resulted in positive response. This format also provides an opportunity to assess the effectiveness of learning arising from the chance to compare one's own judgment model with a criterion model. After comparing the test taker's model with the criterion model and explaining differences, the test taker can be exposed to an additional set of judgment tasks to determine whether the prior model has been adjusted.

Another technology-enabled assessment approach might allow assessment of the doctor's ability to acquire appropriate information in an area of deficit. When the test taker fails to answer one or more questions in a single domain correctly, the test system would make available a variety of reference resources. The examinee would seek information to answer the question. The computer would track the use of information, allowing assessment of the quality of information retrieval and use to answer the initial questions.

Virtual reality techniques offer the potential, particularly in complex psychomotor procedural skills, to test skills not now tested. Endoscopic diagnostic and surgical simulators using virtual reality techniques, including realistic visual and haptic feedback, are now available and ready to be studied for use in training and assessment (Westwood, Hoffman, Mogel, Robb, & Stredney, 2000). With no patient present, the computer-controlled endoscope responds to test taker manipulation by displaying the appropriate visualization drawn from a digital reconstruction of the relevant anatomic structures. This visualization is fully responsive to the device, allowing the technique of the operator to be assessed and the skill in detecting or treating lesions to be evaluated. Using even more complex devices, including VR goggles and haptic feedback surgical 'instruments', the test taker can visualize an operative field that actually is not there and feel instruments encounter tissues that exist only within the computer.

While these virtual reality technologies are available now, more complex virtual reality environments are likely to emerge based on similar environments under development for other purposes. These range from multi-player, internet-based simulated environment games to fully immersive virtual reality environments, such as CAVE™ (cave automatic virtual environment). These technologies offer to provide virtual environments in which interactions among healthcare professionals and patients can be fully simulated. Such high-fidelity simulation may someday allow learning and assessment for healthcare professionals like that now available for pilots in sophisticated flight simulators.

In the not too distant future, most hospitals and many doctors' offices will collect all information in an electronic format. When this is the case, these standardized electronic records can be sampled to provide real life 'transaction lists'. By analyzing the observed behavior of healthcare professionals with real patients, it may be possible to develop reliable and valid measures of actual performance, providing evidence of practice-based learning and guidance for professional development.

Finally, technology makes systematic collection of ratings—whether from peers, coworkers, patients, teachers, or others—more practical. Research indicates that a moderate sized sample of raters can produce stable measures of traits that are otherwise difficult to assess, traits such as professionalism. Touch-tone telephony, web-based forms, and database-driven periodic automated sampling may make rating-based assessments feasible in the near future. The American Board of Internal Medicine is already implementing peer ratings as part of its maintenance of competence initiative (*www.abim.org*).

Thus, technology opens a number of doors that allow more comprehensive assessment of the key competencies for medical practice. The same is likely to be true in most professions. However, implementing these new approaches will challenge many assumptions of our current assessment systems, such as point-in-time testing. As more competencies are assessed, it will become more challenging to establish minimum standards for practice.

This future looms before us—so many opportunities, and so few qualified assessment experts and resources to explore and apply them. However, Shakespeare's advice (*Julius Caesar*, Act IV, Scene iii) is apt: 'There is a tide in the affairs of men, which, taken at the flood, leads on to fortune; omitted all the voyage of their life is bound in shallows and in miseries. We must take the current when it serves, or lose our ventures'. Testing in the health professions must recognize the tide of technology-based assessment and take the current when it serves.

REFERENCES

American Board of Medical Specialties (ABMS). (2002). *2001 Annual report and reference handbook*. Evanston, IL: Author.

American Medical Association. (1997). *Code of medical ethics*. Chicago, IL: Author.

Clauser, B. E., Harik, P., & Clyman, S. G. (2000). The generalizability of scores for a performance assessment scored with a computer-automated scoring system. *Journal of Educational Measurement*, **37**:245–262.

Clauser, B. E., Margolis, M. J., Clyman, S. G., & Ross, L. P. (1997a). Development of automated scoring algorithms for complex performance assessments: A comparison of two approaches. *Journal of Educational Measurement*, **34**:141–161.

Clauser, B. E., et al. (1997b). Developing a scoring algorithm to replace expert rating for scoring a complex performance based assessment. *Applied Measurement in Education*, **10**:345–358.

Clauser, B. E., Subhiyah, R., Nungester, R. J., Ripkey, D., Clyman, S. G., & McKinley, D. (1995). Scoring a performance-based assessment by modeling the judgments of experts. *Journal of Educational Measurement*, **32**:397–415.

Clauser, B. E., Swanson, D. B., & Clyman, S. G. (1999). A comparison of the generalizability of scores produced by expert raters and automated scoring systems. *Applied Measurement in Education*, **12**:281–299.

Derbyshire, R. C. (1969). *Medical Licensure and Discipline in the United States*. Baltimore, MD: Johns Hopkins Press.

General Medical Council (1998). *Good Medical Practice*. London: General Medical Council.

Hubbard, J. P., & Levit, E. J. (1985). *The National Board of Medical Examiners: The First Seventy Years*. Philadelphia, PA: NBME.

Julian, E. R., & Wright, B. D. (1988). Using computerized patient simulations to measure the clinical competence of physicians. *Applied Measurement in Education*, **1**:299–318.

LaDuca, A. (1994). Validation of professional licensure examinations: professions theory, test design, and construct validity. *Evaluation and the Health Professions*, **17**:(2), 178–197.

LaDuca, A., Engle, J. D., Wigton, R., & Blacklow, R. S. (1990). A social judgment theory perspective on clinical problem-solving. *Evaluation in the Health Professions*, **13**:63–78.

LaDuca, A., & Leung, C. (2000, August). Assessment of practicing doctors' clinical judgment. *Proceedings of the Association for Medical Education in Europe*, Beer Sheva, Israel.

LaDuca, A., Taylor, D. D., & Hill, I. K. (1984). The design of a new physician licensure examination. *Evaluation and the Health Professions*, **7**(2):115–140.

Luecht, R. M., & Nungester, R. J. (2000). Computer-adaptive sequential testing. In W. J. van der Linden & C. A. W. Glas, (Eds.), *Computerized Adaptive Testing: Theory and Practice*, (pp. 117–128). Dordecht Kluwer.

Medical Professionalism Project (2003). *Medical Professionalism in the New Millennium: A Physician Charter*. Philadelphia, PA: American Board of Internal Medicine.

Melnick, D. E. (1990a). Computer-based clinical simulation: State of the art. *Evaluation in the Health Professions*, **13**:104–120.

Melnick, D. E. (1990b). Using a computer-based simulation model of assessment: The case of CBX. In S. L. Willis & S. S. Dubin (Eds.), *Maintaining Professional Competence*, pp 147–161 Jossey-Bass: San Francisco.

Melnick, D. E., & Clyman, S. G. (1988). Computer-based simulations in the evalution of physicians' clinical competence. *Machine-Mediated Learning*, **2**:257–269.

Miller, G. E. (1990). The assessment of clinical skills/competence/performance. *Academic Medicine*, **65**:S63–67.

NBME (2003). *USMLE Bulletin of Information*. Philadelphia, PA: NBME.

Novak, J. D. (2003). The promise of new ideas and new technology for improving teaching and learning. *Cell Biology Education*, **2**:122–132.

Platt, C (1999). You've got smell!. *Wired*, **7**:11.

Senger, S. (1998). An immersive environment for the direct visualization and segmentation of volumetric data sets. In J. D. Westwood et al. (Eds.), *Medicine Meets Virtual Reality: Art, Science, Technology: Healthcare (R)evolution*, Amsterdam: IOS Press.

Shryock, R. H. (1967). *Medical Licensing in America, 1650–1965*. Baltimore, MD: Johns Hopkins Press.

Swanson, D. B., Case, S. M., Ripkey, D. R., Clauser, B. E., & Holtman, M. C. (2001). Relationships among item characteristics, examinee characteristics, and response times on USMLE Step 1. *Academic Medicine*, **76**(10 Suppl.):S114–116.

Westwood, J. D., Hoffman, H. M., Mogel, G. T., Robb, R. A., & Stredney, D. (2000). *Medicine Meets Virtual Reality 2000*. Amsterdam: IOS Press.

CHAPTER 10

Issues that Simulations Face as Assessment Tools

Charles Johnson
Competence Assurance Solutions Ltd, UK

In the last few years I have spoken at a number of seminars and conferences about how to get the best out of simulations. One of the features of these events is the way in which simulation seems to have become synonymous with simulators and simulators have become seen as being largely computer-based equipment. Of course, after a few minutes discussion, everyone in these audiences will tell you that they realise this is not true, but it is still interesting how the notion pervades most of the thinking about simulation now.

Not all that many years ago, I was asked to be a member of a steering group for a project commissioned by the Department for Education and Employment (DfEE) in the United Kingdom. The aim of the project was to review developments in computer based assessment and training and to make recommendations on how the DfEE could support desirable developments. The project team concluded that although computer based assessment had promised much, the economic and commercial realities of the world meant little of that promise had been delivered and was unlikely to be in the foreseeable future.

At the time, the steering group concluded that the project team were correct. Personal computers were slow, unreliable, with poor graphics capability and thinly spread around amongst users, whether individuals or organisations. Many companies at the time who would have liked to use computers for assessment concluded that the capital and development costs were far too high to be contemplated. About the same time, I was also part of a team that submitted a bid to the DfEE for funding to develop a crisis management simulator. The funding committee agreed that the aim was worthwhile but did

Computer-Based Testing and the Internet: Issues and Advances.
Edited by D. Bartram and R. K. Hambleton. © 2006 John Wiley & Sons, Ltd.

not give us funding because they had had their fingers burnt on projects of this sort too often in the past and did not believe the project could be delivered successfully. As it happens, we obtained private funding from a client and did deliver the simulator, on time, but it was easy to understand the attitude of the DfEE given their experiences. It is clear that the DfEE were not unusual in their position as evidenced by the description by Melnick and Clauser in Chapter 9 of the trials and tribulations experienced in the development of the MMDS simulation.

Yet, here we are, some 10 years later, in a position where we can all agree with Hornke and Kersting in Chapter 8 that PCs can now be found in every office and most homes and that the quality of the presentation is such as to make simulations very realistic and compelling. Furthermore, we now realise it is difficult to foresee what will be possible in even a few years time. Between the Winchester 2002 ITC conference on computer based testing being announced and my completing the writing of this chapter, the fastest processor speeds on PCs have increased from 1.6 to 3.2 GHz. No doubt by the time this book comes out we will have 4.0 or even 5.0 GHz processors.

HAS COMPUTERISATION DELIVERED VALUE?

Despite the improvements in technology, it is still valid to ask the question of whether the advances in computer technology are associated with commensurate advances in testing and assessment practice and whether these are delivered through simulation. The chapters by Hornke and Kersting and by Melnick and Clauser share an important characteristic, a belief that computer-based simulation is worth the effort. I agree with this up to a point. Simulation can provide significant value if well constructed and well managed. Unfortunately, this is not always the case. In what follows, I explore some of the reasons why simulations may fail to deliver everything they promise, draw some boundaries for their effective use and suggest some necessary next steps in the development of psychometric theory necessary for realising the full benefit of simulation.

ASSESSMENT FRAMEWORKS

Consider first what the defining features of simulations are and how they differ from other forms of assessment. Simulations mimic the real world without having to duplicate it. They can be designed to achieve a high degree of realism but this is not necessary. This differentiates simulations from both work sample exercises, which are slices of real activity, and analogous exercises, which, like simulations, draw on the same set of skills and abilities as real work but do not attempt to mimic real work activities. Simulations do not have to mimic all aspects of real work activities but they have to be recognisable as a simulacrum of real work. The US Navy has developed the notion of scaled simulation, identifying only those features of an activity that must be included to ensure the committed engagement of participants (Ehret, Gray, & Kirschenbaum, 2000). Being a recognisable simulacrum usually requires some degree of skill integration, and it is this that distinguishes most simulations from traditional, single construct, psychometric tests of ability. Achieving a very high degree of realism in simulations often entails huge costs, which are difficult to justify unless the assessment stakes are also very high. Furthermore, a high degree of realism in the activity does not guarantee reliable and valid assessment. Indeed, the need to impose an assessment activity on top of the simulated work activities can often detract from the realism of the simulation and, if poorly integrated into the task, decrease the level of acceptance by participants.

One way to judge the value of simulations, particularly when computer delivered, is to evaluate them against a common assessment framework. For the purposes of this chapter, consider the list in Table 10.1, based on one produced by the EURYDICE Unit at the National Foundation for Educational Research for the Qualifications and Curriculum Authority in the UK (O'Donnell, Sargent, & Andrews, 2003).

In fact, a number of these dimensions need not be considered in detail since they apply equally to simulations, computer-based assessment and other forms of testing. The following sections, therefore, consider only those dimensions, marked with an asterisk in Table 10.1, where specific issues arise.

Table 10.1   Common Assessment Framework (O'Donnell et al., 2003).

Framework dimension	Comments
Control*	Who ensures that assessment conditions are appropriate, sufficiently secure and that confidentiality is maintained, and how is this done?
Purpose of assessment	What are the assessment needs of the client and the candidate and what claims are made for the assessment outcomes?
Participation*	Who gets involved, in what way, and who decides the nature and timing of the participation?
Nature of assessment*	What content is included, what assessment method is used, which version, and how is the assessment delivered?
Administration*	How is it ensured that administration of the assessment is sufficiently standardised and runs smoothly?
Interpretation*	How is the assessment scored, interpreted and matched to assessment requirements?
Consequences	What implications do the results of the assessment have for the client and the candidate?
Use of results	Where in the organisation's competence management system will the results be used, and how will the results be fed back to clients and candidates?
Monitoring and review	How will the technical and operational quality of the assessments be established and checked to ensure that value is still being delivered over time?

At the general level, however, computer-based simulation can benefit from a number of improvements related to the computerisation of tests. There are two main ways in which computerisation has undoubtedly improved assessment practice. The first is in increased efficiency in the delivery and administration of assessment materials and the second is in increased flexibility. Increased efficiency can be achieved in a number of ways:

- Quicker, and more accurate, scoring. You only have to consider the volume of testing reported by Melnick and Clauser to appreciate how expensive and time consuming the hand-marking of test papers can be.
- Providing different types of score, some of which would be difficult or impossible to produce otherwise. For example, Hornke and Kersting refer to formula scores, maximum likelihood scores, person fit indices and others that are only feasible with the advent of computerised scoring.
- Adaptive testing, which, in the right circumstances, can give equally reliable and valid results for significantly less testing effort. Hornke and Kersting report time savings of up to 25%.
- Item banks and form generation can cut down hugely on the time taken to produce parallel versions of tests.
- More rapid evaluation of test quality.

Likewise, flexibility can be achieved in a number of ways:

- On-demand testing.
- Wider distribution of assessment sites and accommodation.
- Greater variety of answer and response formats.
- Greater variety of content presentation formats with greater control of the presentation.

However, all of these have costs. Furthermore, it is not always clear that computer-based simulation results in more sophisticated assessment. One sign that computer-based simulations do not necessarily deliver more sophisticated assessment can be seen in the guidance and standards documents that have been produced on computer-based testing (see for example, the British Standards Institute, 2002; International Test Commission, 2005). The focus is almost entirely on how to ensure the quality of delivery and administration given the constraints of the technology. The sections on psychometric quality could, invariably, have been written about any sort of testing.

Control

Good control of assessment involves a range of activities ranging from control of the assessment event (e.g. timing of the assessment event, choice of test version) through updating or enhancement of assessment materials to test security. As noted above, computerisation generally has advantages where control of the assessment event is concerned, in particular allowing greater standardisation of assessment delivery. However, there are other aspects of control where computerisation results in unique problems.

Candidate Identification

Making sure that the correct person is undertaking an assessment is, of course, a serious issue in all high stakes assessment. However, the flexibility which computer-based assessment offers in terms of distributed assessment locations, testing on demand and adaptive testing, while being one of its greatest advantages, also creates some special problems requiring new solutions. The need to confirm candidate identity has led to the use of biometric devices such as iris scans and fingerprinting as well as login and password protocols. Screen-mounted web cameras with motion and sound detection are used to control cheating in unsupervised locations. Even then, it is clear that fully invigilated testing centres will need to be retained for the highest stakes assessments.

Security of Test Content

Everyone involved in large scale testing or assessment knows the dangers attached to the security of test content. This is why, traditionally, examinations have always been run on the same day at the same time at all assessment centres. Where the same tests are used over extended periods of time, as is often the case in graduate recruitment, it may not take very long before the security of the materials is compromised. When I worked at the Civil Service Selection Board in the 1980s, we were only too aware that there were organised groups of candidates who would each remember one test item and then get together to reconstitute the complete test paper later. There was one bio-data tool that was used for sifting purposes during that time where the average score between its first and second use increased by 50%.

This is where tailored testing and item banking can come into its own in traditional question and answer tests, notwithstanding the costs identified by Melnick and Clauser involved in maintaining item banks. Simulation offers a more interesting solution, but one that also creates special problems. One of the features of even moderately realistic simulations is that the way they unfold can depend on candidate responses and behaviours. It can also depend on the starting conditions for the simulation scenario. Where the underlying model for the simulation allows this, it can result in no two candidates ever having quite the same assessment experience. This can greatly enhance the security of the materials, which can be further improved by the fact that assessment may be continuous in the simulation so that there are no obvious test items for the candidate to remember.

The downside is that it may be difficult to ensure the equivalence of different assessments. Furthermore, it is not clear that common measures of test quality are appropriate. For example, item response theories have a number of underpinning assumptions that are not met in this sort of flexible simulation. The need for local independence of items is clearly broken, since how the simulation unfolds is at least partly determined by previous responses. This does not happen in the same way as in adaptive testing. There, the system chooses what material to present next on the basis of previous answers but the answer to the next item is not usually dependent on previous answers. In simulations, what happens next follows, more or less closely, the natural consequences of the actions the candidate has taken and, unless the chain of events is broken, future responses can often be affected by previous ones. This is acceptable where a simulation is being used for training or development purposes but not for high stakes assessment. In such situations, constraints need to be placed on the way in which scenarios unfold to ensure that the simulation does not get out of hand and that each candidate gets a fair chance to show their capabilities.

The assumption of unidimensionality will also usually be broken in simulations. Most responses require the integrated application of a range of skills, often from quite different cognitive domains. The design of the assessment and scoring regimes needs to be very clever if this problem is to be side-stepped.

Updating and Enhancing Simulations

Historically, this has been regarded as an area of weakness for simulations. Even minor changes in one part of a simulation often entailed major changes elsewhere. Simulators that made use of highly realistic equipment, such as cockpit simulators, might require a complete rebuild if there were changes to their design. As more use is being made of modular designs, graphics rather than video and scaled simulations, this is less of a problem, but the fact is that the costs associated with changing simulations are significantly greater than with traditional tests and this is a major constraint on their widespread use.

The Nature of the Assessment

There are two main areas worth consideration here, the content of assessments and issues concerning standardisation and the equivalence of forms.

Content

A recurring problem in the development of simulations is that far too often simulators are a bit of technology looking for an application. I have lost count of the number of conferences, workshops and seminars I have attended where one or more of the presenters is a representative of an engineering or a video company who, for other reasons, have developed a clever bit of software or a valuable database and then thought what a good idea it would be to use it for running simulations. Then, having designed the simulation, as an after-thought they begin to consider how they might superimpose some sort of assessment regime on the simulation. Usually, in these cases, even less thought is given to whether the assessment has good technical characteristics or to whether the same assessment goal could not be achieved at half the cost in a third of the time using some other method.

With this in mind, it is interesting to note the trials and tribulations Melnick and Clauser report in the development of the MIDS simulation. Almost all of the common lessons for simulator developers are there:

- Don't start with scenarios.
- Do start with what it is possible to assess.
- Think about the volume and quality of evidence that the simulation is capable of providing at the outset.
- Decide in advance how you will score or measure performance.
- Decide how stripped down you can make the simulation without losing quality, credibility or key performance information.
- Don't assess everything you can—the correlations between different measures are often so high that only one measure is needed.
- Optimise the value you get from the simulation:

  - Don't fall back on tired old multiple choice assessment when there is the possibility of obtaining high quality performance evidence.
  - Use the simulation for as many purposes as possible, e.g. training, task rehearsal, recruitment, competence assessment, etc.

Standardisation and Equivalence of Forms

As noted previously, standardisation and equivalence can be a problem for simulation if the scenario underpinning it can unfold in a myriad different ways depending on the candidate. There are a number of ways of controlling this. You can minimise the degree of interaction between the candidate and the simulator. Responses can be recorded but have no effect on how the scenario unfolds. The simulation can be split into short, manageable segments with the status of the scenario being reset at the end of each segment. The cost of each of these solutions is to reduce the reality of the simulation and to restrict the sorts of behaviour that can be observed, for example, how well individuals recover from making sub-optimal decisions or errors. However, it is unnecessary to strive for very high levels of reality. Carefully constructed scaled simulations can cover all the bases while allowing the assessor to maintain a high level of control over assessment conditions.

194   COMPUTER-BASED TESTING AND THE INTERNET

Scoring and Interpretation

Computerisation can bring the benefits of instant scoring, fast comparison against norms or other interpretive guides (cf. Hornke & Kersting) and, if desired, instant feedback. However, again, the experience of Melnick and Clauser in developing the MIDS simulator shows what a complicated task scoring and interpretation can be. There are two major aspects of interpretation to think about.

1. What type(s) of score should you use?
2. How sophisticated a scoring process should you adopt?

Again, just because you can do it does not mean you should. Simulations can involve any or all of the following types of measure:

- Number correct.
- Number of errors.
- Number of omissions.
- Number attempted.
- Appropriateness of decisions/options chosen.
- Goal achievement.
- Success in achieving goals relative to other candidates.
- Speed of response.
- Etc.

However, the nature of the simulation task may preclude some of these or make others undesirable. In particular, you should choose a type of score that does not alter the behavioural or performance aspects of the simulation in undesirable ways. For example, consider the most commonly used of all test scores, the number correct. For many types of simulation this will be an entirely appropriate measure. If you want to be sure that doctors make correct medical diagnoses, it makes sense to present symptoms in a variety of ways and check that the correct conclusions are reached. However, the business game simulation described by Hornke and Kersting does not fit this model. There is a specified goal and evidence of progress towards that goal can be measured, but there are many ways the goal can be achieved. There is no individual action along the way that, in any simple sense, can be said to be correct or incorrect, even though you may be able to track a sequence of goal-oriented behaviours that, taken together, lead to a positive outcome.

The business game highlights a further problem with the scoring of simulations. If the scoring focuses on outputs or the achievement of goals, there may be too little scoreable information at the end of the task to establish the reliability of the measure. Furthermore, in goal-oriented scenarios, candidates may be doing all the right things but then make one big mistake that negates all the good work that has gone before. This may be very like real life, a crucial observation if you are dealing with the assessment of competence in a high risk safety activity, and may be an excellent learning experience for the candidate, but it is less than ideal from an assessment perspective.

Therefore, careful thought has to be given to identifying the best types of score to be used in simulations. They need to provide sufficient evidence to generate reliable measures while also telling you something valuable (i.e. valid) about the candidate without losing the key benefits of the simulation, namely that it involves continuous, realistic performance of integrated tasks.

Consider another example. The developers of simulations can often get carried away with the technical possibilities for scoring that their simulator offers them. Many different scores can be calculated. One computerized work sample test once used by British Rail and later Railtrack plc, though no longer, in the recruitment of signallers produced three test scores measuring anti-cipation, goal achievement and delay minimisation. Unfortunately, it was impossible to maximise your score on all three scales. In particular, the goal achievement and delay minimisation scores were almost always negatively correlated. Yet, the computer generated feedback report clearly suggested that all three scores should be high. The main problem in this case was the candi-date instructions. Left to their own devices, candidates adopted different strategies for tackling the task. No guidance was given to candidates about where or how to focus their attention or efforts. Candidates very soon realized that they had to trade off one aspect of performance against the others and made their own decisions about what mattered most. Not surprisingly, this affected both the reliability and validity of the measures, which is why the test was dropped.

Response speed or speed of performance is another example worth consi-dering. Computers offer excellent opportunities to measure reaction times and, therefore, such characteristics as information processing speed. Now, it may be the case that measures of information processing speed give very good predictions of intelligence scores, and they may be important sources of evi-dence for evaluating different models of information processing, but do they always give value in simulation assessments? Of course, I have posed the question this way because the answer is no. There are situations in which scoring processing speed may actually detract from the performance of candi-dates. The knowledge that speed of response is being measured may cause candidates to behave in atypical or sub-optimal ways. Therefore, again, it is vitally important to determine in advance whether measuring this attribute will provide value in the assessment. Do not measure it just because you can.

PARTICIPATION

There are three aspects of participation that are affected by the use of computer-based simulation:

- Candidate access.
- Candidate selection.
- Equal opportunities.

Equality of access has been an issue for computer-based testing since its earliest days and has become more important with the advent of internet-based testing. Yet, one has to wonder whether it was ever really a problem. The assumption has been that those who can afford their own access will be at an advantage, but it is usually only low stakes testing which is readily available on the internet. As soon as the stakes are higher, controls need to be put in place that constrain access. The highest stakes testing nearly always requires supervision in test administration centres, so offering no access advantage to those with their own equipment. The situation described by Melnick and Clauser for the USMLE tests seems fairly typical, with tests being offered at dedicated, secure testing sites either continuously or during discrete testing windows. This requirement for control tends to be even more apparent for computer-based simulations, which, as well as supervised administration, also often need special equipment.

Access can affect participation in less direct ways, however. There are many examples of tests available on the internet, even if they are of variable quality. Many test publishers provide practice tests on their web sites. Therefore, individuals with ready access to the internet will have many more opportunities to practice a variety of test types. On the other hand, there are not many, if any, practice simulations available on the internet, so there is no direct advantage there. Perhaps the greatest advantage will come in the reduction of anxiety, which Melnick and Clauser note seems to become apparent whenever new computer-based testing programmes are introduced.

These arguments do not extend to all aspects of selection and recruitment. For example, many companies and recruitment agencies now require applicants to apply using electronic forms or to email CVs via the internet. If this is the main or only way of attracting applicants, it is likely that it may be a biased sample of candidates who make it through to subsequent selection stages.

Indirect discrimination is a more serious issue. Experienced users of computers are likely to be at an advantage, particularly with simulations that can make significant demands on skills such as screen navigation, cursor movement, use of graphical interfaces and the like.

More importantly, there are known to be significant differences between groups in their ability to handle and process material on screen. For example, it is well known that females are more likely than males to suffer from pseudo-motion sickness, sometimes called cyber-sickness, particularly where motion is simulated using visual cues that are not supported by full-motion simulation (Kass, Ahlers, & Dugger, 1998; Kennedy and Fowlkes, 1992). Likewise, people who are not good at the mental manipulation of representations of three dimensional objects in two dimensions can have problems coping with screen-based simulations. Often their ability to estimate distances and directions is markedly affected.

When such problems are recognised, the proposed solutions are often ad hoc and only partially successful. One train operating company in the United Kingdom that identified the pseudo-motion sickness problem found that some of the effect was mitigated by leaving the doors of their train driving simulator open, thus, presumably, giving their trainees external visual reference points that helped their brains to compensate for the apparent movement on the simulator screen.

Note that I have not tried to deal with problems associated with disabilities, not because they are unimportant but because there is nothing unique about simulations in this respect. All the same issues that affect both paper and pencil tests and computer-based tests are relevant, such as the need for extra time, spoken rather than written instructions, the need for special equipment, and so on.

ADMINISTRATION

As noted, computer-based administration has some obvious advantages, not the least of which is guaranteed standardisation. However, fully automated administration is difficult to achieve with simulations. It is not unusual for various features of a simulation to require explanation or guided practice. Apart from adding significantly to the administration time, it is difficult to ensure that candidates fully understand the assessment and operating instructions without having an administrator to answer questions or to guide bewildered candidates. The effects on candidate confidence and anxiety levels can be dramatic if something goes wrong or even if it appears to go wrong.

Again, the defining characteristic is whether it is a high or low stakes assessment. Self-administered, automated assessments will be satisfactory as long as nothing too much hangs on the outcome. The most telling moment is when there is a system crash or when the simulation programme hangs. This, you will say, should not happen in a well constructed simulator, but it is remarkable how often circumstances or candidates find ways of conspiring to make the most fail-safe systems fall over. Furthermore, not all systems are built with sophisticated fail-safes. However, the key issue is not recovery of the system, it is being able to console and reassure the poor candidate.

SO, IS SIMULATION WORTH THE EFFORT?

Clearly, Melnick and Clauser and Hornke and Kersting think so, in spite of the difficulties described, and all the validation evidence from the last 50 years suggests that simulations are amongst the most accurate single methods of assessment. Nonetheless, there is a range of potential problems with simulation, some of which have not yet been resolved. Common measures of technical quality, especially those based on item response theory, may not apply to many simulations because the assessment items do not conform to several of the underlying assumptions. The ways in which simulations unfold and the ways in which candidates' interaction with simulations affects that unfolding makes it difficult to guarantee not only equivalence of forms but also equivalence of assessment experience from one candidate to another. Lack of equivalence has immediate implications for equal opportunities, which is further compounded by the fact that various candidate groups may be differentially affected by characteristics of simulations that are irrelevant to the skills under consideration.

It is also important to consider the utility of simulations. In comparison with traditional psychometric tests, simulations can be very expensive to both develop and maintain. So, unlike most tests, where the development costs are relatively trivial compared to the potential benefits as long as there are reasonable numbers of candidates, the evidence for the validity and benefits of simulation must be much clearer cut to justify the up-front costs.

There are a number of criteria that are worth applying before committing to simulation:

• The development costs must be justifiable either because the value of identifying good performers or the risks of poor performance are sufficiently high.
• Real work experience is not available, either because it is too dangerous to let individuals with unproven competence loose in real work or because the scenarios being assessed are too rare in real work.
• Assessment opportunities are not available or relevant behaviour is not easy to observe.
• There is a threshold to cross before undertaking real work.
• Competence is demonstrated through performance involving the integration of skills and it is insufficient to measure single constructs.

It is equally important to address well in advance the key issues of what sorts of assessment opportunity the simulation will provide, the value of the various scores that might be calculated and the effects on candidate engagement of collecting evidence for such scores. Considering these issues only once the scenarios have been created will almost always result in a simulation that fails to deliver the value it should.

REFERENCES

British Standards Institute. (2002). *BS 7988: Code of practice for the use of information technology (IT) in the delivery of assessments*. London: British Standards Institute.
Ehret, B. D., Gray, W. D., & Kirschenbaum, S. S. (2000). Contending with complexity: Developing and using a scaled world in applied cognitive research. *Human Factors, 42*(1):8–23.
International Test Commission. (2005). *International guidelines on computer-based and internet-delivered testing* (Version 1.0). Retrieved June 2, 2005, from http://www.intestcom.org/Downloads/ITC/Guidelines

Kass, S. J., Ahlers, R. H., & Dugger, M. (1998). Eliminating Gender Differences through Practice in an Applied Visual Spatial Task. *Human Performance*, **11**(4):337–349.

Kennedy, R. S., & Fowlkes, J. E. (1992). Simulator sickness is Polygenic and Polysymptomatic: Implications for research. *International Journal of Aviation Psychology*, **2**(1):23–38.

O'Donnell, S., Sargent C., & Andrews, C. (2003). *The international review of curriculum and assessment frameworks*. London: QCA–NFER.

CHAPTER 11

Inexorable and Inevitable: The Continuing Story of Technology and Assessment

Randy Elliot Bennett
Educational Testing Service, USA

This chapter argues that the inexorable advance of technology will force fundamental changes in the format and content of assessment. Technology is infusing the workplace, leading to widespread requirements for workers skilled in the use of computers. Technology is also finding a key place in education. This is not only occurring because technology skill has become a workplace requirement. It is also happening because technology provides information resources central to the pursuit of knowledge and because the medium allows for the delivery of instruction to individuals who could not otherwise obtain it. As technology becomes more central to schooling, assessing students in a medium different from the one in which they typically learn will become increasingly untenable. Education leaders in several States and numerous school districts in the United States are acting on this implication, implementing technology-based tests for low- and high-stakes decisions in elementary and secondary schools and across all key content areas. While some of these examinations are already being administered statewide, others will take several years to bring to fully operational status. These groundbreaking efforts will undoubtedly encounter significant difficulties that may include cost, measurement, technological dependability, and security issues, but most importantly state efforts will need to go beyond the initial achievement of computerizing traditional multiple-choice tests to create assessments that facilitate learning and instruction in ways that paper measures cannot.

Computer-Based Testing and the Internet: Issues and Advances.
Edited by D. Bartram and R. K. Hambleton. © 2006 John Wiley & Sons, Ltd.

THE INEXORABLE

In the business world, almost everywhere one looks new technology abounds—computers, printers, scanners, personal digital assistants, and mobile phones, plus networks for these devices to plug into. Why is this?

First, since 1995 the United States has experienced dramatic improvements in productivity. Although information technology's contribution continues to be debated, evidence suggests that it is responsible for at least some of the effect (Federal Reserve Bank of San Francisco, 2000; McKinsey & Company, 2001; Oliner & Sichel, 2000). Technology may help increase productivity because manipulating information electronically is often cheaper than physically manipulating things (Negroponte, 1995). The following are examples:

- Southwest Airlines expends $10 to sell a ticket through a travel agent, while it pays $1 to make an online sale (Abate, 2001). Because Southwest gets 30% of its passenger revenue through online sales, the savings are enormous.
- GE purchases large amounts of supplies and raw materials through online exchanges, generating an estimated savings of $600 million through lower prices and cheaper transaction costs (De Meyer & Steinberg, 2001).
- Wal-Mart has extensive databases that give real-time information on individual store inventories to the chain's 10,000 suppliers, who can refill inventory as needed (Steinberg, 2001). Among other things, this system saves Wal-Mart the cost of buying and storing more inventory than it can quickly sell.
- Cisco Systems must train thousands of sales and technical support staff each time a new product is launched. Since these employees are deployed worldwide, the travel costs alone are huge. Through e-learning, Cisco has reported savings of 40–60% over instructor-led courses (Cisco Systems, 2001).

Besides aiding efficiency, technology can break down traditional barriers, enhancing the value of products and services. One such barrier was the age-old relationship between richness and reach (Evans & Wurster, 2000). It used to be that a business could either reach many customers with a relatively spare message—say, through broadcast advertising—or engage a few customers in a deeper interaction (e.g. via a showroom encounter). The Internet has fundamentally changed that traditional relationship by permitting companies to reach many individuals in a personalized way. Customers can use the Web to order a computer built to particular specifications (http://www.dell.com), design their own sneakers (http://www.customatix.com), configure office furniture to suit their needs (http://www.hermanmiller.com), or purchase pants to fit (http://www.landsend.com).

The value that technology provides to businesses and consumers is continually increasing. One illustration is Moore's law: since the late 1960s, computational capability has doubled every 1½–2 years (Kurzweil, 1999; Negroponte, 1995). The impact has been to dramatically expand the tasks computers can perform and simultaneously drive down hardware prices. A second illustration is Metcalfe's law, which states that the worth of a network increases by the square of the number of participants (Evans & Wurster, 2000). This means that as more organizations and individuals gain access to the Internet, the more useful that access becomes (e.g., consider e-mail).

So, what is inexorable? The relentless advance of technology, not only in terms of its ever-growing capability but, more importantly, its steady infusion into the world of work.

THE INEVITABLE

Technology and Education

The inexorable (and rapid) advance of technology in business has important implications for the workforce. For one, it suggests that the ability to use technology will become a standard job-entry requirement. In fact, it is estimated that by 2006 almost half of all US workers will be employed by industries that are either major producers or intensive users of IT products and services (Henry et al., 1999).

But learning how to use new technology once is not enough. Businesses that currently use technology routinely upgrade to remain competitive. Those businesses that do not yet use technology eventually will. Thus, job entry requirements are likely to increase continually, as they have for the past several decades (Moe & Blodget, 2000).

In addition to this rise in entry qualifications, the knowledge required to maintain a job in many occupations is changing so fast that 50% of all employees' skills are estimated to become outdated within 3–5 years (Moe & Blodget, 2000). Therefore, those who are not conversant with technology and skilled at rapidly learning the next technology will be at a disadvantage in finding and keeping a job.

Of course, being skilled in a global economy is not simply about knowing how to use new technology. It also concerns knowing how to solve problems; learn new things; work on a team; communicate; and locate, evaluate, and act on information. However, ultimately, it may be most about *combining* those more traditional skills with technological ones to get work done (International ICT Literacy Panel, 2002).

How do we ensure that our population is able to develop and continually renew the competencies needed for success in a global economy? Several blue ribbon panels have recently studied this question and come to similar conclusions. Interestingly, their conclusions are not restricted to workforce training but extend to education generally. The Commission on Technology and Adult Learning (2001), sponsored by the American Society for Training and Development and the National Governors Association, stated the following: 'The Commission . . . encourages governors, CEOs and other leaders to make e-learning the cornerstone of a national effort to develop a skilled workforce for America's digital economy. . . . By embracing e-learning in our states, our communities and our organizations, we can improve our competitiveness and point the way to a new era of unprecedented growth and opportunity for all Americans'. Similarly, the National Association of State Boards of Education (2001) concluded 'E-learning will improve American education in valuable ways and should be universally implemented as soon as possible'. The President's Information Technology Advisory Committee Panel on Transforming Learning (2001) recommended that '. . . the federal government set as a national priority the effective integration of information technology with education and training'. Finally, the bipartisan Web-Based Education Commission's Report to the President and Congress (Kerrey & Isakson, 2000) concluded 'The question is no longer *if* the Internet can be used to transform learning in new and powerful ways. The Commission has found that it can. Nor is the question *should* we invest the time, the energy, and the money necessary to fulfill its promise in defining and shaping new learning opportunity. The Commission believes that we should'.

The statements of these panels certainly have an air of what Alan Greenspan might term 'irrational exuberance'. Is there any indication whatsoever that the e-learning vision implied by these groups has the least chance of coming true?

Maybe there is. For example, with respect to postsecondary education, 35 states now have virtual universities (or other organizations) to deliver or promote Web-based distance learning (Young, 2001). Are students enrolling? Some online institutions, in fact, have already reached traditional on-campus levels: the University of Maryland's University College has 30,000 pupils (*UMUC Institutional Planning, Research and Accountability Fact Sheet*, n.d.), the University of Phoenix Online has 57,000 students (University of Phoenix Online, n.d.), and the SUNY Learning Network reports offering over 2,000 courses to 19,000 individuals (*SUNY Online Learning Network*, 2003).[1]

E-learning's potential to bring postsecondary education to even more diverse audiences is also being explored. The Army recently awarded a $450 million contract to create eArmyU, a consortium of institutions designed to allow soldiers to attain degrees online (Emery, 2001; Schwartz, 2001). EArmyU is now operational, enrolling 12,000 students in its first year (Arnone, 2001). Internationally, the People's Republic of China plans to have 5 million students in 50–100 online colleges by 2005 (Walfish, 2001). Also, the World Bank and Australia have announced plans to spend $750 million to bring Internet distance learning to developing countries (Maslen, 2001; World Bank Group, 2001). Finally, the United Kingdom (UK) has established UKeU, a joint venture between all UK institutions of higher education and the private sector, with government support of £62 million (UKeU, 2003).

---

[1] Institutions sometimes report data as course enrollments (in which the same student may be counted multiple times if he or she is registered for more than one course), and sometimes as unduplicated headcounts. I try to present here unduplicated headcounts. For the University of Maryland's University College, the count is based on the percentage total enrollment that is online only multiplied by the total unduplicated headcount for the university.

Electronic resources are playing a growing role for students attending class *on* campus, too. As of September 2001, 96% of students between the ages of 18 and 24 reported using a computer, with 86% of students indicating that they did so in school (US Department of Commerce, 2002). In fact, most college students (73%) say they use the Internet more than the library for information search (Jones, 2002). And it is no surprise why: the Internet provides virtually instant access to libraries and databases all over the world. This pervasive use on the part of students is not just a matter of personal preference: as early as fall 2000, Web resources were a component of the syllabus in over 40% of all college courses (Campus Computing Project, 2000). Several major institutions are aiding the trend: MIT has begun a 10-year, $100 million effort to put *all* of its course material online, which includes some 2,000 courses (Schwartz, 2001). A 500-course 'pilot' is already underway and several courses are now available.

Given the activity at the postsecondary level, it should be no surprise that e-learning is migrating downward. At least 16 states have established virtual high schools to serve districts without qualified staff, home-schooled students, and children of migrant workers (Ansell & Park, 2003; Carr, 1999; Carr & Young, 1999; Kerrey & Isakson, 2000). Apex, a for-profit virtual high school that specializes in advanced placement courses, claims agreements with 30 states representing 15,000 high schools (*Apex Learning Celebrates Record Enrollments*, 2002).

Not surprisingly, the teaching force is catching on: nationally representative data suggest that, in early 1999, 66% of public school teachers were using computers or the Internet for instruction during class time (National Center for Education Statistics, 2000). In what specific ways were they using them? Teachers said they assigned students work to a large or moderate extent that involved word processing, spreadsheets, or other applications (41% of teachers), practice drills (31%), and research using the Internet (30%). In an early 2001 survey, Quality Education Data found that 90% of K-12 teachers indicated using the Internet as a professional resource (Quality Education Data, 2001). They employed it most frequently for research (89% of teachers), communication with colleagues (85%), and professional development (73%).

What about students? An Education Department survey indicates that, towards the end of 2001, 87% of public-school instructional rooms contained computers connected to the Internet and that the ratio of students to those computers was 5:1 (National Center for Education Statistics, 2002). Are students using those computers? The US Department of Commerce (2002) reports that, as of September 2001, 75% of children aged 5–9 and 85% of those 10–17 used a computer at school.[2] For late elementary through high school, lower, but still considerable, percentages used the Internet—45% of those aged 10–13 and 55% of those 14–17.

---

[2] These figures combine those who use computers only at school and those who use computers at school and home. The values are calculated from Figure 5-4, Computer Use by Age and Location, 2001.

What do students use computers for? In a nationally representative sample taking the 2001 NAEP US History assessment, 82% of 8th grade and 86% of 12th grade students indicated using a word processor to write reports at least to some extent; 73% and 77% of these respective groups reported using the computer for research (Lapp, Grigg, & Tay-Lim, 2002). Similar results appear in *Education Week's* 2001 technology survey, where an overwhelming majority of grade 7–12 students said they employed a computer for school research or for writing papers (*Technology Counts*, 2001). The significant use implied by these various data sources will be further encouraged by the *No Child Left Behind Act of 2001*. Among other things, this landmark legislation appropriates $700 million in fiscal year 2002 to improve student achievement through the use of technology in elementary and secondary schools (US Department of Education, 2002).

To be sure, e-learning and, more generally, educational technology are not without critics and not without failures. Critics have argued that empirical support for the effectiveness of e-learning is inconclusive, that technology has not improved teaching or student achievement, and that continued investment is unjustified (e.g. Cuban, 2000, 2001).[3] Although this argument raises very important concerns, its conclusion does not necessarily follow. First, it may be true that computers have not changed how teachers instruct or how much students learn (at least in the ways we currently measure achievement). However, the tools students use to learn certainly are changing, as the data cited above suggest. There is no question that the need to learn these tools is, in part, driven by their pervasive position in the world of work.[4] But these tools are also becoming part of the equipment of 21st century scholarship and,

---

[3] *No Child Left Behind* authorizes up to $15 million for an independent, long-term study of the effectiveness of educational technology, including the conditions under which it increases student achievement (Educational Testing Service, 2002). The study's final report is due by April 2006.

[4] There is certainly a clear and influential economic dimension to the argument for using computers in schools. This argument has become critical only in the past few decades with the emergence of the global economy. The genesis of the current school reform movement is often linked to the publication of *A Nation at Risk* (National Commission on Excellence in Education, 1983), which opens with these words:

> Our Nation is at risk. Our once unchallenged preeminence in commerce, industry, science, and technological innovation is being overtaken by competitors throughout the world.

Since the publication of this report, the perceived threat has not diminished. In a report titled *School Technology and Readiness*, the CEO Forum on Education and Technology (2001) puts it this way:

> Student achievement must be improved in order to prepare students to succeed in the global economy. Many observers liken the need for a world class, high-quality educational system to a national security issue. The United States can only remain a leading power in the global economy if it continues to ensure students will be prepared to thrive in the future.

The concern of both these reports is in not having a workforce skilled and productive enough to compete with those of other nations. A skilled and productive workforce keeps jobs at home by encouraging both domestic and foreign businesses to invest here. This, in turn, helps us maintain a high standard of living and a tax base strong enough to support an effective national defense. Moreover, as suggested, the ability to use technology in conjunction with other competencies helps make for a skilled and productive workforce.

consequently, necessary for college-bound students generally. Knowing how to do intellectual work *with* technology—to model a problem using a spreadsheet, create a presentation, use data analysis tools, find information on the Internet, or write and revise a paper with a word processor—is becoming a critical academic skill.

Second, even if e-learning is no better than traditional instructional methods it may still make for a wise investment in some circumstances. For instance, many individuals can not get the education they desire from local sources. These individuals include adults whose work or family responsibilities prevent them from physically attending class on a set schedule, as well as younger students whose school districts do not have staff qualified to teach certain specialized courses. For these students, it is either electronic access to a desired educational experience or no access at all.

Besides critics, e-learning has had its share of failures. The speculative dot.com bubble that burst in late 2000 hit online learning ventures, too: Temple University pulled the plug on its for-profit distance learning company; Caliber and Pensare went bankrupt; NYUonline and the US Open University announced that they would shut down; UNext laid off staff; and Columbia's Fathom changed its approach (Arnone, 2002a, 2002b; 'Caliber Files', 2001; Carnevale, 2001; Mangan, 2001a).

Still, it is hard to dismiss the widespread indications that technology is beginning to play an important role in education. At the very least, to quote Bob Dylan, 'Something is happening here...'.

THE IMPLICATIONS FOR ASSESSMENT

Increasingly, people have to know how to use technology to work and to learn. Thus, technology is becoming a *substantive* requirement in its own right. The emergence of technology as a necessary skill means there will be tests of it. For those who specialize in computing, such tests have become common for certifying job proficiency (Adelman, 2000). But as working and learning begin to require technology competence of almost everyone, assessing these skills will become routine.

Perhaps more important for assessment, however, is that technology is also becoming a *medium* for learning and work. The CEO Forum on Education and Technology (2001) suggests '...as schools...integrate technology into the curriculum, the method of assessment should reflect the tools employed in teaching and learning'. At the least, a mismatch between the modes of learning and assessment could cause achievement to be inaccurately estimated (Russell & Haney, 2000). Writing presents a good example: more and more, students are using the computer to complete composition assignments; however, research suggests that testing these students on paper underestimates their proficiency (Russell & Plati, 2001). The bottom line is that, as students come to do the majority of their learning with technology, asking them to express that learning in a medium different from the one in which they routinely work will become increasingly untenable, to the point that much of the paper testing we do today will be an anachronism (Bennett, 2001).

Acting on the Implications

Education leaders in a significant number of US States and numerous school districts have recognized the inevitability of technology-based assessment. As of this writing, 12 states had begun developing or administering some component of their State assessment program online. These States were: Arkansas, Georgia, Idaho, Kansas, Kentucky, Maryland, North Carolina, Oregon, South Dakota, Texas, Utah, and Virginia. Another eight were running or had run pilots without yet committing to operational delivery, including Delaware, Illinois, Indiana, Mississippi, New York, Pennsylvania, Washington, and Washington, DC. Finally, Florida, Massachusetts, and Louisiana had developed online practice tests to help students prepare for their State assessments.

Several points concerning these efforts should be noted. First, States are implementing technology-based tests in elementary and secondary schools and in all of the key content areas (i.e. reading, math, science, English, social studies). For example, Idaho is creating a testing program at both levels, each program covering English/language arts and mathematics (Olson, 2003). Second, states plan to deliver both low- and high-stakes examinations through this medium. Some tests, like Virginia's Algebra Readiness Diagnostic Test, are intended for instructional purposes, whereas its eSOL (Standards-of-Learning) tests will be used for making graduation decisions (Virginia Department of Education, n.d., 2001). Third, some of these examinations are *already* being administered statewide, whereas others will take several years to bring to fully operational status. For instance, Arkansas began administering its Vocational Student Competency Testing Program in 2002–2003 statewide, with 7,000 classrooms participating (Gehring, 2003). Other states, such as Virginia and Oregon, will offer assessments in both Web and paper format until electronic delivery can be made universal (ODE, 2002; Virginia Department of Education, n.d., 2001). Fourth, the tests generally use multiple-choice items exclusively, though the intention typically is to move in later versions to more complex tasks that better represent the instructional uses of technology that schools are moving toward (e.g., Internet research, writing on computer, data modeling). Finally, in some cases it is clear that electronic assessment is part of an integrated state plan to employ technology throughout the educational process. Virginia has as an explicit goal the online delivery of instructional, remedial, and testing services. South Dakota is well along toward realizing a similar vision, having intensively trained over 40% of its teachers to use technology in the curriculum and having connected its schools, libraries, and postsecondary institutions into a high-speed data/video network.

Practical Concerns

These leading-edge States are, of course, not alone in their attempts to move testing programs to computer. Over the past decade, many occupational and professional, as well as postsecondary-education tests, have done so. Examples include the College-Level Examination Program® (CLEP®), Graduate Record Examinations® General Test (GRE®), Graduate Management Admission Test®(GMAT®), National Council of State Boards of Nursing NCLEX® Examination, Test of English as a Foreign Language® (TOEFL®), and United States Medical Licensing Examination™ (USMLE™). The collective experience of these programs is that computer delivery presents considerable challenges (Wainer & Eignor, 2000).

Cost

The early entrants into computerized testing bore the cost of creating a computer-based test-center infrastructure, electronic tools for writing items, presentation software, and the large item pools needed to support continuous high-stakes testing. K-12 education will benefit enormously from the fact that (1) hardware is much cheaper than it was a decade ago, (2) integrated test authoring and delivery software is now readily available, (3) a universal electronic delivery network built with other people's money now exists (the Internet), and (4) because it has broad instructional use, the local-school space, software, hardware, and Internet connections used for testing can be expensed through other budgets. Still, the required investment and operational costs will, at least initially, be large relative to paper testing. Among other things, these costs will include vendor charges for testing software, central servers to house test content, training, and technical support. Some analyses (e.g. Neuburger, 2001) suggest that the savings from eliminating such paper processes as printing and shipping will eventually outweigh these costs. States are, however, saddled with not only budget deficits from recession and the unplanned expense of homeland defense but also the *No Child Left Behind* requirement to test every child once a year in grades 3–8 in reading and math. While the Act provides significant funds for states to implement the required assessments, these monies are expected to be considerably less than the actual cost of implementing the law's testing requirements (GAO, 2003). Given the situation, States may find it hard to justify the extra upfront expenditures associated with computer testing. In fact, in some leading-edge states, online assessment activities are already slowing (Borja, 2003).

How can the additional costs of online assessment be met? Perhaps the least effective approach would be for each state to create it own system, duplicating the efforts of others with similar population characteristics and education needs. Instead, consortia, cooperative agreements, or buying pools for obtaining test questions, telecommunications equipment, computer hardware, testing software, and equipment maintenance should be considered.

Measurement and Fairness Issues

The experience of the early entrants also suggests that there will be non-trivial measurement and fairness issues. For those K-12 agencies that plan to offer the same tests on paper and computer, comparability will be a concern, especially for high-stakes decisions. Although comparability has often been supported (Bridgeman, 1998; Mead & Drasgow, 1993; Schaeffer, Bridgeman, Golub-Smith, Lewis, Potenza, & Steffen, 1998; Schaeffer, Steffen, Golub-Smith, Mills, & Durso, 1995), in some instances it does not hold, as when examinees are tested in a mode different from the one in which they routinely work (Russell & Plati, 2001). Further, while it is desirable from a fairness perspective, comparability may limit innovation by preventing the computer-based version from exploiting the technology to broaden measurement beyond what traditional methods allow. Where feasible, the wise choice may be to eliminate the problem entirely by offering only a computer-based instrument or by delivering in the two modes for as short a period as possible.

Regardless of whether the test is delivered solely on computer, there is a second comparability concern. This concern is for 'platform' comparability. From one school to the next (and even within the same school), monitor size, screen resolution, keyboard layout, connection speed, and other technical characteristics may vary, causing items to appear differently or to take more time to display. (Display-time variations may occur for the same machine as a function of time of day.) Any of these variations may affect scores unfairly. For instance, Bridgeman, Lennon, and Jackenthal (2001) found that lowering the screen resolution, and thus increasing the need for scrolling, diminished test performance on reading comprehension items by a small (but nontrivial) amount. Similarly, Powers and Potenza (1996) presented evidence to suggest that essays written on laptops might not be comparable to those written on desktops having better keyboards and screen displays.

A third measurement issue is differential computer familiarity. Although physical access to computers at school differs little by income and racial group, home-access disparities are still substantial (US Department of Commerce, 2002). Thus, there may be group (or individual) differences in computer experience that affect test performance in construct-irrelevant ways. For multiple-choice tests, the research to date suggests that differences in computer experience have little, if any, effect on test scores (see, e.g., Bridgeman, Bejar, & Friedman, 1999; Taylor, Jamieson, Eignor, & Kirsch, 1998). However, as electronic tests incorporate more performance tasks, the complexity of the mechanisms for responding—and the demands on computer facility—could well increase.

Finally, for States wanting to use online assessment in connection with the accountability requirement of *No Child Left Behind*, there is uncertainty about the appropriateness of adaptive testing. NCLB requires all students in a grade to be assessed against the *same* standards. The US Education Department (ED) has interpreted this requirement as *dis*allowing adaptive testing because, in giving more able students harder items and less able students easier questions, CAT does not, in the ED's view, hold all students to the same grade-level standards (Trotter, 2003). This issue was one factor in South Dakota's decision to use its Dakota Assessment of Content Standards as a voluntary benchmark and diagnostic assessment instead of an accountability test (DECA, 2002), as well as a factor in Idaho's decision to amend its adaptive test to include a linear section (Olson, 2002; Trotter, 2003).

Technological Dependability

As we all know, and as the large, high-stakes testing programs have found, computers do not always work as intended (see, e.g., Mangan, 2001b). Such glitches are conceptually similar to printing and shipping errors in paper programs that cause examinees to receive no test, take an erroneous test, or complete a correctly printed test that never reaches its destination. Though any such event is unacceptable, for paper and electronic programs, these occurrences are, in fact, extremely rare. For K-12 assessment programs, the situation may be initially more troublesome because computer delivery is a new business for most vendors and because schools do not always have ready access to the onsite technical staff needed to fix problems quickly.

Security

High-stakes electronic testing entails security problems that are not very different from those of paper programs; in particular, items can be stolen or examinee data tampered with regardless of delivery mode. Rather, it is more the specific methods of wrongful access and prevention that differ. For example, electronic delivery depends on such preventatives as encryption, firewalls, and controlled software access. In paper delivery, security depends on tracking shipments and keeping materials under lock and key. (In either paper or digital form, once stolen, item content can be shot around the world at the touch of a button. For paper, there is only the extra step of first scanning the pilfered document.) The challenge for K-12 programs, then, is not that security threats will necessarily be greater, but that staff must manage new methods of detection and prevention.[5] Georgia, for example, suspended its Criterion Referenced Competency Testing program (Georgia Department of Education, n.d.) at the end of the 2002–2003 school year after it discovered that secure forms inadvertently included items also in the State's online practice testing system (Jacobson, 2003).

---

[5] Security will be more costly and complex if testing is done continuously. Continuous testing may call for larger item pools, methods of controlling item exposure, and the frequent rotation of pools in and out of service.

CONCLUSION

This paper has argued that the advance of technology is inexorable in at least two ways. First, technological capability is increasing exponentially. Second, new technology is pervading our work, and it is beginning to infuse learning.

The paper also argued that the incorporation of technology into assessment is inevitable because, as technology becomes intertwined with what and how students learn, the means we use to document achievement must keep pace. However, it is similarly inevitable that this incorporation will not be easy. There are still enough open issues, especially of cost and measurement, to ensure that at least some significant setbacks will occur. But even if all of the existing issues were resolved, the history of technology is one of unanticipated consequences that are not always positive.

Given the dangers, one can see why some US States chose to begin the transition with low-stakes assessments. The decisions based on these tests can tolerate lower levels of measurement quality, technological dependability, and security; moving too quickly to high-stakes tests would maximize risk—political, financial, legal, and educational. Similarly, the use of multiple-choice questions is very sensible. They can be easily presented on screen and require little computer skill for responding. Incorporating significant numbers of performance tasks at this stage would raise costs, demand more sophisticated presentation software, and increase the potential for construct-irrelevant variance in responding.

What the US States are doing now, however, must be only a beginning. If all we do is put multiple-choice tests on computer, we will not have done enough to align assessment with how technology is coming to be used for classroom instruction. Sadly, our progress in using the computer to improve assessment has been limited. Almost a decade ago, we moved the first large educational tests to computer, fully intending to use technology to introduce new measurement approaches. These efforts got as far as adaptivity and then, due to cost, technical complexity, the need to maintain scale, and the sufficiency of multiple-choice for summative decision-making, moved no farther. Fortunately, K-12 agencies have educational responsibilities that may force them to go beyond the initial achievement of computerization to create assessments that support learning and instruction in ways that paper tests cannot. Researchers can help them meet this challenge by discovering how to cost-effectively design coherent systems of assessment that have both summative and formative components (Pellegrino, Chudowsky, & Glaser, 2001). These systems might include simulations and other complex performances that not only indicate achievement level, but also offer proficiency inferences with clear instructional implications. Creating such systems will be a difficult challenge, but it is aided by an emerging science of assessment design (see, e.g., Mislevy, Steinberg, Almond, Breyer, & Johnson, 2001; Pellegrino, Chudowsky, & Glaser, 2001).

To be perfectly clear, it is not at all inevitable that we will incorporate technology into assessment in ways that bring lasting educational benefit. The question is no longer *whether* assessment must incorporate technology. It is how to do it responsibly, not only to preserve the validity, fairness, utility, and credibility of the measurement enterprise but, even more so, to enhance it. In this pursuit, we must be nothing less than inexorable.

REFERENCES

Abate, C. (2001, September 1). The smart business 50: Southwest Airlines. *EWeek.* Retrieved April 19, 2002, from *http://www.eweek.com/article/0,3658,s = 1884&a = 10418,00.asp*

Adelman, C. (2000). *A parallel postsecondary universe: The certification system in information technology.* Retrieved April 19, 2002, from the U.S. Department of Education Web site: *http://www.ed.gov/pubs/ParallelUniverse*

Ansell, S. E., & Park, J. (2003). Tracking tech trends: Student computer use grows, but teachers need training. *Education Week,* **12**(35):43–48.

Apex Learning celebrates record enrollments. (2002, June 17). [Press release]. Retrieved May 17, 2003, from *http://apexlearning.com/about/press_room/articles/pr_2002_june17_record_enrollments.asp*

Arnone, M. (2001, December 10). Army's distance-education project seeks more colleges as participants. *The Chronicle of Higher Education.* Retrieved April 19, 2002, from *http://chronicle.com/free/2001/12/2001121002u.htm*

Arnone, M. (2002a, February 5). United States Open University announces it will close in June. *The Chronicle of Higher Education.* Retrieved April 19, 2002, from *http://chronicle.com/free/2002/02/2002020501u.htm*

Arnone, M. (2002b, February 8). Fathom adds corporate training to its distance-education offerings. *The Chronicle of Higher Education.* Retrieved April 19, 2002, from *http://chronicle.com/free/2002/02/2002020801u.htm*

Bennett, R. E. (2001). How the Internet will help large-scale assessment reinvent itself. *Education Policy Analysis Archives,* 9(5). Retrieved April 19, 2002, from *http://epaa.asu.edu/epaa/v9n5.html*

Borja, R. R. (2003). Oregon. *Education Week,* **12**(35):84.

Bridgeman, B. (1998). Fairness in computer-based testing: What we know and what we need to know. In *New directions in assessment for higher education: Fairness, access, multiculturalism, and equity* (GRE FAME Report Series Vol. 2). Retrieved April 19, 2002, from the Educational Testing Service FTP site: *ftp://ftp.ets.org/pub/gre/241343.pdf*

Bridgeman, B., Bejar, I. I., & Friedman, D. (1999). Fairness issues in a computer-based architectural licensure examination. *Computers in Human Behavior,* 15:419–440.

Bridgeman, B., Lennon, M. L., & Jackenthal, A. (2001). *Effects of screen size, screen resolution, and display rate on computer-based test performance* (RR-01-23). Retrieved April 19, 2002, from the Educational Testing Service FTP site: *http://www.ets.org/research/dload/RR-01-23.pdf*

Caliber files for Chapter 11. (2001, June 15). *Baltimore Business Journal.* Retrieved April 19, 2002, from *http://baltimore.bizjournals.com/baltimore/stories/2001/06/11/daily41.html*

Campus Computing Project. (2000). *The 2000 national survey of information technology in U.S. higher education: Struggling with IT staffing.* Retrieved April 19, 2002, from *http://www.campuscomputing.net/summaries/2000/index.html*

Carnevale, D. (2001, November 28). NYUonline will shut down. *The Chronicle of Higher Education.* Retrieved April 19, 2002, from *http://chronicle.com/free/2001/11/2001112801u.htm*

Carr, S. (1999, December 10). 2 more universities start diploma-granting virtual high schools. *The Chronicle of Higher Education,* p. A49.

Carr, S., & Young, J. R. (1999, October 22). As distance learning boom spreads, colleges help set up virtual high schools. *The Chronicle of Higher Education*, p. A55.

CEO Forum on Education and Technology. (2001). *School technology and readiness—Key building blocks for student achievement in the 21st century: Assessment, alignment, accountability, access, analysis.* Retrieved April 19, 2002, from *http://www.ceoforum. org/downloads/report4.pdf*

Cisco Systems, Inc. (2001). *Listen, share, and deliver: 2001 annual report.* Retrieved April 19, 2002, from *http://www.cisco.com/warp/public/749/ar2001/pdf/AR.pdf*

Commission on Technology and Adult Learning. (2001). *A vision of e-learning for America's workforce* (p. 27). Retrieved April 19, 2002, from the National Governors Association web site: *http://www.nga.org/center/divisions/1,1188,C_ISSUE_BRIEF% 5ED_2128,00.html*

Cuban, L. (2000, February 23). Is spending money on technology worth it? *Education Week on the Web.* Retrieved May 30, 2002, from *http://www.edweek.org/ew/ewstory. cfm?slug = 24cuban.h19*

Cuban, L. (2001). *Oversold and underused: Computers in classrooms.* Cambridge, MA: Harvard University Press.

De Meyer, D., & Steinberg, D. (2001, September 1). The smart business 50: General Electric. *EWeek.* Retrieved April 19, 2002, from *http://www.eweek.com/article/0,3658,s = 1884&a = 10319,00.asp*

Department of Education and Cultural Affairs (DECA). (2002). *DACS (Dakota Assessment of Content Standards).* Retrieved April 19, 2002, from *http://www.state.sd.us/deca/ dacs/*

Educational Testing Service. (2002). *The No Child Left Behind Act: A special report.* Princeton, NJ: Author.

Emery, G. R. (2001, July 16). Army project boosts e-learning prospects. *Washington Technology, 16*(8). Retrieved April 19, 2002, from *http://www.washingtontechnology.com/ news/16_8/federal/16859-1.html*

Evans, P., & Wurster, T. S. (2000). *Blown to bits: How the economics of information transforms strategy.* Boston, MA: Harvard Business School Press.

Federal Reserve Bank of San Francisco. (2000, November 10). Information technology and productivity. *FRBSF Economic Letter* (No 2000-34). Retrieved April 19, 2002, from *http://www.frbsf.org/econrsrch/wklyltr/2000/el2000-34.html*

Gehring, J. (2003). Arkansas. *Education Week, 12*(35):63–64.

General Accounting Office (GAO). (2003). *Title I: Characteristics of tests will influence expenses; information sharing may help states realize efficiencies* (GAO-03-389). Washington, DC: Author.

Georgia Department of Education. (n.d.). *Criterion-Referenced Competency Test (CRCT) frequently asked questions.* Retrieved April 19, 2002, from *http://www.doe.k12.ga.us/sla/ ret/crct_faq.html*

Henry, D., et al. (1999). *The emerging digital economy II.* Washington, DC: US Department of Commerce.

International ICT Literacy Panel. (2002). *Digital transformations: A framework for ICT literacy.* Princeton, NJ: Educational Testing Service.

Jacobson, L. (2003). Georgia. *Education Week, 12*(35):67–68.

Jones, S. (2002). *The Internet goes to college: How students are living in the future with today's technology.* Washington, DC: Pew Internet and American Life Project. Retrieved May 29, 2003 from *www.pewinternet.org*

Kerrey, B., & Isakson, J. (2000). *The power of the Internet for learning: Moving from promise to practice: Report of the Web-Based Education Commission to the President and the Congress of the United States* (p. 134). Retrieved April 19, 2002, from *http://interact.hpcnet.org/ webcommission/index.htm*

Kurzweil, R. (1999). *The age of spiritual machines: When computers exceed human intelligence.* New York: Viking.

Lapp, M. S., Grigg, W., & Tay-Lim, B. S.-H. (2002). *The nation's report card: U.S. history 2001*. Washington, DC: US. Department of Education, Office of Educational Research and Improvement.

Mangan, K. S. (2001a, September 13). UNext lays off 135 employees, citing need to spend conservatively. *The Chronicle of Higher Education*. Retrieved April 19, 2002, from *http://chronicle.com/free/2001/09/2001091301u.htm*

Mangan, K. S. (2001b, September 25). Error message leads many who took GMAT to question their scores. *The Chronicle of Higher Education*. Retrieved April 19, 2002, from *http://www.uh.edu/admin/media/topstories/che092501gmat.htm*

Maslen, G. (2001, August 8). Australia will spend $100-million on distance programs for developing countries. *The Chronicle of Higher Education*. Retrieved April 19, 2002, from *http://chronicle.com/free/2001/08/2001080801u.htm*

McKinsey & Company. (2001). *U.S. productivity growth, 1995–2000*. Retrieved April 19, 2002, from *http://www.mckinsey.com/knowledge/mgi/feature/index.asp*

Mead, A. D., & Drasgow, F. (1993). Equivalence of computerized and paper-and-pencil cognitive ability tests: A meta-analysis. *Psychological Bulletin*, **114**:449–458.

Mislevy, R. J., Steinberg, L. S., Almond, R. G., Breyer, F. J., & Johnson, L. (2001). *Making sense of data from complex assessments* (CSE Technical Report 538). Retrieved April 19, 2002, from the UCLA CRESST web site: *http://www.cse.ucla.edu/CRESST/Reports/RML%20TR%20538.pdf*

Moe, M. T., & Blodget, H. (2000). *The knowledge web: People power—Fuel for the new economy*. San Francisco: Merrill Lynch.

National Association of State Boards of Education (NASBE). (2001). *Any time, any place, any path, any pace: Taking the lead on e-learning policy*. Retrieved April 19, 2002, from *http://www.nasbe.org/Organization_Information/e_learning.pdf*

National Center for Education Statistics. (2000). *Teacher use of computers and the Internet in public schools* (NCES 2000-090). Retrieved May 29, 2002, from the U.S. Department of Education web site: *http://nces.ed.gov/pubs2000/2000090.pdf*

National Center for Education Statistics. (2002). *Internet access in U.S. public schools and classrooms: 1994–2001* (NCES 2002-018). Washington, DC: US Department of Education, Office of Research and Improvement, National Center for Education Statistics.

National Commission on Excellence in Education. (1983). *A nation at risk: The imperative for educational reform*. Retrieved April 19, 2002, from *http://www.ed.gov/pubs/NatAtRisk/*

Negroponte, N. (1995). *Being digital*. New York: Vintage.

Neuburger, W. (2001, April). On-line assessments: A state's perspective. In R. E. Bennett (Chair), *The 'Three W's' meet the 'Three R's': Computer-based testing in the schools—Why, what, and how*. Symposium conducted at the annual meeting of the National Council on Measurement in Education, Seattle, WA.

Oliner, S. D., & Sichel, D. E. (2000, March). The resurgence of growth in the late 1990s: Is information technology the story? In *Structural Change and Monetary Policy*. Conference sponsored by the Federal Reserve Bank of San Francisco and Stanford Institute for Economic Policy Research, San Francisco. Retrieved April 19, 2002, from *http://www.frbsf.org/economics/conferences/000303/papers/resurgence.pdf*

Olson, L. (2002, January 23). Idaho to adopt 'adaptive' online state testing. *Education Week*. Retrieved April 19, 2002, from *http://www.edweek.org/ew/newstory.cfm?slug = 19online.h21*

Olson, L. (2003). Legal twists, digital turns: Computerized testing feels the impact of 'No Child Left Behind'. *Education Week, 12*(35), 11–14, 16.

Oregon Department of Education (ODE). (2002). *Technology Enhanced Student Assessment (TESA) system*. Retrieved April 19, 2002, from *http://www.ode.state.or.us/asmt/tesa/*

Pellegrino, J. W., Chudowski, N., & Glaser, R. (Eds.). (2001). *Knowing what students know: The science and design of educational assessment*. Washington, DC: National Academy Press.

Powers, D. E., & Potenza, M. T. (1996). *Comparability of testing using laptop and desktop computers* (RR-96-15). Princeton, NJ: Educational Testing Service.

President's Information Technology Advisory Committee Panel on Transforming Learning. (2001). *Report to the President: Using information technology to transform the way we learn*. Retrieved April 19, 2002, from the National Coordination Office for Information Technology Research and Development web site: *http://www.itrd.gov/pubs/pitac/pitac-tl-9feb01.pdf*

Quality Education Data. (2001). *QED's school market trends: Internet usage in teaching—2001–2002*. Denver, CO: Author.

Russell, M., & Haney, W. (2000). Bridging the gap between testing and technology in schools. *Education Policy Analysis Archives, 8*(19). Retrieved April 19, 2002, from *http://epaa.asu.edu/epaa/v8n19.html*

Russell, M., & Plati, T. (2001). Effects of computer versus paper administration of a state-mandated writing assessment. *TC Record.Org*. Retrieved April 19, 2002, from *http://www.tcrecord.org/Content.asp?ContentID=10709*

Schaeffer, G. A., Bridgeman, B., Golub-Smith, M. L., Lewis, C., Potenza, M. T., & Steffen, M. (1998). *Comparability of paper-and-pencil and computer adaptive test scores on the GRE General Test* (RR-98-38). Princeton, NJ: Educational Testing Service.

Schaeffer, G. A., Steffen, M., Golub-Smith, M. L., Mills, C. N., & Durso, R. (1995). *The introduction and comparability of the computer-adaptive GRE General Test* (RR-95-20). Princeton, NJ: Educational Testing Service.

Schwartz, K. D. (2001). Learning is mandatory; presence is optional. *Mobile Computing Online*. Retrieved April 19, 2002, from *http://www.mobilecomputing.com/showarchives.cgi?145*

Steinberg, D. (2001, September 1). The smart business 50: Wal-Mart. *eWEEK*. Retrieved April 19, 2002, from *http://www.eweek.com/article/0,3658,s=1884&a=10427,00.asp*

SUNY online learning network enrollment up 34%. (2003, January 23). [Press release]. Retrieved May 15, 2003 from *http://www.suny.edu/sunynews/News.cfm?filename=2003-01-23SLN.htm*

Taylor, C., Jamieson, J., Eignor, D., & Kirsch, I. (1998). *The relationship between computer familiarity and performance on computer-based TOEFL test tasks* (TOEFL-RR-61). Princeton, NJ: Educational Testing Service.

Technology counts 2001: The new divides. (2001). *Education Week on the Web*. Retrieved April 19, 2002, from *http://www.edweek.org/sreports/tc01/charts/tc01chart.cfm?slug=35challenges-c10.h20*

Trotter, A. (2003). A question of direction. *Education Week, 12*(35):17–18, 20–21.

UKeU. (2003). *About us*. Retrieved May 17, 2003, from *http://www.ukeu.com/aboutus.shtml*

UMUC institutional planning, research and accountability fact sheet. (n.d.). Retrieved May 15, 2003, from *http://www.umuc.edu/ip/fast.html*

University of Phoenix Online. (n.d.). Retrieved May 15, 2003, from *http://www.uoponline.com/default.asp*

US Department of Commerce. (2002). *A nation online: How Americans are expanding their use of the Internet*. Washington, DC: Author. Retrieved April 19, 2002, from *http://www.ntia.doc.gov/ntiahome/dn/nationonline_020502.htm*

US Department of Education. (2002). *FY 2003 budget summary—February 4, 2002*. Retrieved April 19, 2002, from *http://www.ed.gov/offices/OUS/Budget03/Summary/SectionII/A.html#top*

Virginia Department of Education. (n.d.). *eSOL Web-based assessment*. Retrieved April 19, 2002, from http://www.pen.k12.va.us/VDOE/Technology/soltech/soltech.html

Virginia Department of Education. (2001). *Virginia Algebra Readiness Diagnostic Test (ARDT) participation resources*. Retrieved April 19, 2002, from *http://www.accessardt.com/*

Wainer, H., & Eignor, D. (2000). Caveats, pitfalls, and unexpected consequences of implementing large-scale computerized testing. In H. Wainer (Ed.), *Computerized adaptive testing: A primer* (2nd ed.). Mahwah, NJ: Erlbaum.

Walfish, D. (2001, May 21). Chinese government predicts strong growth in online education. *The Chronicle of Higher Education*. Retrieved April 19, 2002, from *http:// chronicle.com/free/2001/05/2001052101u.htm*

World Bank Group. (2001, August 3). Virtual Colombo Plan. *DevNews*. Retrieved April 19, 2002, from http://www.worldbank.org/developmentnews/stories/html/ 080301a.htm

Young, J. (2001, June 13). Web site tracks statewide virtual university projects. *The Chronicle of Higher Education*. Retrieved April 19, 2002, from *http://chronicle.com/free/ 2001/06/2001061301u.htm*

CHAPTER 12

Facing the Opportunities of the Future

Krista J. Breithaupt, Craig N. Mills and Gerald J. Melican
American Institute of Certified Public Accountants, USA

In the last several decades, there has been an increasing demand for authentic, complex, yet cost-effective ways to assess the competencies and knowledge of school children, college and graduate school applicants, and job and promotion applicants. The measurement profession has responded with numerous innovations in the creation of new types of assessment tasks, new test designs, new assembly, scoring and analysis methods, and new test administration designs. Most of these advances have been made possible thanks to enhanced computer technologies with increased computational speed and power.

The previous chapters in this volume have described many of the recent advances in the application of technology to testing practice. The purpose of this chapter is to build upon those chapters by placing the advances in the context of the growing set of requirements and expectations of consumers. We also offer a review of some current trends in assessment and the implications of these trends to test and system design requirements, while identifying some existing obstacles. Finally, we identify additional innovations evolving from current work to improve consumer satisfaction with assessment devices, scoring, and reporting. Most of these examples are drawn from our experiences with the Uniform CPA examination, with references to other relevant work.

We will focus on three broad areas in this chapter:

- Test Development.
- Test Design and Administration.
- Score Interpretation.

Within each of these three areas, we will propose a vision of the future including a discussion of work being done today to support that vision, and

Computer-Based Testing and the Internet: Issues and Advances.
Edited by D. Bartram and R. K. Hambleton. © 2006 John Wiley & Sons, Ltd.

identify some challenges to be overcome if the vision is to be achieved. The final section of the chapter will provide examples of some work we are doing in the areas covered in the chapter.

TEST DEVELOPMENT

Future Vision and Current Work

Dramatic innovations appeared in the last decade in the incorporation of complex performance tasks into assessments (Drasgow & Olson-Buchanan, 1999). Given the success of testing programs in designing and scoring such tasks, it is reasonable to assume that the demand for more (and more complex) assessments will increase. Among the more striking examples of these innovations are those introduced in the licensing programs of the National Council of Architectural Registration Boards (NCARB), United States Medical Licensing Examinations (USMLE), and American Institute of Certified Public Accountants (AICPA). In these programs, candidates are expected to use Computer Assisted Design software to provide complete architectural drawings (NCARB), use medical simulation software to evaluate, diagnose, and treat patients (USMLE), or review financial information and use a variety of financial tools, including searchable databases, to evaluate a client's financial information and make auditing/financial recommendations (AICPA).

Examples of high-fidelity assessment for educational and certification programs can also be found in a variety of other settings (Tekian, McGuire, & McGaghie, 1999). These settings include information technology industries (Red Hat, Cisco, Microsoft, Hewlett-Packard, and others) and specialized training programs (e.g. flight simulations for pilots, defense and combat simulations, aptitude and management assessments).

The complexity of these assessments leads to psychometric challenges such as multi-dimensionality of the underlying construct being tested and increases in the amount of time per unit of measurement collected, which affect reliability and validity. Also, the cost in time from subject matter and technology experts, and systems designers to support the administration and scoring of these remains high when compared to traditional assessments.

It is currently the case that many of these complex assessments are generated in accordance with traditional test development processes. That is, a content blueprint that describes the knowledge and skills to be tested is provided to test developers. They then apply their knowledge and creativity to design appropriate tasks to measure the skills and content defined in the blueprint. The result is an exercise that retains content validity, and high fidelity to the practice or performances in a realistic environment where the candidate would normally demonstrate skills.

While this development process, allowing the author creativity in response format and question generation as well as the content of the measurement task, is intended to assure realism in the exercise, it also introduces some unique challenges. First, the test takers may find preparation for the test a problem given the variation in tasks. In addition, since the open-ended exercises allow candidates to consider and incorporate a wider range of practical information in their responses, response time can be lengthy, resulting in limited numbers of tasks within a given period of time. Further, the amount of time required to respond can vary dramatically across exercises. In the worst case, the response information collected from the test taker is too sparse to produce a reliable score. These assessment tasks, while they have substantial relevance to practice, limit the breadth of content that can be covered in a given amount of time, thus threatening the generalizability of the interpretation of the results and the comparability of scores across examinees.

In addition to the variability in content and item type current test development procedures often do not constrain examinee responses sufficiently to prevent test takers from providing unique and unexpected, but correct, responses. The creative test developer may not (and probably can not) envision every behavior candidates will evince. These issues might be viewed as a natural tension between the need to present realistic exhibits, and the desire to collect as much pertinent response data as possible from the candidate in a restricted time period. However, responses to realistically complex tasks can lead to a need to engage in lengthy, error-prone manual review of large numbers of unanticipated responses to tasks.

An emerging alternative, described elsewhere in this volume (Chapter 5), is that of 'principled design'. A principled design process is intended to focus the test developer's creativity on the key assessment goals of an exercise while limiting the introduction of irrelevant variation in the tasks. Principled design begins by considering the interpretation of the score and keeps that perspective paramount in task design and content development. A series of questions illustrates how the sequence of the development process would be changed from the standard blueprint-based approach:

- What conclusions do I want to draw about the test taker's knowledge and skills?
- What would constitute evidence that the test taker has or does not have that knowledge and skill?
- Can I ask the test takers to give an answer or perform a task that would require them to provide the evidence I seek?
- What static and/or interactive information will the candidate require (e.g. description of client or patient situation, relevant financial or medical information, etc.)?
- What tools (e.g. spreadsheet, word processor, and calculator) are required for the candidate to provide the information and how robust do these tools need to be?
- Is there any non-relevant knowledge or skill required to answer the question or perform the task?
- Can I develop many different questions to measure this task that are equivalent?

- Do the questions provide sufficient information for the time it takes the test taker to respond, and leave time so that I can ask more questions to ensure confidence in the decision made using their scores?
- Can I evaluate the responses consistently, quickly, and accurately?

By following the principled design sequence, test developers become more than subject matter experts. They now participate in the realm of test engineers and software architects. The answers to the questions above should provide the specifications for assessment task design. Among the specifications that can result from a principled design are the tools (exhibits, calculators, spreadsheets, word processors, search engines, etc.) that need to be available to the test taker to provide the necessary information, limitations on the length of the task based on the amount of information to be generated from it, the range, breadth, and depth of content that is appropriate for the task, and the rubrics, keys, and rules to evaluate of the response (single key, lists of acceptable keys, algorithms, etc.). In other words, principled design will produce assessment templates that both enable and constrain test development.

A principled design can also provide standardized specifications for the tools. For example, there may be sufficient overlap across different financial situations that several entire classes of tasks can all be supported by one, two, or three standard spreadsheet templates. Properly designed, these templates would be large enough to allow the creation of useful measurement tasks, but would ensure that the test developer does not introduce unnecessary and time-consuming complexity into the task.

Benefits from this design process should be decreased complexity of task development, increased quality and consistency across tasks, which aids both the developers and the candidates, known task characteristics (e.g. unidimensional or multidimensional), known response characteristics, comprehensive scoring specifications, and reduced costs of both development and scoring. An important intended longer-term benefit from a rigorous principled design is the development of tasks with known statistical properties. Once the features of the task have been stabilized and the essential format of the item or task has been administered to test takers, the empirical difficulty of scored elements can be estimated. An example of the usefulness of collateral information in the prediction of statistical properties of new items is available from Keller (2002). These estimates could be useful in scoring (or calibration with smaller samples) when new tasks are based on the same template. Such a result would dramatically reduce the time between the development of a task and its use in an operational test (by eliminating the need for pretesting or post-administration analyses) and allow faster scoring and reporting.

Additional benefits of a principled design include automated, or semi-automated, task generation and review, thus further reducing development time and expense (see, e.g., Brittingham et al., 2000).

In order to meet consumer needs, performance exercises of the future will need to measure a combination of skills and content, be template based, and ultimately be mass producible. A template would constrain the performance within a specified range, including the number and size of exhibits, the number and types of responses captured, the available tools for creating a solution, and scoring rubrics. One logical approach to this problem of task design has been offered by Mislevy, Steinberg, and Almond (1999). A generalization of this method can be extended to tasks in a variety of contexts. For example, each template for a set of tasks could be designed to measure performances based on a special sub-set of the content and skills of interest.

We envision a future in which the development process will be automated to the point that as soon as an author creates an assessment task the task will be batched and routed for electronic and, if needed, human subject matter expert review. Once the reviewers have certified the appropriateness and accuracy of the task and the questions associated with the task, multiple versions will be automatically generated and routed for automatic and/or human review to ensure the task conforms to specifications, does not contain errors, and is unique. These versions will vary in the degree to which they are clearly related to the original and to one another.

Under this methodology, the scoring would also be based on, and incorporated into, the original template. This is necessary to ensure that the original and automatically generated version of the task do not require lengthy review or development of additional scoring templates. The scoring rules and keys must be developed prior to or concurrent with the development of the task elements in the template. We believe the discipline that results from using these templates, coupled with new developments in the calibration of individual tests questions and 'families' (a collection of questions written from the same task and scoring templates) of questions will allow the generation of operationally useful statistics for an entire family of performance tasks with very small samples. This reduction in the number of candidates required for calibrations will result in greater test security and shorter time between the development of a task and its operational use.

Traditional test question formats (e.g. multiple choice) could also benefit from principled development models. In essence, the traditional question format is just a very simple performance task. An example of this kind of design is the rules-based approach to item development, the Automated Item Generation, AIG, software developed at Educational Testing Services. Although AIG will undoubtedly evolve and become more sophisticated in its generation of test questions, it can already be used not only to create many similar versions of a single item, but also to generate substantially different questions that (theoretically) measure the same content. It is inevitable that we will gain additional experience with AIG, or other automated item generating paradigms, in response to the increasing need for efficient generation of valid test items for computer-based administration (Irvine & Kyllonen, 2002). We will necessarily employ a more principled design for test questions. As a consequence, it is reasonable to imagine there may be future tests for which items will not even exist prior to test administration. Rather, the rules for item and test generation and scoring will reside on the computer along with libraries of resource materials that will be incorporated into the completed item (elements of the fact patterns, correct keys, and distracters).

In this scenario, when the examinee signs on to the testing session, the administration software and underlying system will dynamically create items and build the test in real time. At the conclusion of the test, the items would be reduced to their parts and disappear (although the specifications will be retained so the test can be recreated if necessary). In time, as advances are made in test translation, these test generation systems may also have the capability to translate items into a language of the examinee's choice or to modify the test in response to the particular needs of an examinee with disabilities.

These examples of principled development, templating, and dynamic construction also offer opportunities to adjust test content quickly in response to changing educational and professional contexts. Such tests would be tightly coupled to the appropriate authoritative literature, eliminating the typical lag between the generation of new knowledge or practices, and the generation of appropriate exercises to measure performances. The generation of learning lists and study aids based on poorly answered questions would be a natural extension of this dynamic model.

Test Development Challenges

The present and future of test development theory and practice is exciting to contemplate as the consumer need for innovative measurement continues to grow. The challenges are many, but the potential improvements in interpretation of test results will be substantial. One of the major challenges to any evolving testing program is the commitment of resources, time, and money to set a course for the future. Navigating this course requires us to conceptualize and confirm the content and mode of assessment, to develop and verify the method of establishing and maintaining templates, and to build the required technology. These strategic activities are legitimate research projects. As a consequence, accurately estimating the necessary time and expense is difficult.

Budgeting strategic development work involves managing and balancing opposing kinds of risk. On one hand, the demand for visible results can lead the program to implement innovations too quickly. Developers who produce a viable prototype case study or simulation often will be faced with pressure to implement it in production before validation and certification of the systems and procedures required to support operational work. This intermediate step might be missed in response to the pressure to move ahead rapidly. However, it is this phase of development, between innovation and production versioning, that allows program management to develop the processes necessary to ensure sustainability. Instantiation of the prototypes will require careful attention to content and construct validity, beginning at the templating stage. On the other hand, the desire to resolve all issues prior to implementation can lead to excessively long research and development timelines. Experience shows us that every program will encounter unexpected results when introducing a new assessment format, regardless of how much research is conducted ahead of time. Therefore, balancing these two opposing risks, while difficult, is necessary.

Reduction of one kind of risk can be accomplished by improving our understanding of how the new assessment will perform when it is introduced. Subject matter experts and systems designers can identify a great variety of ways that test takers might respond to the assessment. It is also true that any complex performance task has a potentially limitless combination of possible response sets. As a consequence, new assessments will not always generate the expected responses from test takers. Pretesting new item types, content derivatives, and technological tools with appropriately prepared candidates is a costly, yet valuable risk reduction strategy.

Pretesting is an efficient way to identify useful items and cull out inappropriately difficult, non-discriminating, or coachable items, while trouble-shooting new administration and scoring systems in a low stakes environment. Equally valuable is the feedback that can be obtained from the pretest participants. Reactions to the demands of the new assessment can identify modifications or improvements to the performance task. An investigation of the responses and sources of variance can also provide important guidance for the development of materials to facilitate candidate preparation. Evaluation of pretest results across many tasks built using a principled design can lead to improvements in task design templates, reducing irrelevant variation. Finally, a pretest program can build support among program stakeholders in educational, regulatory, or industry settings for the proposed innovation in the test.

The AICPA conducted a pretesting program in universities and colleges during the development of the computer-based Uniform CPA Examination. Significant program resources (staff and money) were required to coordinate the overall program. However, there was extensive reliance on collaboration with the accounting faculties. As a result, this endeavor not only provided important information about the new assessments, but also engendered professional support for the new test. The pretest program allowed our assessment to be given at over 200 different schools across the country in just the initial two years. The experiences that students had with the new assessment and the 'buzz' on university campuses about the new test were invaluable in reducing anxiety and dispelling misconceptions about the changes to the testing program as well as in generating excitement and support for the new test design. Faculty and students alike gained an understanding of what the new test was like and became spokespersons in support of the innovations.

TEST DESIGN AND ADMINISTRATION

Future Vision and Current Work

Consumers desire assessment programs that will meet a wide variety of demands that are often contradictory. For example, licensure examinations must provide the most precise measurement at the pass/fail point for accurate classification decisions. At the same time, these examinations should provide accurate diagnostic study aids for failing candidates. Program managers must meet both needs in their content development, the construction of the test, the administration format, and the scoring and score reports, and all at the lowest possible cost to the examinee.

Frequent or continual testing is a growing expectation among the computer literate generations. Annual, semi-annual, or quarterly administrations are no longer viewed as acceptable in many situations. It is also true that frequent test administrations are not usually cost efficient. Test development costs increase as test security and exposure concerns require larger banks of test questions. The test forms are administered to smaller numbers of test takers at a given time. When continuous administration is implemented for high stake testing programs, test center facilities with permanent staff are required. The modern versions of these secure tests are delivered by dedicated computer stations in brick-and-mortar test centers, often using custom software and internal networks that offer high speed data transfers.

Additional expenses are involved in ensuring that candidates are familiar in advance with the mode of testing. Researchers have demonstrated an important interaction between computer familiarity and performance on the required tasks (Taylor, Kirsch, Eignor, & Jamieson, 1999). The context and the underlying trait to be assessed must be recognized explicitly. NCARB, for example, distributed software to all test registrants to allow them to learn the computer assisted design software used in their test. Candidate preparation tools must be readily available and cost effective. The purpose of this material is to allow for self-training and, if appropriate, some feedback that is helpful and straightforward for future test takers.

These exercises must contain realistic content and generalizable tasks to exercise all aspects of the functionality built into the computerized test. They are carefully designed and quality tested to provide the range of experiences that the test taker will have in the actual testing situation. Maintaining fidelity to the actual examination can be difficult. This is because these tutorials usually require unique software and delivery methodology (e.g. web delivered, or on compact disks) that differs from the actual administration software used for the computerized test they represent. Of course, the content in these training tests are disclosed to the public and will not be useful for operational test forms.

Many of these issues can be addressed in the future through a seamless process of preparation, assessment, diagnosis, remediation, re-assessment, and summative evaluation. This test design and administration model has its roots in responsive educational paradigms (see, e.g., Mager, 1962; Popham, 1973).

An initial movement toward such a paradigm might be the incorporation of formative evaluations into education and career planning. Examples of current practice in this area come from employee selection instruments (Chapter 1). It is conceivable that these evaluations would become dynamic and continual. Samples of real work stored electronically could be periodically evaluated and feedback provided to the practitioner to tailor training and career planning. As such, these evaluations might also serve as pre-testing opportunities to ensure the performance assessment tasks are of high quality prior to their use in any classification or summative evaluation decision. The realism and dynamic nature of these formative evaluations would help to ensure the currency of test material before the items are used on high stake tests.

It is extremely likely that assessments will be integrated into the work place and classroom, in evaluative and formative low stake assessment situations. Workers and students who receive assignments electronically may have assessment tasks assigned to them as if they were actual assignments. Alternately, an intelligent agent might be directed to search a student's computer to select a representative set of files for evaluation as part of a portfolio assessment. As individuals rely more and more on technology to investigate issues, complete their work, and store their work products, they are creating a database that contains information about their knowledge and skills, their command of the tools needed to do their work, and efficiency. Other information, such as date-stamps on files, may provide insights into individuals' ability to prioritize competing demands, work on multiple tasks, or collaborate with team members.

Building on some of the comments of Wim van der Linden (Chapter 2), one can envision analyses that capitalize on the availability of collateral information. This information might be of direct interest as indication of a skill or knowledge area, or might be used to inform statistical models of response data used for scoring (see, e.g., Keller, 2002). Examples might be records of time spent on task and the order in which certain activities were conducted, as well as specific details about the complexity of the solutions.

Conclusions might be drawn from non-intrusive assessments concerning individuals' competence and expertise. Advice could be formulated to guide training. Improvements or efficiencies in later performance could also be measured. A next logical development would be to completely synchronize and automate job or practice analyses, with the assessment experience. Work samples would be selected, reviewed, and evaluated semi-automatically to identify new job tasks that would need to be incorporated into the assessment.

New models of test design and administration will be required to bring to life the innovations we envision. Some new test designs have emerged over the past decade. For example, several adaptive administration models have been introduced operationally since the advent of computerized administration. These include fixed and variable length adaptive computer-based tests. Luecht's discussion (Chapter 5) of multi-stage or computer-assisted sequential testing represents some recent developments in this area. An excellent summary of advances in adaptive computer-based models is available from van der Linden and Glas (2000).

Along with the development of adaptive testing models, important contributions are available from the cognitive modeling theorists who are already using neural network or novice/expert approaches to test design

(Mislevy, Steinberg, Russell, Breyer, & Johnson, 2001). These approaches might be extended to elicit meaningful diagnostic information from response data obtained from complex performances. Alternatively, it is possible to create test modules designed specifically for the purpose of extracting useful feedback for the test taker. These diagnostic modules could be embedded within a larger, comprehensive assessment, such as a credentialing examination.

Although adaptive testing designs have not been used in this way, they offer promise. In the example of a certification examination, an adaptive design with diagnostic models offers a solution for usually contradictory requirements, Specifically, an adaptive design may be created to provide an accurate pass–fail decision in the passing score zone, and to provide good diagnostic information for candidates who may obtain scores well below the passing score.

Test Design and Administration Challenges

One of the greatest obstacles to introducing complex testing models in operational testing programs is obtaining public acceptance. Despite significant emphasis on testing throughout the developed world, stakeholders are usually not well informed about even basic psychometric practices. As a result, test takers and even executives responsible for promoting policy that will impact testing programs often have generally naïve perceptions of how testing actually works.

A common perception encountered among stakeholders is the misconception that standardized testing means that all test takers take the same test under the same circumstances. Many people view even the long used tool of equating traditional tests with skepticism when they first learn that different people take different tests. The notion that two test takers could receive the same reported score even if they answered a different proportion of questions correctly on different forms of a test is initially counter-intuitive. Any perception of unfairness raised by these impressions is heightened when the concept of adaptive testing, or modern approaches to scoring, is introduced.

A key public relations issue for the AICPA during the development of its CBT was explaining test administration, assembly, and scoring in such a way as to dispel misconceptions. The computerized administration makes use of a multi-stage testlet (MST) design (based on the work of Luecht & Nungester, 1998, and described by Luecht, Brumfield, & Breithaupt, 2002). The AICPA selected this design for a variety of reasons, including the expected benefit of precision with shorter test lengths and good diagnostic information. Sets of multiple-choice questions (testlets) are administered together. There are testlets of different difficulty available during the test experience and the administration of moderate or difficult testlets depends on the performance of the test taker up to that point in the test. The selection of this semi-adaptive design (routing occurs at two points during the test) was desirable because the MST offers test takers a chance to review and revise answers within a testlet, whereas some administration models prohibit review. An important initiative in our program was to communicate the adaptive design to stakeholders, while demonstrating that the adaptation was fair to candidates at different ability levels.

Communicating the technical aspects of the MST design was crucial in order to dispel the misperception that all candidates might not have comparable test experiences or be graded fairly. The blueprint for the examination was expressed on two dimensions, namely skills and content (AICPA, 2002). Most of the controversy was related to the scoring method used for the examination (item response theory, IRT), whereby objectively scored responses are weighted in part by the difficulty of the question. This was complicated by the MST design, where it was apparent that some test takers would have more difficult testlets compared with other candidates. In order to properly convey the fairness of scoring, it was necessary to convey a non-technical understanding of IRT scoring to stakeholders.

IRT scoring is common to high stake testing programs (GRE, NCSBN, USMLE, and others), yet a challenge in communicating on the fairness of scoring persists. Adaptive models for administration have also gained a significant history since computerized testing began, and this adds to the existing responsibility for clear and accurate communications to a variety of audiences. Many stakeholders will continue to lack a good understanding of these psychometric topics despite our best efforts. However, the onus is on the community of testing professionals to make available appropriate and timely information on the design and scoring of their assessments (AERA, APA, & NCME, 2000). Although the development of testing theories is established within our community of testing professionals, it is important to remember that the public attempts to understand our innovations through the filter of their (often flawed) understanding of traditional assessments. It is likely that the widespread use of traditional designs, historically, is the foundation for past acceptance and the obstacle modern testing programs must overcome.

As the measurement profession responds to the call for more realistic assessments, there is a need to substantiate and apply more sophisticated psychometric models to the test design and scoring procedure. This means we will have to demonstrate confident interpretation of responses from complex assessment tasks. For example, there is usually a requirement to interpret a set of tasks as intrinsically measuring a construct that requires a single classification decision. The component tasks are often measuring along a range of underlying skills and content. As a consequence, mathematical properties such as multidimensionality must be accounted for in selecting appropriate scoring and assembly techniques. If the vision of unobtrusive, multi-dimensional, multi-purpose assessments outlined above is to be achieved, psychometric models for data must also evolve. In turn, the measurement profession will need to develop clear, non-technical explanations of these test designs to avoid the risk that old, possibly inappropriate, techniques persist while improved methods are available.

SCORE INTERPRETATION

Future Vision and Current Work

Imagine the following vignette:

> Consumer: 'We need to know if examinees can conduct a good interview. Wouldn't it be neat if we could include interviews on the test? Maybe we could have videos of clients responding to interview questions and have the examinee answer questions based on the video.'
>
> Psychometrician: 'That wouldn't tell you much about their interview skills.'
>
> Consumer: 'Of course it would. It's the kind of thing they have to do every day in the office and, if they aren't good at it, they don't tend to stick around very long.'
>
> Psychometrician: 'That may be, but, at best, you would be testing listening skills. To test interview skills, you'd have to have the examinee ask the questions.'
>
> Consumer: 'Oh, you're right. But that's important, too.'
>
> Psychometrician: 'Well, there may be other...'
>
> Consumer: 'Wait a minute! I've seen that speech recognition software. We could use that to have them ask the question. Then we could have a whole bunch of answers already recorded. The computer could analyze the question they asked, select an answer, and then have them answer questions from the response. That would be awesome.'

This exchange demonstrates one source of tension between test users and the measurement profession. Many users focus on surface features of the test, and what it requires the examinee to do. The vignette also suggests the power that the consumer brings to the process, the knowledge of what must be measured and imagination from a person intimate with the applied field of the task to be measured. Measurement professionals must direct these strengths to focus on what interpretation can be drawn from the responses to the test and how to obtain valid information as efficiently as possible. Test users tend to distrust assessments that do not mimic the actual work or educational environment while measurement professionals tend to view assessments more as experiments from which they can draw reasonable inferences from the data obtained. In order to draw inferences with good certainty, there must be sufficient evidence in the form of response data. Thus, the measurement professional is inclined to design a test that, while artificial in appearance, provides many opportunities for the examinee to respond (provide data for the experiment). These responses are interpreted in the context of real-world situations. The tension might be better understood if we characterize the user as focused on what the test asks and the measurement professional as focused on what response means.

The tension between what people are asked to do in a testing situation and what the responses mean can lead to productive innovation in the future.

As technology makes it possible to ask more complex questions and easily capture the responses, users will become more insistent on the use of these technologies in assessments. This will, in turn, require advances in test design, development, scoring, and interpretation. As discussed previously, principled test design can lead to innovative and informative assessments that make use of current technology and realistic representation of natural tasks.

Future assessments will almost certainly rely less on recall than traditional tests. Given the wide availability of electronic resources, memorization of information is already less important to success in most professions. For example, the ability to quickly locate information and apply it correctly in a given situation has already become more important than recall of facts in the work of CPAs. It is fair to say that in educational and professional settings, successful individuals rely more on their ability to properly find and use organized information resources including public information, proprietary information, and their own prior work on similar tasks than on memorization of laws, rules, formulas, etc. As a result, future assessments will likely include a greater number of tasks that call for activities such as research of reference databases, revision to a prior work product to customize it for a new situation, or interpretation of available resource material.

We also envision more reliance on the evaluation of work products in the future. In recent years, portfolio assessments have been popular in the United States for assessing public school students' progress, and for advanced placement in university programs. However, portfolios are difficult to grade and often consist of special projects or only good examples of the students' work. Scoring rules are often subjective and holistic. There is promise, however, that work being done on the automated evaluation of written material is motivating the design of systems that can score work products that exist in electronic form (Shermis & Burstein, 2003). If so, the evaluation of these work products could be quickly and efficiently integrated with other assessment results to provide a more robust, objective, and replicable evaluation of knowledge and skills.

As we have described above, it is reasonable to imagine that assessments will be integrated into the work place and the classroom. Workers and students who receive assignments electronically could have certain standard exercises assigned to them as if they were actual assignments. Portfolio assessment may evolve to a system whereby an intelligent agent enters a students' computer and selects a representative sample of work based on file tags and assesses its quality. In either case, one can envision analyses that incorporate records of time on task, the order in which certain activities were conducted, and the sophistication of the solutions. From these non-intrusive assessments, conclusions would be drawn concerning individuals' competence, how expert they are, and what types of training are likely to improve their performance. We can also envision the development of automated job and practice analyses where work samples are selected, reviewed, and analyzed automatically (at least in part) to identify job tasks.

Current speech recognition technology is at a rudimentary level; however, this is an area that is going to grow and evolve. As it does, we envision that spoken responses (such as recordings of discussions, verbal presentations, or negotiations) will be incorporated into assessments and scored automatically. Meanwhile, some progress has been made in creating and automatically scoring written responses (see e.g., Martinez & Bennett, 1992).

While it is easy to imagine these types of assessment, it is not clear at this point how to score them and obtain meaningful information from the resulting scores. Natural language processing has been successfully applied to the scoring of written communications in several contexts. It is reasonable to assume that these technologies will be extended to be able to replicate holistic human ratings assigned to even more complex texts. However, being able to reproduce a score does not necessarily imply that we understand what that score means. The typical portfolio assessment involves a small number of judges evaluating a unique set of work products. It is not clear that these judges all use the same weighting of the different components of the portfolio. Nor is it clear that the judges, faced with a different portfolio, would use the same weighting as was used for the first one.

Both theoretical and practical developments will be required for our vision of unobtrusive assessment to become reality. The intelligent agents that select the work will need to have the capability to assess the content of the work sufficiently to select a representative set of materials with the proper mix of content to meet the multi-dimensional profile needed for the desired inter-pretation. Substantively meaningful objective scoring methods will be required to produce accurate, standardized, and generalizable results. Finally, we agree with van der Linden (Chapter 2) that ancillary information such as time to complete a task, order of operations, and complexity of solution have great promise for richer interpretations of examinee work.

Score Interpretation Challenges

One of the biggest challenges in the interpretation scores from complex assessments is related to the development of scoring specifications. This process is often inefficient and prone to error. Specifications or rubrics are used to award credit for correct responses to performance tasks. Content experts who use their understanding of the problem usually develop these rubrics and how candidates will respond to define possible correct responses (keys). After this initial development, rubrics are often modified as a result of committee reviews of the tasks and keys. The scoring specifications might also be changed when samples of responses have been analyzed.

At each point in the rubric development process the universe of possible correct responses is increased. This is a natural consequence from realistic tasks where candidates construct responses (compared with traditional objec-tive assessment such as the multiple choice question, where all of the response options are supplied by the test itself, and are fixed). Creative responses to complex tasks can come in an infinite variety, at least in principle. A valid rubric will need to award credit for all expected correct values and ensure fairness to candidates.

The common method of uncovering this universe of correct responses usually requires post-administration analysis of results. Iterative reviews and analyses and the evolving rubrics that result from decisions must be tightly controlled and versions tracked to ensure scores can be re-created at any time to examine validity. The current methodology for generating and refining the rubrics necessary for scoring these tasks is cumbersome, requires a long development cycle and is hard to implement in a continuous testing environment. Scores can be released only after all the validation steps in the rubric development have been completed. This means some expected benefits from computerization are not realized. Automated objective scoring and continuous reporting are simply not possible when rubrics are developed in this fashion.

It bears emphasis that even the development process for rubrics described above has no formal criteria for establishing validity. In most programs, subject matter experts evaluate responses to these complex tasks. Automated scoring systems will then credit responses where merit is indicated by human judges. The emphasis is then necessarily on logical and subjective judgment. Some progress is being made in establishing standards for performance-based assessment (e.g. guidelines, standards and best practices are available from the International Test Commission, 2000; the AERA, APA, & NCME, 1999; and the Performance Testing Council, 2004). However, at the time of this writing, formal criteria specific to computer-administered complex assessments are lacking.

It also is important to consider the unique properties of the results when statistical methods are applied to score these tasks. Traditional and modern scoring methods have specific assumptions that must be examined. For example, some item response theory (IRT) scoring models require the assumption of unidimensionality (Hulin, Drasgow, & Parsons, 1983). Another way of expressing this statistical assumption is that the scoring model requires that irrelevant aspects of the task are not important to the solution. In reality, complex assessments are typically multi-dimensional. The series of tasks that form the assessment is designed to reflect a variety of different content and skill areas. An example of advances in statistical treatments for calibration of linked tasks, or testlets, is available from Wainer, Bradlow, and Du (2000). The challenge remains to identify an appropriate model for scores, or a new methodology for scoring, when the assumptions required for existing statistical models for data might not be met.

A consequence of the need to examine response data from unique assessments carefully, and to refine automated scoring processes after test administration, is potential impact on any pass or fail decisions. The methodology available for setting passing scores, and application of these decisions to performance-based assessments, is evolving accordingly (see, e.g., Hambleton & Pitoniak, 2002). Analytic approaches to setting passing scores based on multiple-choice items are not easily adapted to complex linked tasks, whereas work-sample-based methods require large samples of responses.

Typically, responses that are judged as representative of the ability of the cut-score group must be scored to determine the placement of the passing score. This means that post-administration scoring might be required prior to the adoption of a cut score by the policy makers in the testing program. In any testing program in transition to performance-based testing, this requirement is one additional factor to be considered in a complex and changing environment. Ensuring the validity of passing scores established in this manner is an area in which additional research is sorely needed.

Luecht (Chapter 5) offers some approaches to deal with the kinds of responses that arise when complex performance assessments are used. Luecht emphasizes the benefits to be gained from item authoring and prototyping that ultimately would simplify scoring. Using a template design, item components can be independently constructed and then assembled according to rules. These steps would standardize the scoring of each component and control variation across the set of tasks.

Some scoring issues remain from traditional forms of assessment. The assessment of written communication has long been incorporated into assessments. In the context of computerized administration we benefit from a standardized input mode (word processors), but we struggle with a historically subjective approach to scoring. A particular challenge to score interpretation for writing skills is the confounding of different elements in the response supplied. The quality of the response from candidates is a reflection of at least two factors. The writer's familiarity with the subject matter about which they are required to write will be a limitation of their capability to express their writing skill. Many testing programs have addressed this issue by recognizing these factors, and sometimes training human graders to consider both (e.g. 'a score of 5 indicates excellent writing and full understanding of the subject matter . . .'). However, this kind of holistic scoring relies on subjective judgment and it is not yet clear how an automated scoring system would enforce an equivalent appraisal.

Apart from some specific solutions in specialized testing programs, there is little to guide developers who must create these scoring systems. Clearly, there are implications for the design of systems, the supporting policies governing the testing program, and the role of subject-matter experts. Evaluations to enforce scoring rules are finalized based on professional judgment and logical analyses. A decision on whether to give partial credit for a set of tasks, to score all components individually, or to score only the final answers might depend on statistical properties of the responses and substantive understanding of the relative importance of task components. This problem is exacerbated by the need to inform the test takers of the basic rules for scoring in advance of administration, particularly when there are high stake consequences from score interpretations (AERA, APA & NCME, 1999).

Much more work is required to understand the cognitive processes of the candidate required for multi-step problems in different contexts. The logical connections between the presentation of tasks, the intellectual solution from the responder, and the psychometric appraisal of the results must be better understood to support decisions made from test scores. This holistic approach to establishing the entire development, scoring, and consequential aspects of score interpretation is consistent with current conceptions of validity (Messick, 1989). Scoring technologies and procedures are only valid to the extent that these are guided by a clear understanding of what responses mean in their context, and what are appropriate mathematical models to apply to response data.

EXAMPLES FROM THE UNIFORM CPA EXAMINATION

The Uniform CPA Examination (UCPAE) is a national test developed by the American Institute of Certified Public Accountants and administered in 54 jurisdictions (all 50 states of the USA, the District of Columbia, the US Virgin Islands, Puerto Rico, and Guam) as one of the requirements for obtaining a license to practice as a CPA. There are four sections to the test, and, historically, over 300,000 examinations have been given each year. The examination has been revised and was administered via computer beginning in 2004. The impetus for the revision and computerization of the examination was the rapidly changing business and financial environment in American and global business, the increasing need for CPAs to exercise judgment in the interpretation and application of accounting standards and principles, and the emphasis on the application of technology to the work of CPAs.

An oversight group, the Board of Examiners (BOE), makes policy decisions regarding the CPA examination. The BOE has traditionally included CPAs who have volunteered to participate on a committee to oversee the development of the UCPAE to ensure content validity. Several subcommittees support the work of the BOE. Single purpose task forces are also empanelled on an as-needed basis to recommend BOE action on specific issues. As part of the development of the computerized examination and in recognition that psychometric expertise was needed to augment the auditing and accounting expertise of BOE members, psychometricians were added to the BOE and to several of its committees and task forces.

The testing program at AICPA provides an illustration of some challenges and innovations discussed in the early sections of this chapter. The future we envision for testing will only materialize as a result of maturation and innovation in all aspects of the testing profession. This maturation requires some time. It will evolve in the future as small, incremental improvements and innovations are successfully implemented and as errors help us identify our mistakes and identify solutions. In this section of the chapter, we document some of the steps we have taken over the few years leading up to the introduction of the computerized Uniform CPA Examination. Below is a brief description of some solutions we pursued and the lessons we learned along the way.

Test Development: Innovations and Lessons Learned

Principled Test Development and Templates

The AICPA developed item and task templates in order to implement a principled test design orientation to the examination. These templates helped constrain the complexity of systems development, simplified the psychometric analysis of the results, and allowed automated item generation to build a large item inventory quickly. This was particularly important to the development of our simulations, case-based scenarios with a variety of performance assessments embedded in them. Using the discipline of templates, we found that we could work with subject matter experts to develop a single, large simulation, codify its features in a template, and then generate multiple versions of that simulation that incorporated some or all of the features of the template.

Figure 12.1 depicts the constrained user interface we developed for all simulations. A familiar tab metaphor was used to allow candidates to move through the exhibits and input fields at their own pace and in any order. The tabs that require a candidate response have a pencil graphic that is grayed out only after a candidate has responded to any part of the tab. The candidate can then see at a glance if any tab has been left unanswered.

There is also a generic help screen, calculator, spreadsheet function, and screen split available at all times within the simulation. In Figure 12.1, the balance sheet task is in the foreground. In the spreadsheet the candidate may only operate on valid input fields. The cell accepts both formulae and numerical answers. If the candidate had split the screen, all input fields would be on the lower half and tabs containing exhibits would appear above.

Further work is needed to define templates more rigorously. We found that creative subject matter experts could use our templates to develop new, unanticipated kinds of question. Since we had not anticipated such questions, the scoring specifications that supported the development templates were inadequate. We also learned that it is very difficult to anticipate how different competent candidates will solve the same problem. During each administration, we discover additional, unanticipated, correct responses to tasks within our simulations. While better definition of the templates will reduce this problem, it is also clear that, until we are confident we understand the full range of acceptable responses, pretesting is a critical part of the development process.

Use of Authoritative Reference Material

CPAs routinely have to prepare written communications to clients concerning the results of their work. These communications often rely heavily on the specifications provided in professional standards ('authoritative literature'). We successfully developed a task that demonstrates test takers' ability to research the authoritative literature to create these communications. This task requires the test takers to conduct a search in the authoritative literature, select the appropriate exemplar text, and construct a client letter.

An example of the searchable database is provided in Figure 12.2. The search engine is the same as that available from the vendors of the authoritative literature tool as it is used in industry and academia. The result of the search can be copied and then pasted into the input field on the response tab.

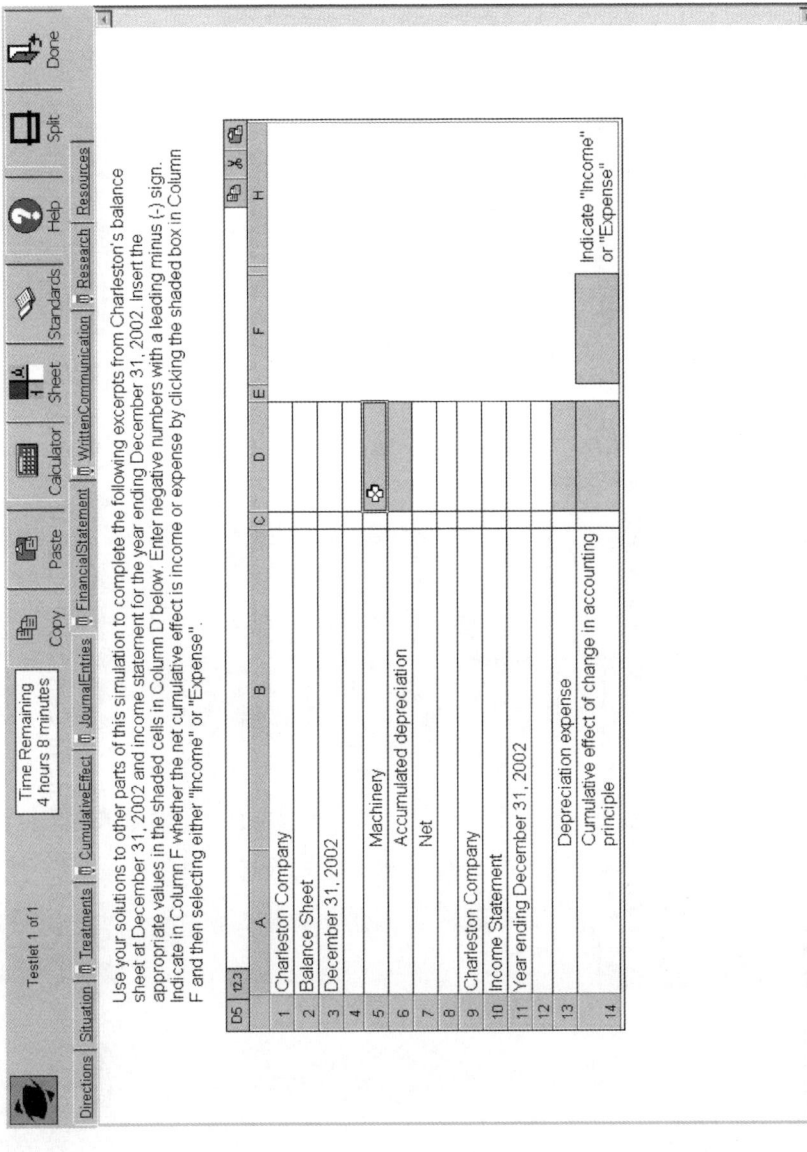

Copyright © 2003 by the American Institute of Certified Public Accountants, Inc. Reprinted with permission.

Figure 12.1 Simulation interface template.

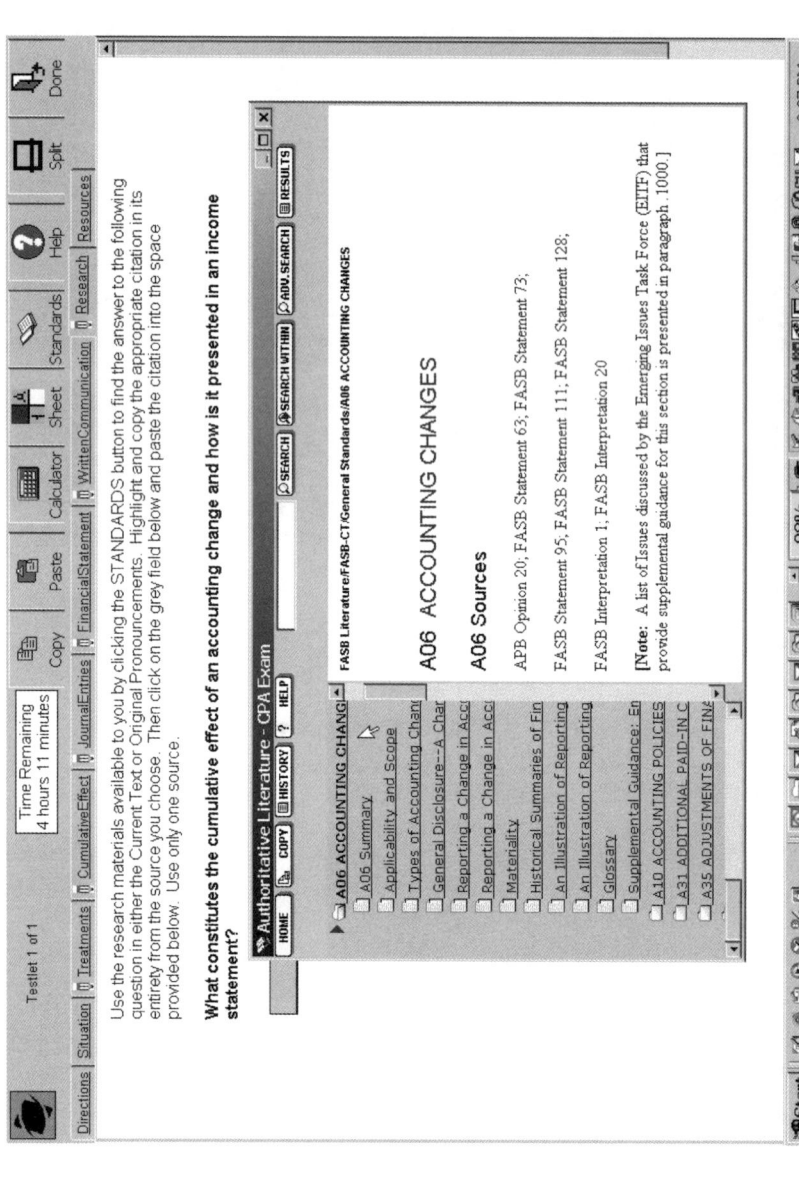

Copyright © 2003 by the American Institute of Certified Public Accountants, Inc. Reprinted with permission.

Figure 12.2 Searchable database interface.

Where paragraphs are to be copied, these are selected as a single unit in order to constrain the universe of possible correct answers that might be supplied in the input field. The copy-and-paste functionality was developed to work at the paragraph level only; that is, a full paragraph would be pasted in the tab to eliminate the possibility that a candidate would make a copy-and-paste mistake by including partial sentences or paragraphs.

Response functionality needs to be more tightly controlled by the software we use to administer the test. The examination includes other performance tasks that require independent generation of prose. We discovered that test takers sometimes used the response interface for the written communication task as a staging area for the development of their response for the author-itative literature task. They did not use the response interface provided and produced responses that were correct, but did not match the electronic key for the item in our scoring rubric. Candidates also substituted copies of author-itative literature for the generation of their own prose in the other performance task. It was unclear from our scoring specifications when this constituted a correct answer or plagiarism. This is true because entry-level CPAs are frequently called upon to generate first drafts of memorandums using canned material and excerpts from authoritative literature. Deciding when a candi-date is doing this appropriately as opposed to trying to 'beat the test' is a challenge. It is apparent that a close collaboration between system designers and subject matter experts is needed to resole problems when test takers give unexpected, and sometimes correct, responses.

Automated Item Generation

Multiple-choice item developers and case study or performance task authors are limited resources. It is important to capitalize on the skills and time of these subject matter experts and disciplined or principled approaches are designed to allow this. After templates had been established the next major innovation we attempted was the automatic generation of variants of multiple-choice items and simulations so the subject matter experts could concentrate on generating new material. The variants would have surface features of items changed, and could be considered clones of their parent source.

In the case of multiple-choice items, it was possible to generate a large number of variants. However, the new items often were so similar to the original item that they could not be considered as additions to the item inventory in the same way as entirely new items. Because of the rules for assembly that limit the presence of similar items on a complete test form, if one of these were selected the other variants would not be eligible for inclusion. Although these 'enemies' could appear in different test forms, they could not be used within a form to ensure full coverage of a topic area. The likelihood of enemy item conditions was increased dramatically due to the practice of generating many item variants.

The need for additional expert reviews of completed forms has the effect of decreasing the amount of time the subject matter experts could devote to the generation of unique item templates. While the work that Bennett (1999) and others have done to create operationally useful item generation machines is remarkable, our experience indicates that the work is far from complete.

Efficient Estimation of Statistical Properties

Statistical estimates of item properties are used as part of the specifications to create our testlets and panels, and are required for IRT scoring. Estimation of these statistics is traditionally based on reasonably large samples. This means a pre-tested item would normally need to be tested with 300–500 candidates before stable estimation of statistical properties is useful for building test forms or for scoring operational items. One strategy we are pursuing is to capitalize on the adaptive nature of the MST in calibration of multiple-choice items (van der Linden & Mead, 2004). A judgment of item difficulty will allow the pre-test item to be placed in a testlet that will be presented to candidates with ability in the appropriate range.

In an effort to cut the time required from development to operational scoring of simulations, we plan to make use of the fact that principled development has been used for the performance tasks. To the extent that the exercises (tasks or items) are similar, it is likely possible to generalize item statistics across questions that have the same development and scoring templates. A possible future extension of this is to retain scoring decisions made from responses to another example of the same template for new performance tasks. If successful, this will reduce the time and expense associated with pretesting, and will allow scoring to occur without the need for a large sample post-administration analysis.

Our experiences with the first year of computerized testing raised some concern that even seemingly subtle variations to tasks and items will have unexpected impact on statistical properties. Although collateral information related to the item might be used to reduce the required sample size for estimation, and generalizations may be acceptable for assembly purposes, it is premature to use estimates of this kind for scoring. Until we understand more thoroughly the consequences of task variations, and constrain the range of correct responses that result from our templates, a post-administration analysis is still warranted for any new content in the examination. In the early phase of development, there is too much variation in test taker responses for this innovation to be implemented.

Test Design and Administration

Interpretation-Based Design

Focusing on interpretation reduces test development constraints. This is an important advance over tests that might have been constructed along a single dimension (e.g. content ranges from a blueprint). One of the most important reasons for the AICPA to move to computerized administration was the requirement to test new skills in addition to understanding, judgment, and evaluation, which were the skills assessed in the paper-based examination. Specifically, the test is balanced to meet content specifications in addition to skill specifications (now including written communication, and research skills). A focus on interpretation allows us to develop test forms to satisfy the margins of these two levels of specification (content and skills) for the computerized examination.

For the paper-based examination, due to the small number of forms to be administered each year, tests were assembled one item at a time to meet content specifications, only. Under CBT, which required the assembly of many test forms to meet the two-dimensional specification for computer administration, we sought out experiences from other testing programs.

The National Board of Medical Examiners and the Nursing Boards are examples of programs where the complexity of constraints has had significant consequences for automated assembly and administration of computerized tests. In the present computerized CPA examination, the content and skill requirements (along with statistical and other design properties) are expressed as mutual requirements in the assembly process. The resulting testlets and panels match all dimensions of our test specifications (Breithaupt, Ariel, & Veldkamp, 2004).

Due to the accelerated pace at which professions are changing to meet real world challenges, traditional practice analysis and job analysis methods that determine the content required for high stake testing programs are becoming less appropriate. Despite our success in making the content specifications more general, our program must become more responsive to rapid changes in the accounting profession. The interpretation-based design offers some generality. However, the time needed for formalizing policy, delivering timely communications to stakeholders, and developing new test content introduces unacceptable delays when test content must change. There is some efficiency to be gained by focusing expert reviews on the broad features needed for validity in the domain of test specifications, with less emphasis on the subtopics that may lie within these domains. At the same time, we need a faster or different process to respond to changes in the profession that have a substantive impact on the content of the examination. Performing focused practice analyses and using the Internet to collect practice analysis information are two possible areas of improvement.

Internet Testing

Internet delivery of tests is convenient and flexible, and sometimes no special software or hardware is required. Through a version of secure Internet testing, we were able to implement a relatively low cost university-based field test program for the computerized examination. This afforded us a mechanism for obtaining pretest data in a non-operational setting and created an invaluable opportunity to connect us to one of our most important stakeholder groups, newly graduating accounting students.

Feedback from the participants was very positive, and provided an unexpected source of support for the innovations in the new test. It was possible to retain secure delivery of new test content outside of brick-and-mortar testing centers, at the convenience of the students, and on their own campuses. There are many challenges in this area, such as speedy delivery of complex content via the Internet and through local area networks that only meet minimum requirements for hardware and software.

Internet testing is not a mature technology. Despite the flexibility of computer languages and platforms, we experienced significant difficulties when changes were made to the commercially available software to represent our test content and complex performances. Server availability, delays caused by Internet traffic, and other variations in 'standard' installations sometimes led to slow screen refresh rates, and even termination of the field test event for a given student. However, the technologists working in this area have made good progress. Secure Internet testing is becoming a reality and we continue to rely on this important resource to maintain our testing program into the future. Internet testing already provides splendid diagnostic and practice opportunities for assessment.

Functioning Work Tools

Fidelity with real-world practice requirements is feasible. When NCARB computerized the architectural licensing examination, they embedded current building codes into the examination. Similarly, the AICPA incorporated accounting standards, tax laws, and other authoritative literature into the new CPA exam. This enabled the incorporation of a variety of assessment tasks that would have been logistically impossible in a paper-based format. The inclusion of this material in the test is a closer representation of the daily work required from entry level CPAs in their natural working environment. In turn, educational programs where students are trained for accounting have also evolved to train students using the relevant work tools. This can be seen as an unexpected positive consequence of modernizing the CPA examination; in some educational programs there was a positive impact on test taker preparation. License agreements for software and other products used normally in business must be redefined for situations where these tools form part of an assessment. These tools (e.g. spreadsheet software) are typically licensed for a specified number of users. In an assessment context, this is prohibitively expensive. In addition, there are often competing software and informational products that might be used in practice. It was necessary to ensure the test made use of products that were commonly used in education and in practice without giving a competitive advantage to one or more companies.

Storage requirements for large databases can also be problematic. Computerized test delivery center servers have a finite capacity and there is a business need to limit the space devoted to databases for a single testing program. This problem, however, should pose the briefest of obstacles in building modern, authentic tests. Versioning of reference material is also an important issue. Ensuring that the databases are both up to date and consistent with test content and scoring keys is a challenge. The content of the databases is dynamic, changing as rules and regulations change. Distribution to test centers, however, is periodic as is distribution of test content. Ensuring that all test questions conform to the current database and coordinating the release of new database content is a balancing act. In accounting, updating these tools must be coordinated with both the timing of regulatory changes and the retirement of obsolete test content.

Multi-Stage Adaptive Test Models

The Uniform CPA Examination was launched using a computerized semi-adaptive design based on testlets (a special case of the CAST model proposed by Luecht and Nungester, 1998). This represents the first operational testing program to make use of the model in a large volume certification program. The selection of the model was based on expected gains controlling item exposure, providing useful feedback information, ensuring score accuracy at shorter test lengths, and allowing examinees a limited opportunity for review and revision of their responses (Luecht et al., 2002). The main purpose of the CPA examination is to identify candidates with sufficient knowledge and skills to protect the public interest. A secondary purpose is to provide accurate information to failing candidates to help guide further study to retake the examination. The MST targets the administration of appropriately difficult items to lower or higher scoring candidates, while ensuring a broad range of content for diagnostic scoring and precision of the passing score decision (Breithaupt & Hare, 2004).

There are pragmatic issues that limit the usefulness of the adaptive model. Key among these are limitations of the item banks, administration software and scoring validation methods. Equally, or perhaps more, important is the burden on the testing program to communicate to stakeholders accurately and gain acceptance of the administration method from the profession. A number of questions were raised by the oversight boards and candidates when the AICPA announced its decision to implement an MST design. Examples are 'How can making high scoring candidates take harder questions be fair to them? Won't giving easier items to low scoring candidates afford them a better chance to pass than if they were forced to take the same items as the higher scoring candidates?' and 'Do you mean that two candidates may answer the same number of items correctly and one may pass while the other one fails?'. While the administration and scoring models might be established among testing professionals, it is important to recognize and address the misconceptions of each stakeholder group. A lack of support from stakeholders may result in the rejection of a sound test design and the validity of score interpretations may be questioned.

Scoring Complex Performances

An extension of traditional scoring methods was required for the case-based performance component in the CPA examination. Input from systems architects, subject matter experts, and psychometricians was critical in defining a workable automated scoring system. Consider a performance task that requires the examinee to select N correct responses from a list of Y options. Designing a scoring rubric for this task requires specification of whether the task will be scored as Y 'yes–no' tasks or as a single task in which credit is given only if the N correct responses are chosen. There could also be partial credit solutions. In this example, there are Y 'measurement opportunities', or responses from the examinee.

Analysis of candidate responses is usually necessary to determine whether each measurement opportunity is also a 'scoring opportunity' or whether it is more appropriate to combine several (or all) measurement opportunities into a single scoring opportunity. A template design for this performance task for the Uniform CPA Examination was incorporated into the scoring rubric for the items. The combination of scoring rules can be replicated and used for any performance task that has the same template. The scoring rules can be Boolean and can make use of formulas for evaluating the candidates' responses. The evaluation defined in the rubric assigns credit or no credit for each scorable part of the task. When new tasks are written, the evaluation performed by the rubric is incorporated into the template. Authors need only specify the correct measurement opportunity value for each component of the task.

An example of the scoring rule applied to a spreadsheet task is provided in Figure 12.3. The author of the simulation creates the rubric dynamically with the simulation itself. All spreadsheet cells that are open to responses from candidates appear on the response ID list. The author selects one cell and defines the parameters of the correct response. These may include allowing formulae, numerical, or alpha characters, and tolerances around target values. A more complex scoring rule would include references to cells in other worksheets where previous work has to be carried over (thus avoiding penalizing an examinee for a computational error that was previously evaluated). It is also possible to add scripting functions to any scoring rule to accommodate more complex logic in the rubrics. The rubric and scripting are specific to each response field, and are applied by an intelligent computer program called an 'evaluator'.

The kinds of evaluation applied by the rubrics we use to score our complex performances are novel in the testing field and merit additional discussion. Complex performances might give the candidate an opportunity to supply sets of linked responses. Suppose an examinee is required to complete five cells in a spreadsheet. Each cell is a measurement opportunity. A decision is required whether to score the contents of each cell or only the cell or cells that represent final calculations. If only final results are to be scored, then decisions must be made whether to penalize the examinee for errors in cells that are not scored. Once the decision is made, the scoring rubric can be built to evaluate

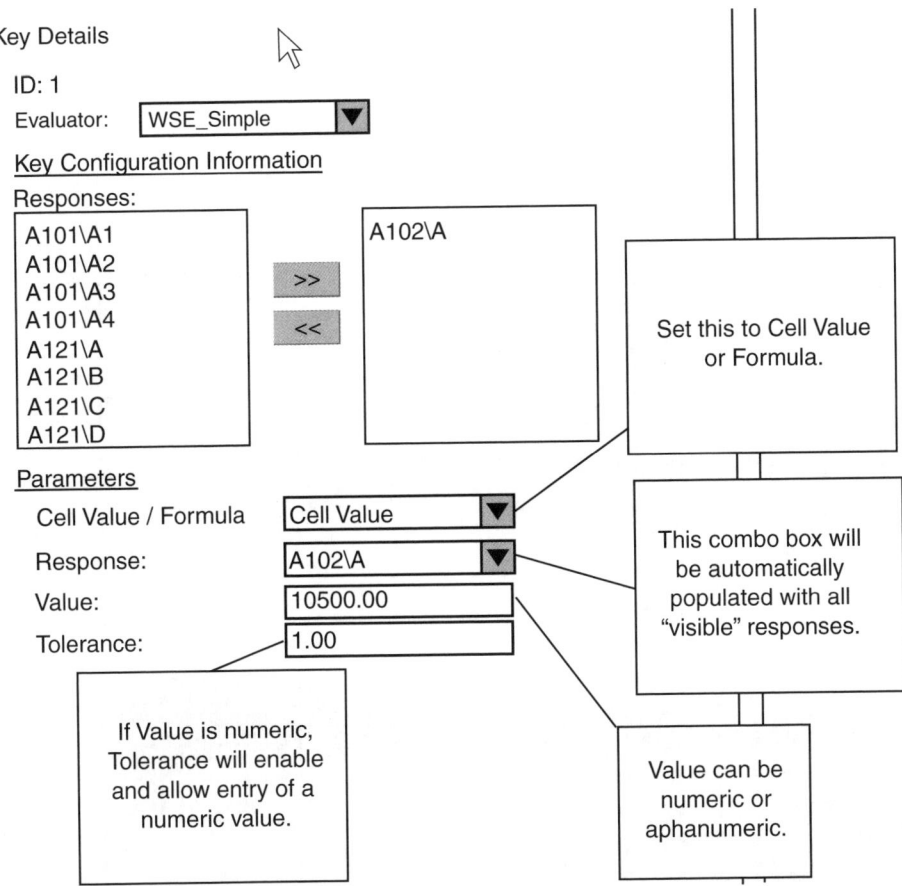

Key Details

ID: 1

Evaluator: WSE_Simple ▼

Key Configuration Information

Responses:

A101\A1
A101\A2
A101\A3
A101\A4
A121\A
A121\B
A121\C
A121\D

\>\>
\<\<

A102\A

Set this to Cell Value
or Formula.

Parameters

Cell Value / Formula   Cell Value ▼

Response: A102\A ▼

Value: 10500.00

Tolerance: 1.00

This combo box will
be automatically
populated with all
"visible" responses.

If Value is numeric,
Tolerance will enable
and allow entry of a
numeric value.

Value can be
numeric or
aphanumeric.

Figure 12.3   Scoring a spreadsheet task

the supplied response and to apply the scoring rule consistently across multiple tasks.

In the example above, the evaluator in the rubric reads and calculates a summary value using a formula provided in one cell and a value provided in another cell. The item author needed to enter the reference values in the rubrics. An example of the task and rubrics is presented in Figure 12.4. (The test taker does not see the lists at the bottom of the screen; these are the sets of formulae that are used by the scoring system to evaluate test taker responses.) A response in the target cell that results from applying any of the formulae assigned to that cell would receive credit as a correct response.

Of course, a limitation of this scoring design is the time and effort required to recognize and assign credit for the universe of possible responses. At the current time, most of the responses received can be scored automatically using predefined rubrics. However, because of the importance of the decision

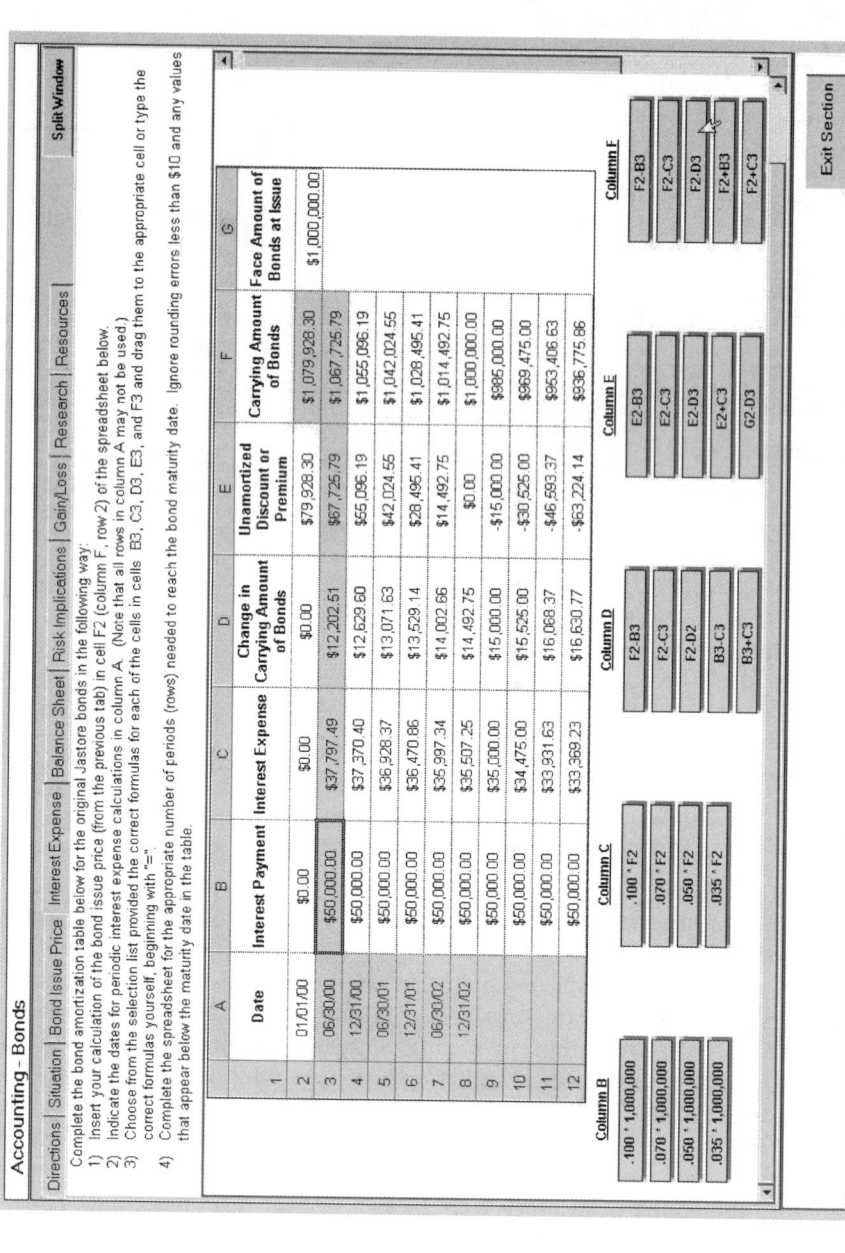

Accounting – Bonds

Directions | Situation | Bond Issue Price | Interest Expense | Balance Sheet | Risk Implications | Gain/Loss | Research | Resources | **Split Window**

Complete the bond amortization table below for the original Jastore bonds in the following way:

1) Insert your calculation of the bond issue price (from the previous tab) in cell F2 (column F, row 2) of the spreadsheet below.
2) Indicate the dates for periodic interest expense calculations in column A. (Note that all rows in column A may not be used.)
3) Choose from the selection list provided the correct formulas for each of the cells in cells B3, C3, D3, E3, and F3 and drag them to the appropriate cell or type the correct formulas yourself, beginning with "=".
4) Complete the spreadsheet for the appropriate number of periods (rows) needed to reach the bond maturity date. Ignore rounding errors less than $10 and any values that appear below the maturity date in the table.

	A	B	C	D	E	F	G
	Date	Interest Payment	Interest Expense	Change in Carrying Amount of Bonds	Unamortized Discount or Premium	Carrying Amount of Bonds	Face Amount of Bonds at Issue
2	01/01/00	$0.00	$0.00	$0.00	$79,928.30	$1,079,928.30	$1,000,000.00
3	06/30/00	$50,000.00	$37,797.49	$12,202.51	$67,725.79	$1,067,725.79	
4	12/31/00	$50,000.00	$37,370.40	$12,629.60	$55,096.19	$1,055,096.19	
5	06/30/01	$50,000.00	$36,928.37	$13,071.63	$42,024.55	$1,042,024.55	
6	12/31/01	$50,000.00	$36,470.86	$13,529.14	$28,495.41	$1,028,495.41	
7	06/30/02	$50,000.00	$35,997.34	$14,002.66	$14,492.75	$1,014,492.75	
8	12/31/02	$50,000.00	$35,507.25	$14,492.75	$0.00	$1,000,000.00	
9		$50,000.00	$35,000.00	$15,000.00	-$15,000.00	$985,000.00	
10		$50,000.00	$34,475.00	$15,525.00	-$30,525.00	$969,475.00	
11		$50,000.00	$33,931.63	$16,068.37	-$46,593.37	$953,406.63	
12		$50,000.00	$33,369.23	$16,630.77	-$63,224.14	$936,775.86	

Column B
.100 * 1,000,000
.070 * 1,000,000
.050 * 1,000,000
.035 * 1,000,000

Column C
.100 * F2
.070 * F2
.050 * F2
.035 * F2

Column D
F2-B3
F2-C3
F2-D2
B3-C3
B3+C3

Column E
E2-B3
E2-C3
E2-D3
E2+C3
G2-D3

Column F
F2-B3
F2-C3
F2-D3
F2+B3
F2+C3

Exit Section

Copyright © 2003 by the American Institute of Certified Public Accountants, Inc. Reprinted with permission.

Figure 12.4 Compensatory scoring of a spreadsheet task.

resting on the total examination score and our inability to be confident that we have pre-identified all possible correct answers, all responses and scores are currently verified to ensure that all candidates who should receive credit for their responses are treated fairly.

Combining Scores from Different Item Types

The simulation component is just one of three types of performance that are required from candidates for the CPA examination. In three of the four separate sections of our examination, there are constructed responses measuring written communication, simulations, and multiple-choice items. Sections of the CPA examination are Audit and Attestation, Regulation, Financial Accounting and Reporting, and Business Environment and Context (which contains only multiple-choice questions at the time of this writing). Each section has an aggregate score, and an associated passing score based on performances on all the included item types.

Two particular challenges existed in determining how to arrive at a single score scale when different item types were combined. These were the need to report scores on a scale that could be understood by our stakeholders (accustomed to a 0–99 scale, with a passing score of 75), and the need to establish a reasonable metric for IRT calibrations across item types. Our stakeholders settled on a policy of transforming the IRT-based ability estimation to an expected number correct scale for objective portions of the exam (multiple-choice items and simulations). The weighted sum of the holistic written communication score and the estimated number correct scores was then transformed to the reported score scale of 0–99.

The selection of an initial IRT calibration design was made with consideration of the new content and scoring methods used for the computer-administered examination. The portions of the examination sections with the highest weight in the total score are the multiple-choice testlets. A decision was made to scale the objective simulation scores to the multiple-choice bank as a result of research on the fit of the paper-based multiple-choice response data to the IRT model, and caution in interpreting the new simulation components (Luecht, 2003). As we gain experience with the new test and item formats and as examinees become familiar with the novel item formats, we will need to research alternative designs for scaling (including multidimensional IRT models, partial credit scoring, and separate calibration for simulations).

Setting Passing Scores on Complex Performances

One of the challenges faced by the AICPA was the establishment of new passing scores for the computer-based test. Not only had the test changed substantially through the incorporation of complex performance tasks or simulations, but also many of the administrative constraints on the licensure process were changed. Prior to the implementation of the new examination, most candidates had to take all sections of the examination in a single two-day period and receiving credit for an examination section was conditioned not only on performance on that section, but also performance on other sections. Under CBT, candidates are allowed to take as many or few sections as they desire and performance on other sections has no bearing on the granting of credit for a given section.

These factors created two issues that had to be resolved. First, how could a standard setting study be conducted that would provide appropriate information on the new item formats? Second, how should the policy-makers (the Board of Examiners) consider the standard setting data along with other relevant information to establish the passing standards?

One study was conducted (Hambleton & Pitoniak, 2002) to identify and select standard setting methods. The results of the studies supported the use of standard setting techniques that required expert panelists to evaluate both the content of the test and representative performance of examinees. Thus, the operational standard setting studies were based on methods that provided panelists with examples of actual examinee performance on specific assessment tasks. However, the data provided to panelists was either (1) collected in the paper-based program under the prior administrative regulations or (2) based on low stakes, pretest administrations of the new item formats. As a result, even though the design and conduct of the studies was appropriate (i.e. there was a satisfactory answer to the first issue), the extent to which the results could be expected to represent performance of minimally competent candidates in the new administrative environment was unclear. Therefore, there was no clear direction for the policy makers' deliberations on how to incorporate the standard setting results with other relevant information. This dilemma is not new in high stake testing, as evidenced by the special issue of *Educational Measurement: Issues and Practices* in 1991 and the work of Glass (1978).

Ultimately, the policy body charged with setting the final passing scores, the Board of Examiners, used the standard setting study results as the basis of its decision. However, it adjusted the study-based standard substantially based on other information including, but not limited to, the expected stakeholder perceptions of the validity of the examination if passing rates varied dramatically from prior experience. This is a dilemma that will undoubtedly be faced by more and more test sponsors as consumer demands result in significant changes to tests and testing conditions. Further research is essential to provide policy groups with guidance concerning how to responsibly set passing standards that incorporate multiple information sources in a manner that, while arbitrary, is not capricious.

CONCLUSIONS

In this chapter, we have attempted to provide one vision of the future of assessment. In doing so, we have used the material in the other chapters in this volume as a basis for hypothesizing the evolution of measurement and the application of technology to address the desires of test users. We have also provided examples of some of the innovations in measurement today and attempted to show how those innovations can be indicators that the future we envision is realistic. Our vision of the future is very different from the profession we have today. It suggests that virtually every aspect of testing will change and that testing itself will become more seamlessly integrated into work and educational processes. Advances in psychometrics, integration of expertise from a variety of fields, and the deployment of sophisticated technological solutions will drive these changes.

Our vision is undoubtedly flawed, as are all predictions of the future. However, the work being done today has the potential to lead to dramatic developments in assessment. Millions of high stake tests are being administered on computer around the globe. Internet testing is growing and is on the verge of challenging the current limited use brick and mortar test centers. New item formats are being developed and implemented. Fascinating research is underway to mine the new kinds of data that are being collected from these tasks. A wide range of professions is contributing to these new types of assessment. The work reported in this volume is a compelling indication of the speed at which our field is changing.

The future that we achieve may be quite different from the one we envision. However, it is undeniable that assessments of the future will be richer, more complex, and more targeted than those of today. That these assessments will utilize technology extensively in all aspects of the endeavor is also undeniable. The assessments of the future will be more aligned with client desires, have better fidelity with emerging cognitive understanding, and provide an even better service than the assessments we know today.

REFERENCES

American Educational Research Association (AERA), American Psychological Association (APA), & National Council on Measurement in Education (NCME). (1999). *Standards for educational and psychological testing.* Washington, DC: American Educational Research Association.

American Institute of Certified Public Accountants (AICPA). (2002). *Structure, length, and examination content specifications for the Uniform CPA Examination.* Jersey City, NJ: AICPA.

Bennett, R. E. (1999). Using new technology to improve assessment. *Educational Measurement: Issues and Practice,* **18**(3):5–12.

Breithaupt, K., Ariel, A., & Veldkamp, B. (2004, April). *Balancing item exposure and optimality in automated assembly for multi-stage testing* (AICPA Technical Report, Series II, 2). Jersey City, NJ: AICPA.

Breithaupt, K., & Hare, D. (2004, February). *Automated simultaneous assembly of multi-stage testlets for the Uniform CPA Examination.* Invited paper presented at the ATP Conference, Palm Springs, CA.

Brittingham, P., et al. (2000). *The mathematics test creation assistant: A tool for automated item generation.* Retrieved *http://www.ncme.org/about/awards/bennett.html,* 11th August 2004.

Drasgow, F., & Olson-Buchanan, J. B. (1999). *Innovations in computerized assessment.* Mahwah, NJ: Erlbaum.

Embretson, S. E. (1999). Generating items during testing: Psychometric issues and models. *Psychometrika*, **64**:407–433.

Glass, G. V. (1978). Standards and criteria. *Journal of Educational Measurement*, **15**:237–262.

Hambleton, R. K., & Pitoniak, M. J. (2002). *Setting passing scores on the CBT version of the Uniform CPA Examination: Comparison of several promising methods* (AICPA Technical Report, Series II, 7). Jersey City, NJ: AICPA.

Hulin, C. L., Drasgow, F., & Parsons, C. K. (1983). *Item response theory: Applications to psychological measurement*. Homewood, IL: Dow Jones Irwin.

International Test Commission. (2000). *International guidelines for test use*. Retrieved http://www.intestcom.org, 11th August 2004.

Irvine, S. H., & Kyllonen, P. C. (Eds.). (2002). *Item generation for test development*. Mahwah, NJ: Erlbaum.

Keller, L. (2002). *Using collateral information for IRT parameter estimation*. Paper presented at the International Conference on Computer-Based Testing and the Internet, Winchester, UK.

Luecht, R. M. (2003). *Calibration and scoring the computerized Uniform CPA Examination* (AICPA Technical Report, Series II, 14). Jersey City, NJ: AICPA.

Luecht, R., Brumfield, T., & Breithaupt, K. (2002). *A testlet assembly design for the Uniform CPA Examination* (AICPA Technical Report, Series II, 12). Jersey City, NJ: AICPA.

Luecht, R. M., & Nungester, R. J. (1998). Some practical applications of computerized adaptive sequential testing. *Journal of Educational Measurement*, **35**:229–249.

Mager, R. F. (1962). *Preparing instructional objectives*. Palo Alto, CA: Fearon.

Martinez, M. E., & Bennett, R. E. (1992). A review of automatically scorable constructed-response item types for large-scale assessment. *Applied Measurement in Education*, **5**:151–169

Messick, S. (1989). Validity. In R. Linn (Ed.), *Educational measurement* (3rd ed.; pp. 13–103). Washington, DC: American Council on Education.

Mislevy, R. J., Steinberg, L. S., & Almond, R. G., (1999). *On the roles of task model variables in assessment design* (CRESST Technical Report). Los Angeles, CA: UCLA, CRESST. Retrieved *www.cse.ucla.edu/CRESST/Reports/TECH500.pdf*, 8 November 2004.

Mislevy, R. J., Steinberg, L. S., Russell, R. G., Breyer, F. J., & Johnson, L. (2001, March). *Making sense of data from complex assessments* (CRESST Technical Report). Los Angeles, CA: UCLA, CRESST.

National Council on Educational Measurement. (1991). Standard-setting [Special Issue]. *Educational Measurement: Issues and Practice*, **10**(2).

Performance Testing Council. (2004). *Best practices*. Retrieved *http://www.performancetest. org/bestpractices.html*, 11 August 2004.

Popham, W. J. (1973). *Evaluating instruction*. Englewood Cliffs, NJ: Prentice-Hall.

Shermis, M. D., & Burstein, J. (Eds.). (2003). *Automated essay scoring: A cross disciplinary perspective*. Mahwah, NJ: Erlbaum.

Taylor, C., Kirsch, I., Eignor, D., & Jamieson, J. (1999). Examining the relationship between computer familiarity and performance on computer-based language tasks. *Language Learning*, **49**:219–274.

Tekian, A., McGuire, C., & McGaghie, C. (Eds.). (1999). *Innovative simulations for assessing professional competence*. Chicago, IL: Department of Medical Education, University of Illinois at Chicago.

van der Linden, W. J., & Glas, C. A. W. (2000). *Computerized adaptive testing; Theory and practice*. Boston, MA: Kluwer.

van der Linden, W. J., & Mead, A. D. (2004, April). *Optimal calibration design for multi-stage adaptive testing*. Paper presented at the meeting of the National Council on Measurement in Education, San Diego, CA.

Wainer, H. (1993). Some practical considerations when converting a linearly administered test to an adaptive format. *Educational Measurement: Issues and Practice*, **12**:15–20.

Wainer, H., Bradlow, E. T., & Du, Z. (2000). Testlet response theory: An analog for the 3pl model useful in testlet-based adaptive testing. In W. J. van der Linden & C. A. W. Glas (Eds.), *Computerized adaptive testing: Theory and practice.* Boston, MA: Kluwer.

Wainer, H., & Kiely, G. L. (1987). Item clusters and computerized adaptive testing: A case for testlets. *Journal of Educational Measurement,* **24**:185–201.

Index